STUDIES IN THE ANTIQUITIES OF STOBI

GENERAL EDITORS

DJORDJE MANO-ZISSI   JAMES WISEMAN

Frontispiece. Interior of Stobi Museum, August, 1972.

STUDIES IN THE ANTIQUITIES OF STOBI

VOLUME I

EDITED BY
JAMES WISEMAN

BEOGRAD 1973

Published by the University of Texas at Austin and the National Museum of Titov Veles with a publication grant from the Smithsonian Institution.

FOR THE PUBLISHER

TIHO NAJDOVSKI

EDITORIAL ASSISTANT

ŽIVOJIN RADOŠEVIĆ

Copyright by James Wiseman, 1973.

PRINTED IN YUGOSLAVIA
„NAUČNO DELO," BEOGRAD

TABLE OF CONTENTS
САДРЖАЈ

Foreword	VII
Предговор	X
Preface	XIII
Увод	XV
Staff of the Stobi Project	XVII
Чланови екипе пројекта Стоби	XVII
List of Abbreviations	XIX
Списак скраћеница	XIX
Michael H. Crawford, The Stobi Hoard of Roman Republican Denarii	1
Мајкл Крофорд, Остава римских републиканских денара пронађена у Стобима	22
E. Mott Davis, D. Srdoč, and S. Valastro, Jr., Radiocarbon Dates from Stobi: 1971 Season	23
Е. М. Дејвис, Д. Срдоч и С. Валастро јуниор, Старосно одређивање узорака методом С—14	35
Robert L. Folk, The Geologic Framework of Stobi	37
Роберт Фолк, Геолошки оквири Стоба	58
Ivan Mikulčić, The West Cemetery: Excavations in 1965	61
Иван Микулчић, Западно гробље: Ископавање у 1965. години	93
Al B. Wesolowsky, Burial Customs in the West Cemetery	97
Ал Везаловски, Обичаји сахрањивања у Западном гробљу	138
James Wiseman, Gods, War and Plague in the Time of the Antonines	143
Џејмс Вајзман, Богови, рат и куга у време Антонина	184
Djordje Mano-Zissi, Stratigraphic Problems and the Urban Development of Stobi	185
Ђорђе Мано-Зиси, Проблеми стратиграфије и урбани развој Стобија	225
Žika Radošević, The Stobi Bibliography	233
Жика Радошевић, Стоби: Библиографија	233
Plan of the Site. Surveyed and drawn by Paul Huffman (1971) and David B. Peck (1972)	at end of book

Cover design by *Žika Radošević*

FOREWORD

Three years of a joint collaboration at Stobi encouraged us to initiate *Studies in the Antiquities of Stobi* which will appear in a series. The Stobi Project was arranged by the Yugoslav Institution for International Technical Cooperation and the Smithsonian Institution in 1970. Since then, the sponsoring institutions, the National Museum of Titov Veles and the University of Texas at Austin, have been successfully collaborating. The two principal investigators, who direct the excavations at Stobi with the help of several talented Yugoslav and American scholars, are honored to be co-editors of this series. We are grateful to the government of Macedonia and the Town Hall of Titov Veles for their significant contributions and sincere encouragement. We are also grateful to the Smithsonian Institution, not only for the large funds used for excavations, but for securing means for this publication.

Publication in such a series as ours is not a novelty. Not to mention famous world editions concerned with large archaeological sites, I would remind the reader of examples from the territory of Yugoslavia, Salona and Sirmium. In our opinion, the archaeology and history of Stobi deserve a similar treatment.

The site of ancient Stobi has been known to the world for more than 100 years. Ever since the beginning, excavations were of an international interest and significance. From 1924 until 1940 excavations were performed by the National Museum of Beograd. After the war, from 1955 to 1957, the Archaeological Museum at Skopje investigated the site. During the 1960s the Conservation Institute of Macedonia performed small-scale excavations at the site. In the process, a late antique horizon was uncovered while the problems regarding earlier phases of the urban life were only initiated.

The new excavations (hopefully by 1975) will not only uncover larger urban surfaces, but also investigate chronological extensions of the city, and research geologic, ecological, anthropological, ethnic, economic, social and cult characteristics of different historical phases and formations. We hope also to gain an understanding of the development both of culture and art in this region. The great significance of the city of Stobi as a crossroads between the Aegean World and the Central Balkans is confirmed more and more as the new excavations progress, and we may understand more clearly the relations among the native Paeonians and Hellenized Macedonians and Greeks, as reflected in life, habits, culture, and arts. On the other hand, the relations between Hellenism and Rome, between Mediterranean slaveholding civilizations and autochtonous civilizations, and finally between later Gothic and Slavic ethnic formations and Christian Byzantine culture are nowhere so dialectically distinguished.

The city offers a number of problems for detailed study, including urban development and a variety of architectural structures: theater, baths, synagogue, residences and Christian cult buildings. Many local industries and crafts are already known: mint and foundry, stone-dressing, fresco and mosaic workshops, fulling workshops, and trade in ceramics, glass, sea-shells, fish and salt. Large areas for investigation, unoccupied since mediaeval times, offer to future generations the opportunity for gradual, systematic research. The position of the ancient site on the modern thoroughfare makes it a very convenient place for a base for general studies of Macedonia itself and its relations with Greek and Danubian lands, and even with Adriatic and Pontic regions.

Besides historical and archaeological questions, *Studies* will be concerned with natural sciences and technical, technological, physical, chemical, documentation, and organizational problems: conservation and restoration will have a special place. We are very interested in the presentation of the site. With joint efforts of all concerned we hope to create a research center at Stobi.

We are proud to say that in 1972 a museum was opened on the site. The exhibits of the contextual material are intended to reflect life at Stobi in all its periods. We hope that the excavations will eventually become an Archaeological School, where throughout the year scholars and students may pursue the study of the antiquities. We strongly wish to have their contributions published in future *Studies*.

I here express my gratitude to all authors and collaborators in this work. To my dear colleague, I express my gratitude and recognition of the work that he performed while editing Volume I.

Beograd, March 1, 1973					Djordje Mano-Zissi

ПРЕДГОВОР

Три године колегијалне сарадње у Стобима дале су нам храбрости да покренемо едицију *Проучавање старина у Стобима*. Стоби пројект организовали су 1970. године Југословенски завод за међународну техничку сарадњу и Smithsonian институција. Од тада се успешно развија сарадња између Народног музеја у Титовом Велесу и Универзитета Тексаса у Остину, институција које су носиоци пројекта Стоби. Два главна истраживача, који уз подршку угледних југословaнских и америчких стручњака руководе ископавањима у Стобима, имају част да буду ко-едитори ове едиције. Захваљујемо се влади СР Македоније и Скупштини Титовог Велеса на значајним доприносима и срдачним подстицајима. Smithsonian институција је поред великих инвестиција уложених у теренска истраживања омогућила излажење ове публикације.

Као замисао, оваква едиција није новина. Не помињући чувене светске едиције које се баве изучавањем великих археолошких локалитета сетимо се примера у Југославији, Салоне и Сирмијума. Мислимо да наш покушај ни у чему неће бити мање занимљив.

Локалитет Стоби познат је већ више од сто година светској јавности, а изучавање и ископавање града било је од интернационалног значаја и интереса већ од почетка. Од 1924. до 1940. године ископавања је изводио Народни музеј у Београду. После рата, од 1955. до 1957. Археолошки музеј у Скопљу испитивао је локалитет. Током 1960их година Завод за заштиту споменика Македоније вршио је ископавања мањих размера. Током ових радова откривен је касноантички хоризонт града, док су проблеми градског живота у старијим фазама само начети.

Нова ископавања (која ће према очекивањима трајати до 1975.) не само да ће открити већа урбана пространства, већ ће пронаћи хронолошке границе града и истражити геолошке, еколошке, антрополошке, етничке, економске, социјалне и култне карактеристике разних историјских фаза и формација. Тако са дубоким интересом желимо да откријемо развој културе и уметности овога краја. Даља ископавања све више потврђују велики значај античког града — раскрснице између Егеје и Централног Балкана; такође помажу да јасније сагледамо однос аутохтоних Пеонаца са Хеленизованим Македонцима и са самим Грцима, онако како се одразио у животу, обичајима, култури и уметности. С друге стране, односи између Хеленизма и Рима, медитеранске робовласничке цивилизације и аутохтоних цивилизација, и најзад између хришћанске византијске културе и етничких формација Гота и Словена нигде нису тако дијалектички обележени.

Поред тога град се истиче својим урбанистичким проблемима, ретким архитектонским облицима (театар, терме, синагоге, стамбене зграде, хришћански култни објекти...), својом ковницом и ливницама, каменорезачким, мозаичким и фреско радионицама, ваљаоницом и бојаџиницом текстила, трговином керамике, стакла, морских шкољки и соли. Многи од тих проблема за сада се само назиру. Велики слободан простор за истраживања, нетакнут још од раног средњег века, даје могућност будућим генерацијама за поступна, систематска истраживања. Положај античких Стоба крај ауто-магистрале и жељезнице представља згоду за прерастање локалитета у базу за општа истраживања Македоније и њених односа са Грчком и Подунављем, шта више са Јадраном и Црним морем.

Поред историјско-археолошких питања Студије ће се бавити природословним, техничким, технолошким, физичко-хемијским, документационим и организационим проблемима. Конзервација, рестаурација и презентација ископина заузимаће посебно место. Тако би удруженим напорима свих заинтересованих могло доћи до градње једног истраживачког центра на самом локалитету.

Са поносом можемо да кажемо да је 1972. године отворен на самом терену музеј са систематским збиркама контекстног материјала. Надајмо се да ће истраживања временом прерасти у археолошку школу, где ће научници и студенти проучавати старине током целе године. Желели бисмо да свима њима буду доступни ступци наших *Студија* и да резултати њиховог рада нађу пре свега у њима одјека.

Захваљујем се свим ауторима и сарадницима на овом послу. Свом драгом колеги изражавам признање на уложеном труду вршења прве редакције.

Београд, 1. март 1973.   Ђорђе Мано-Зиси

PREFACE

This volume is the first in a series of studies in the antiquities of Stobi. The series will include articles of the following types: 1) reports of special, limited excavations; 2) technical studies and reports on methodology; 3) special studies on archaeological, historical, or art historical topics. The articles published in the series will normally be too detailed to be included in the annual preliminary reports. Some of the articles, additionally, will deal with material that is not suited to the proposed design of the forthcoming series on the final results of the excavations at Stobi; other articles will present discoveries deemed to be of such scholarly significance that their publication should not be delayed.

Studies will be concerned chiefly, but not exclusively, with the work of the Stobi Project. The Project was inaugurated in May, 1970, as an archaeological excavation sponsored jointly by the University of Texas at Austin and the National Museum of Titov Veles, Yugoslavia, under the auspices of the Smithsonian Institution. The Staff is made up of scholars, students, and technicians from a number of nations, chiefly Yugoslavia, England, and the United States. Co-Directors of the Project are Djordje Mano-Zissi of the University of Belgrade and the undersigned, who also serves as Field Director. The senior archaeologists constitute an Advisory Council and the Administrative Director is Tiho Najdovski who succeeded Todor Gruev in that post in August, 1972.

The Project has been funded largely through the U. S. Foreign Currency Program, administered by the Smithsonian Institution.

Other funds have been generously provided by the Ford Foundation (Archaeological Traineeships for graduate students, 1970—1972), the University of Texas at Austin, a number of private American donors (especially Texans), and the city of Titov Veles. Various items of equipment have been lent or donated to the Project by the University of Texas at Austin, the National Museum of Titov Veles, the National Museum of Prilep, the Archaeological Museum of Skopje, and several members of the Stobi Project.

The Stobi Project has now completed three summer seasons of excavation. Previous archaeological work at Stobi by the National Museum of Belgrade and the Conservation Institute of Macedonia has been summarized by Ernst Kitzinger (see Bibliography) and by the undersigned in the recent *Stobi. A Guide to the Excavations*. Additional details will be found in this volume in the article by Djordje Mano-Zissi.

Publications of the Stobi Project are under the general editorship of the Co-Directors. Žika Radošević, who compiled the Bibliography published here, has been especially helpful in the preparation of this volume. Most importantly, he translated into English the contributions of Ivan Mikulčić and Djordje Mano-Zissi, and translated into Serbo-Croatian the Résumés of all the other articles. It is a pleasure to acknowledge his conscientious assistance in the varied tasks of publication, including seeing this volume through the press in Belgrade. The photographs reproduced here were provided by several members of the staff: Tom Eals, Figs. 3-22, 25, 91 and the Frontispiece; Robert Folk, Figs. 26-29; Marilyn Huffman, Figs. 74, 84-85, 87-90; Djordje Mano-Zissi, all photographs in his article; Ivan Mikulčić, all photographs in his article; Žika Radošević, Fig. 83; Richard Trimble, Figs. 1, 2, 30; Al Wesolowsky, Figs. 66-73, 75-78; the undersigned Editor, Figs. 79, 81, 86. The final form of the English translations was the responsibili.y of the undersigned Editor, who is grateful to Carolyn Snively for her assistance in this and other editorial tasks. My thanks also for advice and for assistance with various manuscripts to B. O. Davis and Lucy Wiseman. Finally, special thanks for many kindnesses are owed to Tiho Najdovski, Director of the National Museum of Titov Veles and the Administrative Director of the Stobi Project.

Austin, Texas
January, 1973

James R. Wiseman

УВОД

Ово је прва из серије књига проучавања старина у Стобима. Серија ће садржавати чланке следећих типова: 1) извештаје о нарочитим, ограниченим ископавањима; 2) техничке студије и извештаје о методологији; 3) нарочите студије о археолошким, историјским или историјско-уметничким темама. Обично ће чланци публиковани у овој серији бити сувише детаљни да би ушли у годишњи прелиминарни извештај. Накнадно ће се појавити и неки чланци о материји која не одговара предложеном изгледу будуће серије о крајњим резултатима ископавања у Стобима, а биће и чланака који ће приказати таква научна открића са чијим се публиковањем не сме чекати.

Студије ће се углавном, али не и искључиво, бавити радовима пројекта Стоби. Пројект је инаугурисан месеца маја 1970. године, као заједнички подухват Универзитета Тексаса у Остину и Народног музеја у Титовом Велесу, а под покровитељством Smithsonian институције. Екипа је састављена од научника, студената и техничара из низа држава, углавном Југославије, Енглеске и Сједињених Америчких Држава. Ко-директори пројекта јесу Ђорђе Мано-Зиси са Београдског универзитета и доле потписани, који такође ради као директор теренског рада. Старији археолози конституишу савет а административни директор је Тихо Најдовски који је наследио Тодора Грујева августа 1972. године.

Пројекту фондове обезбеђује Smithsonian институција из Програма страних средстава америчке владе. Друге фондове несебично су обезбедили: Фордова фондација (археолошке стипендије за студенте трећег степена, 1970—1972.), Универзитет Тексаса у Остину, известан број Американаца дародаваца (нарочито Тексашана) и Скупштина општине Титовог Велеса. Различите делове опреме позајмили су или поклонили пројекту Универзитет Тексаса у Остину, Народни музеј у Титовом Велесу, Народни музеј у Прилепу, Археолошки музеј у Скопљу и неколицина чланова пројекта Стоби.

Пројект Стоби има данас за собом три сезоне ископавања. Претходни археолошки рад у Стобима, Народног музеја из Београда и Завода за заштиту споменика Македоније, сумирали су Ернст Кицингер (види Библиографију) и доле потписани у недавно штампаној књизи *Стоби, водич кроз антички град*. Још неки детаљи могу се пронаћи у овој књизи у чланку Ђорђа Мано-Зисија.

Публикације пројекта Стоби су у редакцији ко-директора. Жика Радошевић, који је саставио овде публиковану Библиографију, нарочито ми је помогао у припремању ове књиге. Најважније, он је превео на енглески језик прилоге Ивана Микулчића и Ђорђа Мано-Зисија а на српскохрватски закључке свих осталих чланака. Задовољство ми је да објавим његову савесну помоћ на различитим пословима приликом публиковања ове књиге укључујући техничку редакцију извршену у Београду. Овде репродуковане фотографије добијене су захваљујући неколицини чланова екипе: Том Илс, Сл. 3-22, 25, 91 и фронтиспис; Роберт Фолк, Сл. 26-29; Мерилин Хафман, Сл. 74, 84-85, 87-90; Ђорђе Мано-Зиси, све фотографије у чланку; Иван Микулчић, све илустрације у чланку; Жика Радошевић, Сл. 83; Ричард Тримбл, Сл. 1, 2, 30; Ал Везаловски, Сл. 66-73, 75-78; доле потписани уредник, Сл. 79, 81, 86. Коначна форма енглеских превода била је одговорност доле потписаног уредника, који је захвалан Каролини Снајвли на овом и другим пословима редакције. Много хвала на саветима и помоћи у вези разних рукописа Б. О. Дејвис и Луси Вајзман. Коначно, нарочито се захваљујем Тихи Најдовском, директору Народног музеја у Титовом Велесу и административном директору пројекта Стоби.

Остин, Тексас
јануара 1973.   Џејмс Р. Вајзман

STAFF OF THE STOBI PROJECT

ЧЛАНОВИ ЕКИПЕ ПРОЈЕКТА СТОБИ

Blaga Aleksova, Archaeological Museum, Skopje, 1970.
Stevo Andov, National Museum, Titov Veles, 1970—72.
Harriett Blitzer, Indiana University, 1971.
Duca Božović, University of Belgrade, 1972.
Marko Camaj, University of Skopje, 1972.
John Cherry, University of Texas at Austin, 1971—72.
Milorad Ćorluka, Conservation Institute of Macedonia, 1970.
Dorothy Crawford, Cambridge University, 1972.
Michael H. Crawford, Christ's College, Cambridge University, 1972.
Boško Damjanovski, Belgrade Academy of Arts, 1972.
Beth O. Davis, Austin, Texas, 1972.
E. Mott Davis, University of Texas at Austin, 1970—72.
Phyllis Della Croce, University of Texas at Austin, 1970.
Nina Dimčeva, Archaeological Museum, Skopje, 1970—71.
William B. Dinsmoor, Jr., Athenian Agora Excavations, Greece, 1970—71.
Tom Eals, University of Missouri, 1972.
Ranko Findrih, Serbian Conservation Institute, 1972.
Robert L. Folk, University of Texas at Austin, 1971.
Elizabeth Gebhard, University of Illinois at Chicago Circle, 1970—71.
Djordje Georgijevski, Conservation Institute of Macedonia, 1970—72.
Geraldine Gilligan, Tufts University, 1970—71.
Todor Gruev, National Museum, Titov Veles, 1970—72.
A. G. Grulich, University of Oregon, 1970.
Margie Grulich, Eugene, Oregon, 1970.
Marilyn Huffman, Denver, Colorado, 1971.
Paul Huffman, Denver, Colorado, 1971.

Radmila Ivanišević, National Museum, Prilep, 1971—72.
Apostol Keramidčiev, Archaeological Museum, Skopje, 1970—71.
Blagoja Kitanovski, National Museum, Prilep, 1971—72.
Ruth Kolarik, Harvard University, 1972.
Kiro Krstevski, Archaeological Museum, Skopje, 1970—72.
Clive Luke, University of Texas at Austin, 1972.
Djordje Mano-Zissi, National Museum, Belgrade, and University of Belgrade, 1970—72.
Virginia Anderson McKeen, University of Texas at Austin, 1971—72.
Ivan Mikulčić, University of Skopje, 1970—72.
Ankica Milošević, University of Belgrade, 1972.
Tihomir Najdovski, National Museum, Titov Veles, 1972.
James Parkey, University of Texas at Austin, 1971.
Sharon Parkey, Austin, Texas, 1971.
David B. Peck, Yale University, 1972.
Diane G. Peck, New Haven, Connecticut, 1972.
Eleonora Petrova, University of Skopje, 1972.
Momčilo Petrovski, Conservation Institute of Macedonia, 1972.
Thomas Poyner, University of Texas at Austin, 1970.
Nada Proeva, University of Belgrade, 1971—72.
Žika Radošević, University of Belgrade, 1970—72.
G. Kenneth Sams, University of North Carolina at Chapel Hill, 1972.
Saržo Saržovski, Conservation Institute of Macedonia, 1971.
Susan Schaffner, Bryn Mawr College, 1971.
Ellen C. Schwartz, Institute of Fine Arts, New York University, 1972.
Elizabeth Shropshire, University of Texas at Austin, 1970.
Timothy Shropshire, University of Texas at Austin, 1970.
Carolyn Snively, University of Texas at Austin, 1971—72.
Viktoria Sokolovska, Archaeological Museum, Skopje, 1970—71.
Veljo Tašovski, Academy of Arts, Ljubljana, 1972.
Richard Trimble, University of Texas at Austin, 1971.
Dragan Vergovski Alpi, Skopje Academy of Arts, 1972.
Marija Vinčić, Skopje Academy of Arts, 1970.
Živojin Vinčić, Conservation Institute of Macedonia, 1970.
Wendy Webb, State University of New York at Buffalo, 1970.
Al B. Wesolowsky, University of Texas at Austin, 1970—72.
James R. Wiseman, University of Texas at Austin, 1970—72.
Lucy Wiseman, Austin, Texas, 1970—72.
Paul Worman, Hampshire College, 1972.
Marija Zojeva, University of Skopje, 1971.

LIST OF ABBREVIATIONS
СПИСАК СКРАЋЕНИЦА

AA	Jahrbuch des deutschen archäologischen Instituts. Archäologischer Anzeiger.
AJA	American Journal of Archaeology.
AJP	American Journal of Philology.
AM	Mitteilungen des deutschen archäologischen Instituts. Athenische Abteilung.
BCH	Bulletin de correspondance héllenique.
BIABulg	Bulgarska akademia na naukite Sofia. Arkhelogicheski institut. Izvestiia Bulletin.
BRGK	Berichte der römisch-germanischen Kommission.
CIG	Corpus Inscriptionum Graecarum.
CIL	Corpus Inscriptionum Latinarum.
CISB	Atti del V Congresse Internazionale di Studi Bizantini.
CSHB	Corpus Scriptorum Historiae Byzantinae
DenkschrWien (phil hist Kl.)	K. Akademie der Wissenschaften, Wien. Philosophisch-historische Klasse. Denkschriften.
Der 6. Kongress	Bericht über den 6. Internationalen Kongress für Archäologie, Berlin 21—26 August, 1939.
DOPapers	Dumbarton Oaks Papers.
Glasnik	Glasnik Skopskog naučnog društva.
Glasnik Sarajevo	Glasnik zemaljskih muzeja u Sarajevu.
Godišnjak	Godišnjak Srpske Akademije Nauka.
IG	Inscriptiones Graecae.
IGRR	Inscriptiones Graecae ad Res Romanas Pertinentes.
JÖAI	Jahreshefte des österreichischen archäologischen Instituts.

Kitzinger, Survey	Kitzinger, E., "A Survey of the Early Christian Town of Stobi," *Dumbarton Oaks Papers* 3 (1946) 83—161.
MGRD	Papazoglu, Fanula, *Makedonski Gradovi u Rimsko Doba* (Skopje 1957).
MP	Kanatsoulis, Demetrios Konstantinos, Μακεδονική Προσοπογραφία (Thessalonica 1955).
MusN	American Numismatic Society Museum Notes.
NC	Numismatic Chronicle.
NE	Narodna enciklopedija srpsko-hrvatsko-slovenačka.
PIR	Prosopographia Imperii Romani.
RA	Revue archéologique.
RBN	Revue belge de numismatique.
RE	Pauly-Wissowa-Kroll, Real-Encyclopädie der Klassischen Altertumswissenschaft.
REG	Revue des études grecques.
RM	Mitteilungen des deutschen archäologischen Instituts. Römische Abteilung.
SEG	Supplementum Epigraphicum Graecum.
SIG³	Dittenberger, Wilhelm, *Sylloge Inscriptionum Graecarum* (1898).
Spomenik	Spomenik Srpske Akademije nauka.
Starinar	Starinar. Organ Srpskog arheološkog društva.
Wiseman, *Guide*	Wiseman, James, *Stobi. A Guide to the Excavations* (Beograd, 1973).
W-MZ (1971)	Wiseman, James, and Dj. Mano-Zissi, "Excavations at Stobi, 1970," *American Journal of Archaeology* 75 (1971) 395—411.
W-MZ (1972)	Wiseman, James, and Dj. Mano-Zissi, "Excavations at Stobi, 1971," *American Journal of Archaeology* 76 (1972) 407—424.
W-MZ (1973)	Wiseman, James, and Dj. Mano-Zissi, "Excavations at Stobi, 1972," *American Journal of Archaeology* 77 (1973). 391—403.
WJh	Wiener Jahreshefte.
Zbornik	Zbornik Narodnog Muzeja u Beogradu.
Zbornik Skopje	Godišen Zbornik na filozofskiot fakultet na univerzitetot vo Skopje.
ZNTW	Zeitschrift für die neutestamentliche Wissenschaft.
ŽA	Živa Antika.

THE STOBI HOARD OF ROMAN REPUBLICAN DENARII[1]

by

MICHAEL H. CRAWFORD

The hoard was found in 1971 in a pit in a gravelly deposit below where the Synagogue later stood.[2] It was contained in two ceramic vessels and consisted of one Athenian tetradrachm, one anonymous victoriatus[3] and 504 denarii. Of the Roman coins all were struck in Rome, except for one denarius struck in Sicily (no. 15) and eight denarii struck at uncertain Italian mints (nos. 16—17, 25—29 and 57). The distribution of the coins over the two pots (see List below) makes it clear that we are dealing with a single hoard. When found the coins, especially in the large pot, were congealed together by corrosion (Figs. 1 and 2); they were separated and cleaned and it is not now possible to say whether or not coins of the same date were close together in the hoard.

I

The hoard is typical, as far as composition goes, of Italian hoards of the same period (see note 4 below); it contains a very full representation

---

[1] I should like to express my warmest thanks to Professor James R. Wiseman for entrusting the publication of the hoard to me, not least because of the opportunity this provided of spending a most congenial month at Stobi.

[2] W-MZ (1972) 410—411; the gravelly deposit antedates the deposition of the hoard, on which see below. For the location, see Plan of Site, no. 4.

[3] This is struck on a broad flan and presumably passed as a denarius.

Figure 1. Coins as found in the larger of the two vessels (C-71-131) after removal of the (broken) neck of the jug.

of issues from 158 to 125 B. C., the closing date of the hoard, together with a sprinkling of earlier issues back to the start of the denarius coinage in 211 B. C. (these early issues, of course, did not arrive in Stobi till many years later); in the period 158 to 125 B. C. only a few very rare issues are not represented. The issue of M. Porcius Laeca, the latest in the hoard, is under-represented, which is not surprising in the case of an issue that only just got into the hoard.

As far as the Republican coinage is concerned, the hoard confirms the chronological conclusions which may be drawn from the Riccia, Maserà and San Giovanni Incarico hoards.[4] The Athenian tetradrachm stands by itself and it is impossible to say after its cleaning whether the degree of wear which it displays supports the high or the low dating of

---

[4] M. H. Crawford, *Roman Republican Coinage* (Cambridge 1973) pp. 47 and 55—65.

Figure 2. Congealed mass of coins from the larger vessel.

the Athenian new-style coinage.[5] I regard the low chronology as preferable on other grounds and would date the tetradrachm to the 120s rather than 153/2 B. C.[6]

Two coins are particularly interesting. No. 78 is an anonymous denarius with Victory in biga as reverse; the head of Roma on the

---

[5] See D. M. Lewis, "The Chronology of the Athenian New Style Coinage," *NC* 2 (1962) 275—300; Margaret Thompson, "Athens Again," *NC* 2 (1962) 301—333; M. J. Price, "The New Style Coinage of Athens: Some Evidence from the Bronze Issues," *NC* 4 (1964) 27—36; Tony Hackens and Edmond Levy, "Trésor hellénistique trouvé à Délos en 1964," *BCH* 89 (1965) 503—566; Margaret Thompson, "A Hoard from Northern Greece," *MusN* 12 (1966) 57—63; M. J. Price, "Greek Coin Hoards in the British Museum," *NC* 9 (1969) 1—14; Harold B. Mattingly, review of Margaret Thompson, *The Agrinion Hoard* (Numismatic Notes and Monographs No. 159, New York, 1967), *NC* 9 (1969) 325—333.

[6] The coin must be no. 540f in Margaret Thompson, *The New Style Silver Coinage of Athens* (New York 1961); cf. W—MZ (1972) 410, note 17.

obverse has a necklace of pendants, not beads, a variant previously not known to me. This decorative feature is not otherwise attested before the issue of C. Titinius and the question must be raised whether or not

Anonymous coins with Victory in biga

Figure 3. Coin 63. Figure 4. Coin 78.

this anonymous piece (and perhaps a few others) belongs later than the main block of anonymous Victory in biga denarii.[7]

Issues of L. Opeimius

Figure 5. Coin 419. Figure 6. Coin 425.

No. 425 is a denarius of L. Opeimius with a quite aberrant style. In the period to which the issue of L. Opeimius belongs, there were two engravers working, each responsible for the whole of one out of two series.[8] The coin in question displays the style of the other series than that to which the issue of L. Opeimius belongs; the stylistic cross-fertilization involved confirms the view that the two series are parallel and not successive.

---

[7] See *Roman Republican Coinage*, no. 197 with p. 54; the evidence of the hoards makes it clear that the main block of anonymous denarii with Victory in biga comes at the beginning of the Roman resumption of the production of a silver coinage in the early 150s.

[8] *Roman Republican Coinage*, pp. 62—65.

II

Paeonia, the area in which Stobi is situated, was definitively part of Macedonia from 217 B.C.;[9] the population was presumably largely Paeonian, with a Macedonian admixture; it was doubtless becoming Hellenized through the reigns of Philip V and Perseus. In 168 B.C. there was evidently also a category of population, Gallic and Illyrian in origin, without political rights.[10]

Issues of C. Cassius

Figure 7. Coin 487.   Figure 8. Coin 488.

Figure 9. Coin 489.   Figure 10. Coin 490.

Figure 11. Coin 491.   Figure 12. Coin 492.

Figure 13. Coin 493.

---

[9] Polybius v. 97; cf. Livy xxxiii.19 for the defeat of marauding Dardani in this area. Stobi was the frontier town to the territory of the Dardani in the Roman settlement of Macedonia in 168; for Paeonia and Dardania see the basic study of J. G. Droysen, *Kleine Schriften* I, 48—79 (still localizing Stobi too far to the north).
[10] Livy xlv.30.5.

Issues of T. Quinctius

Figure 14. Coin 494.

Figure 15. Coin 495.

Figure 16. Coin 496.

Figure 17. Coin 497.

The area as a whole was not unused to silver coinage; the Paeonian kings had struck an extensive silver coinage from 359 B. C. into the third century. A large hoard of these coins was found before 1969, presumably in the area of Stobi.[11] Later silver hoards from the area are also known.[12]

Issue of N. Fabius Pictor

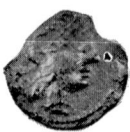 

Figure 18. Coin 498.

Issue of C. Metellus

Figure 19. Coin 499.

It is surprising, however, to find a large hoard of Republican silver coins at Stobi.[13] One can only guess that its owner was in contact with

---

[11] Sale catalogue of Sotheby and Co. of April 16, 1969; the hoard also included gold and silver of Macedonia, of Philip II, Alexander III, and Philip III.

[12] See Sidney P. Noe, *An Inventory of Greek Coin Hoards*, Numismatic Notes and Monographs No. 78 (New York, 3rd ed.) nos. 399, 447, 448; note also the following hoards or parts of hoards: Alexander and Lysimachus tetradrachms with Athenian new-style tetradrachms in Prilep Museum, Alexander tetradrachms in Bitola Museum, silver of Apollonia and Dyrrhachium in Ohrid Museum.

[13] The Bitola and Ohrid Museums contain only a few worn Republican denarii, which presumably arrived in the area during the Empire; there is a small

Greece, as a trader or mercenary or pirate — the first possibility is perhaps the least likely.[14] The evidence from Greece for Republican coins circulating in the second century B. C. is increasing; apart from

Issues of M. Porcius Laeca

Figure 20. Coin 500.   Figure 21. Coin 501.

the Kalaureia and Agrinion hoards, there is now a single denarius from a hoard from Thebes and a small hoard of denarii from Naupactus.[15] As remarked above, the Stobi hoard is absolutely typical of Italian hoards of the same period and presumably derives ultimately from a lot taken from circulation in Italy in the 120s and brought across the Adriatic to Greece and then, exceptionally and by chance, to Stobi.

III

The latest coins in the hoard are of 125 B. C. and I believe that the hoard was deposited not long thereafter. The latest coins show little sign of wear (see Figures 7—21, nos. 487—501) and although it is conceivable that the hoard was kept in Stobi for a long time without circulating, I do not regard this as very likely.[16] The area was used to silver coinage and four denarii were the equivalent of an Attic tetradrachm; one of these was in the hoard and their weight standard was that to which the area was accustomed.

---

hoard of denarii going down to 48 B. C. from 15 km. south of Stobi, clearly to be associated with the Civil War between Caesar and Pompey (information from A. Keramidčiev).

[14] For Macedonians as mercenaries with Rome see G. T. Griffith, *The Mercenaries of the Hellenistic World* (Cambridge University Press 1935) 234—235; note also the Macedonian propensity for piracy in the time of Philip II, H. A. Ormerod, *Piracy in the Ancient World* (Liverpool and London 1924) 117—119.

[15] Tony Hackens, "Le Trésor de Thèbes 1965," *BCH* 93 (1969) 712—729; Manto Karamesine-Oikonomidis, "Νομισματικὴ ϲυλλογὴ 'Αθηνῶν," *Archaiologikon Deltion* 23 (1968) B 1, 12—15.

[16] The present low weight of some pieces is the result of cleaning.

The burial of the hoard was in an area of at least local destruction.[17] Paeonia under the Romans seems in normal times to have been regarded

Athenian tetradrachm

Figure 22. Coin 506.

as a peaceful area; it was the only one of the four Macedonian regions not allowed a militia in 168 B. C., on the grounds that it did not have hostile neighbours.[18] It is tempting, therefore, to associate the non-recovery of the hoard with the raid of the Scordisci in 119 B. C. which was finally repelled in this area.[19]

LIST

The following list gives for each coin a running number, name of magistrate, reference to M. H. Crawford, *Roman Republican Coinage*, excavation inventory number and weight; it should be noted that all coins were weighed after cleaning and that many coins have pieces broken off (cf. note 16 above). Excavation inventory numbers 709 to 775 cover the coins in the small pot, 776 to 1215 the coins in the large pot. Coins marked * are illustrated at a scale of 1:1 in Figs. 3 to 22.

| 1 | Anonymous | 44/5 | 1092 | 3,55 |
| 2 | Anonymous | 44/5 | 1203 | 2,96 |

[17] W—MZ (1972) 411. I am not convinced that the equine remains have anything to do with the hoard.

[18] Livy xlv. 29. 14; the neighbours were the Dardani.

[19] *SIG*³, no. 700; W—MZ (1972) 411, note 20. The arguments of H. B. Mattingly, *NC* 9 (1969) 331—332 for Amphilochian rather than Macedonian Argos as the site of the decisive battle involve some very special pleading.

3	Anchor	50/2	858	3,48
4	Anonymous	53/2	1039	4,05
5		53/2	1159	3,78
6		53/2	1201	3,49
7		53/2	1107	3,44
8		53/2	1065	3,20
9		53/2	805	3,02
10		53/2	1186	3,02
11		53/2	969	2,82
12	— subsidiary variety	54/1	1137	2,32
13	Crescent	57/2	741	3,94
14	Cornucopiae	58/2	1000	3,68
15	Corn-ear	72/3	993	3,61
16	C	107/1 b	998	3,49
17	Wreath	110/1	798	3,65
18	Star	113/1	729	3,08
19		113/1	1108	3,00
20	*Rostrum tridens*	114/1	721	3,39
21		114/1	825	3,29
22	Rudder	117A/1	811	3,56
23		117A/1	796	3,22
24	Dog	122/2	1157	1,75
25	QLC	125/1	930	3,66
26	Pentagram	129/1	734	3,40
27		129/1	1168	2,66
28	Staff and feather	130/1	1177	3,48
29		130/1	772	2,92
30	Owl	135/1	723	3,68
31	Annius or Aurelius	136/1	854	3,41
32	Anonymous	139/1	1084	3,56
33		139/1	916	3,49
34		139/1	1126	3,44
35		139/1	1048	3,40
36		139/1	968	3,28
37		139/1	980	3.09
38		139/1	1095	2,93
39	Cn. Domitius	147/1	1070	3,49
40		147/1	986	2,45
41	Sx. Q	152/1 b	961	3,45
42		152/1 c	727	3,45

43	Cn. Calpurnius	153/1	927	3,56
44	L. Coilius	154/1	761	3,57
45		154/1	823	3,38
46	Prawn	156/1	997	3,51
47	Matienus	162/2 a	791	3,05
48		162/2 a	926	2,71
49	Feather	163/1	866	2,89
50	Anonymous	164/1 a	833	2,79
51		164/1 a	1160	2,63
52	Anchor	165/1 b	972	3,31
53	Anonymous victoriatus	166/1	1113	2,65
54	Anonymous denarius	167/1	795	3,34
55		167/1	1209	2,96
56		167/1	1205	1,70
57	D	171/1	1119	2,54
58	Gryphon	182/1	1178	3,77
59	Purpureo	187/1	1195	3,84
60		187/1	1162	3,62
61		187/1	1187	3,45
62		187/1	1143	3,22
63 *	Anonymous with Victory in biga	197/1 a	1071	3,87
64		197/1 a	934	3,73
65		197/1 a	730	3,64
66		197/1 a	846	3,57
67		197/1 a	1097	3,44
68		197/1 a	1066	3,36
69		197/1 a	1110	3,36
70		197/1 a	1018	3,34
71		197/1 a	899	3,30
72		197/1 a	1127	3,10
73		197/1 a	819	3,02
74		197/1 a	1151	2,69
75		197/1 a	1194	2,62
76		197/1 a	943	2,49
77		197/1 a	1206	2,42
78 *		197/1 a var.	808	3,75
79	Anonymous with Dioscuri	198/1	1083	3,63
80		198/1	828	3,48
81		198/1	1179	2,44
82	Saranus	199/1 a	814	3,74

83		199/1 a	996	3,40
84		199/1 a	931	2,96
85	Natta	200/1	1085	3,64
86		200/1	1031	3,59
87		200/1	994	3,54
88		200/1	870	3,46
89		200/1	1086	3,41
90		200/1	1026	3,30
91		200/1	1153	3,27
92		200/1	792	3,26
93		200/1	1128	3,16
94	C. Scribonius	201/1	759	3,88
95		201/1	829	3,71
96		201/1	1081	3,63
97		201/1	764	3,60
98		201/1	1014	3,39
99		201/1	735	3,36
100		201/1	884	2,87
101		201/1	1067	2,19
102		201/1	1170	1,73
103	C. Talna	202/1 a	1035	3,75
104		202/1 a	780	3,54
105		202/1 a	978	2,89
106	C. Maianius	203/1 a	768	3,70
107		203/1 a	1045	3,51
108		203/1 a	933	3,45
109		203/1 a	1003	3,44
110		203/1 a	839	3,29
111		203/1 a	990	3,25
112		203/1 a	1117	3,08
113		203/1 a	900	2,97
114		203/1 a	1025	2,94
115		203/1 a	1181	2,90
116		203/1 a	1115	2,33
117	L. Saufeius	204/1	751	3,65
118		204/1	758	3,60
119		204/1	778	3,49
120		204/1	1147	3,39
121		204/1	1184	3,34
122		204/1	918	3,33

123		204/1	793	3,31
124		204/1	1078	2,98
125		204/1	906	2,91
126		204/1	1123	2,46
127		204/1	1211	1,50
128	P. Sula	205/1	977	3,67
129		205/1	940	3,66
130		205/1	963	3,46
131		205/1	746	3,39
132		205/1	910	3,17
133		205/1	843	3,15
134		205/1	1174	3,04
135		205/1	781	2,03
136		205/1	1068	1,73
137	Safra	206/1	713	3,93
138		206/1	1030	3,59
139		206/1	975	3,29
140		206/1	1091	3,05
141	Flaus	207/1	709	4,11
142		207/1	765	3,69
143		207/1	1138	3,66
144		207/1	782	3,46
145		207/1	748	3,36
146		207/1	952	3,25
147		207/1	1058	3,03
148		207/1	893	2,91
149	Natta	208/1	1074	3,75
150		208/1	1079	3,62
151		208/1	788	3,56
152		208/1	932	3,47
153		208/1	1207	3,42
154		208/1	821	3,38
155		208/1	988	3,06
156		208/1	1077	2,98
157	C. Iunius C.f.	210/1	1088	3,59
158		210/1	1158	3,58
159		210/1	745	3,37
160		210/1	911	3,28
161		210/1	959	3,22
162		210/1	1185	2,74

163	M. Atilius Saranus	214/1 b	890	3,68
164		214/1 b	1142	2,72
165	Q. Marcius Libo	215/1	877	3,08
166		215/1	1140	3,00
167		215/1	1112	2,81
168		215/1	991	2,67
169		215/1	1172	2,51
170	L. Sempronius Pitio	216/1	1155	3,77
171		216/1	999	3,48
172		216/1	912	3,43
173		216/1	938	3,21
174		216/1	976	2,86
175		216/1	889	1,81
176	C. Terentius Lucanus	217/1	1089	3,89
177		217/1	1193	3,65
178		217/1	954	3,57
179		217/1	929	3,54
180		217/1	919	3,46
181		217/1	1135	3,10
182		217/1	1101	2,93
183		217/1	861	2,43
184		217/1	1036	2,19
185	L. Cupiennius	218/1	953	3,74
186		218/1	804	3,54
187		218/1	830	3,54
188		218/1	987	2,47
189		218/1	1034	2,34
190	C. Antestius	219/1 a	984	3,41
191		219/1 a	718	2,55
192		219/1 a	1111	1,74
193		219/1 d	797	3,29
194		219/1 e	946	3,96
195		219/1 e	747	3,48
196		219/1 e	970	3,42
197		219/1 e	1200	3,42
198		219/1 e	971	3,33
199		219/1 e	855	3,32
200		219/1 e	1037	3,26
201		219/1 e	710	3,03
202		219/1 e	1189	2,99

203		219/1 e	719	2,94
204		219/1 e	967	2,91
205		219/1 e	1152	2,66
206		219/1 e	1114	2,59
207		219/1 e	754	2,56 (plated)
208		219/1 e	1043	2,41
209	M. Iunius	220/1	1082	3,77
210		220/1	763	3,56
211		220/1	748	3,49
212		220/1	818	3,33
213		220/1	733	3,08
214	Annius Rufus	221/1	901	2,82
215		221/1	1164	2,66
216	Anonymous	222/1	834	3,65
217		222/1	1050	3,36
218		222/1	913	3,22
219	C. Curiatius Trigeminus	223/1	742	3,75
220		223/1	752	3,73
221		223/1	847	3,50
222		223/1	820	3,38
223		223/1	1198	3,33
224		223/1	1053	3,08
225	L. Iulius	224/1	989	3,67
226		224/1	1041	3,51
227		224/1	1016	3,29
228	C. Valerius C. f. Flaccus	228/1 a	1076	3,44
229		228/1 a	1060	1,96
230		228/1 b	957	3,65
231		228/1 b	789	3,60
232	A. Spurilius	230/1	924	3,72
233	C. Renius	231/1	1180	3,85
234		231/1	728	3,80
235		231/1	1100	3,78
236		231/1	896	3,72
237		231/1	992	3,71
238		231/1	1094	3,69
239		231/1	1087	3,64
240		231/1	1072	3,62
241		231/1	1006	3,53

242		231/1	1202	3,53
243		231/1	787	3,49
244		231/1	1163	3,45
245		231/1	1167	3,44
246		231/1	806	3,40
247		231/1	1129	3,31
248		231/1	905	3,30
249		231/1	941	3,27
250		231/1	1132	3,27
251		231/1	873	3,25
252		231/1	882	3,20
253		231/1	803	3,15
254		231/1	1012	3,09
255		231/1	786	2,93
256		231/1	1171	2,67
257	Cn. Gellius	232/1	842	3,66
258		232/1	875	3,63
259		232/1	1080	3,61
260		232/1	1075	3,58
261		232/1	886	3,55
262		232/1	840	3,41
263		232/1	785	2,55
264	P. Paetus	233/1	753	3,82
265		233/1	826	3,47
266		233/1	979	3,41
267		233/1	1125	3,32
268		233/1	903	3,03
269	Ti. Veturius	234/1	923	3,69
270		234/1	1049	3,55
271		234/1	949	3,51
272		234/1	964	3,35
273		234/1	1033	3,26
274		234/1	799	3,24
275		234/1	1054	3,05
276		234/1	1010	2,63
277	Sex. Pompeius	235/1 c	731	3,93
278		235/1 c	1146	3,84
279		235/1 c	942	3,78
280		235/1 c	1182	3,67
281		235/1 c	922	3,55

282		235/1 c	1150	3,47
283		235/1 c	1148	3,30
284		235/1 c	874	3,10
285	(SEX. PMO)	235/1 b	1196	3,03
286	M. Baebius Q. f. Tampilus	236/1	773	3,97
287		236/1	1197	3,80
288		236/1	1042	3,67
289		236/1	1191	3,61
290		236/1	1047	3,56
291		236/1	947	3,52
292		236/1	1020	3,40
293		236/1	1169	3,26
294		236/1	1064	3,03
295		236/1	1144	2,79
296		236/1	848	3,61
297		236/1	770	3,82
298		236/1	1099	3,77
299		236/1	1190	3,74
300		236/1	917	3,67
301		236/1	740	3,64
302		236/1	974	3,63
303		236/1	1102	3,62
304		236/1	1120	3,62
305		236/1	831	3,61
306		236/1	985	3,59
307		236/1	774	3,53
308		236/1	894	3,50
309		236/1	904	3,39
310		236/1	813	3,27
311		236/1	887	3,22
312		236/1	1011	2,97
313		236/1	960	2,95
314		236/1	908	2,79
315		236/1	883	2,36
316		236/1	1017	1,44
317	Cn. Lucretius Trio	237/1 a	915	3,83
318		237/1 a	1023	3,79
319		237/1 a	1141	3,69
320		237/1 a	1173	3,68
321		237/1 a	807	3,60

322		237/1 a	937	3,57
323		237/1 a	824	3,52
324		237/1 a	862	3,46
325		237/1 a	878	3,46
326		237/1 a	1001	3,23
327		237/1 a	1032	3,09
328		237/1 a	1059	2,97
329		237/1 a	1149	1,92
330	L. Antestius Gragulus	238/1	945	3,75
331		238/1	920	3,72
332		238/1	812	3,70
333		238/1	925	3,64
334		238/1	836	3,63
335		238/1	845	3,56
336		238/1	857	3,51
337		238/1	1002	3,43
338		238/1	1093	3,42
339		238/1	838	3,38
340		238/1	771	3,30
341		238/1	869	3,30
342		238/1	810	3,27
343		238/1	939	3,22
344		238/1	879	3,16
345		238/1	876	3,15
346		238/1	1130	3,09
347		238/1	956	3,05
348	C. Serveilius M. f.	239/1	1044	3,72
349		239/1	950	3,71
350		239/1	849	3,54
351		239/1	783	2,87
352		239/1	757	2,17
353		239/1	1161	1,84
354	C. Curiatius f. Trigeminus	240/1 a	1051	3,81
355		240/1 a	852	3,33
356	(TRIGE)	240/1 b	895	3,65
357	L. Trebanius	241/1 a	844	3,62
358		241/1 a	856	3,44
359	C. Augurinus	242/1	801	3,79
360		242/1	1124	3,61
361		242/1	1098	3,15

362		242/1	1057	3,12
363	Ti. Minucius C. f. Augurinus	243/1	809	3,86
364		243/1	951	3,86
365		243/1	995	3,69
366		243/1	756	3,67
367		243/1	850	3,64
368		243/1	1183	3,51
369		243/1	860	3,49
370		243/1	732	3,47
371		243/1	891	3,41
372		243/1	863	3,16
373	C. Aburius Geminus	244/1	966	3,71
374		244/1	914	3,63
375		244/1	892	3,61
376		244/1	717	3,55
377		244/1	1204	3,45
378		244/1	1029	3,38
379		244/1	711	2,98
380		244/1	1013	2,41
381	M. Marcius Mn. f.	245/1	762	3,72
382		245/1	1046	3,14
383		245/1	1162	2,70
384		245/1	1038	2,59
385		245/1	880	2,52
386	P. Calpurnius	247/1	1073	3,37
387	L. Minucius	248/1	716	3,78
388		248/1	864	3,67
389		248/1	1056	3,47
390		248/1	1106	3,29
391		248/1	907	2,96
392		248/1	1005	2,93
393		248/1	955	2,12
394	P. Maenius Antiaticus M. f.	249/1	1104	3,89
395		249/1	775	3,78
396		249/1	1027	3,77
397		249/1	841	3,72
398		249/1	769	3,68
399		249/1	921	3,60
400	(brockage)	249/1	1192	3,58
401		249/1	1105	3,46

402		249/1	777	3,30
403		249/1	1062	3,30
404		249/1	1199	2,96
405		249/1	881	2,48
406	M. Aburius Geminus	250/1	958	3,78
407		250/1	1154	3,72
408		250/1	794	3,65
409		250/1	1136	3,41
410		250/1	1103	2,76
411		250/1	1212	0,62
412	L. Postumius Albinus	252/1	715	3,40
413		252/1	1061	2,83 (plated)
414		252/1	1131	2,22
415		252/1	779	2,14
416		252/1	776	1,49
417		252/1	1069	1,71
418	L. Opeimius	253/1	888	3,71
419 *		253/1	897	3,69
420		253/1	1176	3,44
421		253/1	928	3,41
422		253/1	1139	3,25
423		253/1	1133	3,07
424		253/1	871	1,65
425 *		253/1 var.	1096	3,55
426	M. Opeimius	254/1	724	3,86
427		254/1	790	3,80
428		254/1	885	3,51
429		254/1	867	2,89
430		254/1	1118	2,62
431	M. Acilius M. f.	255/1	750	3,83
432		255/1	962	3,69
433		255/1	851	3,61
434		255/1	822	3,56
435		255/1	973	3,48
436		255/1	983	3,32
437		255/1	1055	3,31
438		255/1	720	2,91 (plated)
439	Q. Metellus	256/1	744	3,80

440		256/1	982	3,53
441		256/1	1109	2,48
442		256/1	868	2,02
443	M. Vargunteius	257/1	816	3,75
444		257/1	1188	3,45
445		257/1	817	3,02
446		257/1	872	3,00
447		257/1	760	2,73
448		257/1	853	2,59
449	Q. Pilipus	259/1	1165	3,92
450		259/1	935	3,91
451		259/1	749	3,80
452		259/1	815	3,72
453		259/1	832	3,69
454		259/1	898	3,52
455		259/1	737	3,49
456		259/1	755	2,68
457		259/1	1156	2,33
458	T. Cloulius	260/1	743	3,83
459		260/1	827	3,60
460		260/1	859	3,25
461		260/1	865	3,14
462		260/1	981	3,07
463		260/1	1015	3,04
464		260/1	1024	2,96
465		260/1	726	1,93
466		260/1	1009	1,43
467		260/1	1121	1,00
468	Cn. Domitius	261/1	944	3,89
469		261/1	1052	3,74
470		261/1	1122	3,70
471		261/1	738	3,45
472		261/1	1022	3,45
473		261/1	712	3,29
474		261/1	909	2,49
475	Anonymous with elephant's head	262/1	965	3,67
476		262/1	739	3,25
477	M. Metellus Q. f.	263/1	1145	3,90
478		263/1	1019	2,68
479		263/1	1007	2,55

480	C. Serveilius	264/1	1166	3,68
481		264/1	802	3,66
482		264/1	1175	2,41
483	Q. Maximus	265/1	722	3,82
484		265/1	714	3,81
485		265/1	725	3,52
486		265/1	1004	3,45
487 *	C. Cassius	266/1	948	3,77
488 *		266/1	736	3,69
489 *		266/1	835	3,51
490 *		266/1	902	3,37
491 *		266/1	767	3,25
492 *		266/1	1134	2,94
493 *		266/1	1213	1,29
494 *	T. Quinctius	267/1	800	3,93
495 *		267/1	1090	3,85
496 *		267/1	837	3,45
497 *		267/1	1021	3,17
498 *	N. Fabius Pictor	268/1 a	1008	2,67
499 *	C. Metellus	269/1	1028	3,61
500 *	M. Porcius Laeca	270/1	936	3,62
501 *		270/1	1040	2,36
502	Uncertain early Dioscuri denarius		766	1,64
503			1063	1,36
504			1214	0,98
505			1215	0,90
506 *	Athenian tetradrachm (see note 6)		1208	15,13

The hoard contains in addition five tiny fragments of Dioscuri denarii, doubtless broken off coins listed above.

ОСТАВА РИМСКИХ РЕПУБЛИКАНСКИХ ДЕНАРА ПРОНАЂЕНА У СТОБИМА

МАЈКЛ КРОФОРД

Ова остава састоји се од једне атинске тетрадрахме, једног викторијатуса и 504 денара. Остава не потиче од новца који је у нормалним приликама циркулисао у овој области током другог века пре н. е. Оставу треба сматрати хрпом сребрњака која се овде нашла изузетно и случајно, и која потиче из Грчке односно Италије. Губитак оставе може се повезати са пустошењима Скордиска 119. године пре н. е.

RADIOCARBON DATES FROM STOBI: 1971 SEASON[1]

by

E. MOTT DAVIS, DUŠAN SRDOČ, and S. VALASTRO, Jr.

During the 1971 season at Stobi, 38 samples of charcoal and wood were collected for radiocarbon analysis. Of these, eleven were selected for age determinations.

Many of the samples were large enough to be divided in two, and in these cases one part was sent to the radiocarbon dating laboratory of the Rudjer Bošković Institute in Zagreb (hereafter referred to as the Zagreb laboratory) and the other part to the laboratory of The University of Texas at Austin (the Austin laboratory). The dating thus served the needs of both the Stobi Project and the dating laboratories, since in the latter case it provided cross-checks between different counting systems: proportional counting of methane at Zagreb and liquid scintillation counting of benzene at Austin.

The purpose of this paper is to present the dates from the 1971 season, to discuss agreements and discrepancies between the measurements made by the two laboratories, to examine the significance of the

---

[1] The radiocarbon measurements reported here were accomplished by research teams at the two laboratories involved: at Rudjer Bošković, by Dušan Srdoč (in charge), Josip Planinić, Branko Breyer, Adela Sliepčević, Bogomil Obelić, and Elvira Hernaus; at the University of Texas at Austin, by S. Valastro, Jr. (in charge), Alejandra Varela, and Teresia Lopez-Cepero. The actual writing of this report was done by E. Mott Davis, aided by frequent discussions with personnel of both laboratories and of the archaeological staff of the Stobi Project.

dates in the light of the archaeological evidence and *vice versa*, and to suggest directions for future dating work at Stobi.

The areas and structures cited in this article may be located on the Plan of the Site at the end of this volume.

COLLECTION

An organized plan to collect radiocarbon samples was drawn up late in the 1971 season when it became apparent that radiocarbon dating might help solve some of the chronological problems at the site. Arrangements were made to have dating done at the Zagreb and Austin laboratories, and the staff at Stobi was instructed as to proper collecting procedures. A number of samples had already been collected, and in these cases the methods of collection varied, but in most cases the dates do not appear to have been significantly affected by the collecting procedures, as will appear in the following discussion. The matter is examined here to validate the dates and to provide readers with guidelines for collecting samples.

In most cases the Stobi samples were of charcoal; a few were of wood. Most of them were collected by hand or with small tools. In hand collection, body oils may adhere to the specimen and could make a date falsely recent, but such oils are usually removed in laboratory pre-treatment. In the cases where Stobi radiocarbon dates are younger than the corresponding archaeological dates it is possible that hand collection played a part in the discrepancies, but since some hand-collected samples produced dates older than the archaeological dates, laboratory procedures seem to have been adequate for removing such contaminants.

The samples were stored in polyethylene bags, and in most cases were sealed immediately. When they were opened later for inspection, some were found to be moist, and were dried to prevent formation of mold that would cause modern contamination. Ideally, they should have been dried at the time of collection, and in a few cases this procedure was followed in the field by leaving the bag open to the wind during the day. This is not a desirable practice, because modern dust is a possible contaminant. Laboratory pre-treatment can ordinarily be expected to eliminate dust, but it is best to avoid the dust problem as much as possible. It may be significant that in every case where Stobi samples were dried in the wind (certain samples from the West Cemetery) the radiocarbon dates tend to be more recent than the archaeological dates.

SELECTION

At the end of the season the samples at hand were reviewed in terms of their amount, quality, archaeological significance, and the need for the dates. The selection of eleven samples for dating took into account a number of problems concerning the use of radiocarbon dates, which will be reviewed here.

To date an archaeological context, four or five radiocarbon samples should be counted. A single date is not an adequate basis for establishing the age of a context because the "date" is in reality only a statement of probability concerning a time range (often more than a hundred years) rather than being a specific statement of a finite age. If a number of specimens can be dated rather than one, the age of the context becomes much more certain. In the dates reviewed here only the Episcopal Basilica has a group of samples. The present series, therefore, must be regarded as preliminary.

There are a number of variables, beyond those already mentioned, that can cause discrepancies between radiocarbon ages and actual ages. Principal among these, as far as the present series of dates is concerned, is the possibility of intrusion of older or younger material into the sample as it lies in the ground. Laboratory pre-treatment is designed to remove routine contaminants such as rootlets and humates, just as it is intended to eliminate the oils and dust previously mentioned. If there is a good chance that other contaminants are present, it is best not to date the sample at all. As yet, we have not seen signs of significant contamination of this sort in samples from Stobi, but the possibility is always present and every precaution must be taken in field and laboratory.

Uncertainties such as these make it evident that at a site such as Stobi other dating methods are often more appropriate than the radiocarbon technique: methods such as the use of ceramic or architectural styles for which the time ranges are already known, or even more specific evidences such as coins, or inscriptions that include dates.

Finally there is the matter of archaeological association, a problem that radiocarbon samples share with all other kinds of chronological evidence in archaeology, and one that is of vital importance in selecting samples for dating and in interpreting the dates once they have been determined. If, for example, charcoal is dated from the ruins of a building such as the Episcopal Basilica at Stobi, one might assume in appraising the results that the original wood was part of the building. However, it is also possible, and the possibility must be examined, that the charcoal represents a later intrusion, not related to the structure. Further, if the wood was indeed part of the building, some effort should be made to determine whether the date applies to inner rings from the youth of the tree, or outer rings from the time it was cut and used in construction. In the dates from the Episcopal Basilica it appears that the dates are from inner rings, as will be seen.

The dating of burials provides another instance of associational problems. When a burial is dated there should be evidence that the material collected for dating is directly related to the interment, since otherwise it is possible that the material was included in the earth used to fill the grave and thus could be appreciably older than the burial itself. Special care has been taken with this problem in the samples from the West Cemetery at Stobi.

Problems of this sort are familiar in archaeology, but they are sometimes ignored when material is collected and submitted to a radiocarbon laboratory, as if the magic of radiocarbon might somehow eliminate the troublesome intricacies of archaeological association and dating. Unfortunately, radiocarbon dating does not solve chronological problems by itself. A radiocarbon "date" should be taken only for what it is, a measurement of C^{14} content in relation to C^{12}. It does not really become a *date* until it is viewed in the light of the archaeological information on which it bears.

THE DATES

The basic data on the eleven samples from the 1971 season are presented here, and the dates are expressed graphically in Fig. 23. A discussion follows this listing. Except where otherwise noted, all samples are of charcoal and were collected by hand and put in polyethylene bags for storage.

In the listing, numbers beginning with R- or MF- are the identification numbers of the samples in the inventory of the Stobi Project. Sample numbers beginning with Z- are catalog numbers given samples by the Zagreb laboratory, and numbers beginning with Tx- are Austin laboratory sample numbers. Ages are calculated before A. D. 1950 and time ranges are within one standard deviation (1σ); that is, the chance is 67% that the radiocarbon age falls somewhere within the range indicated, and 33% that it is outside that range.

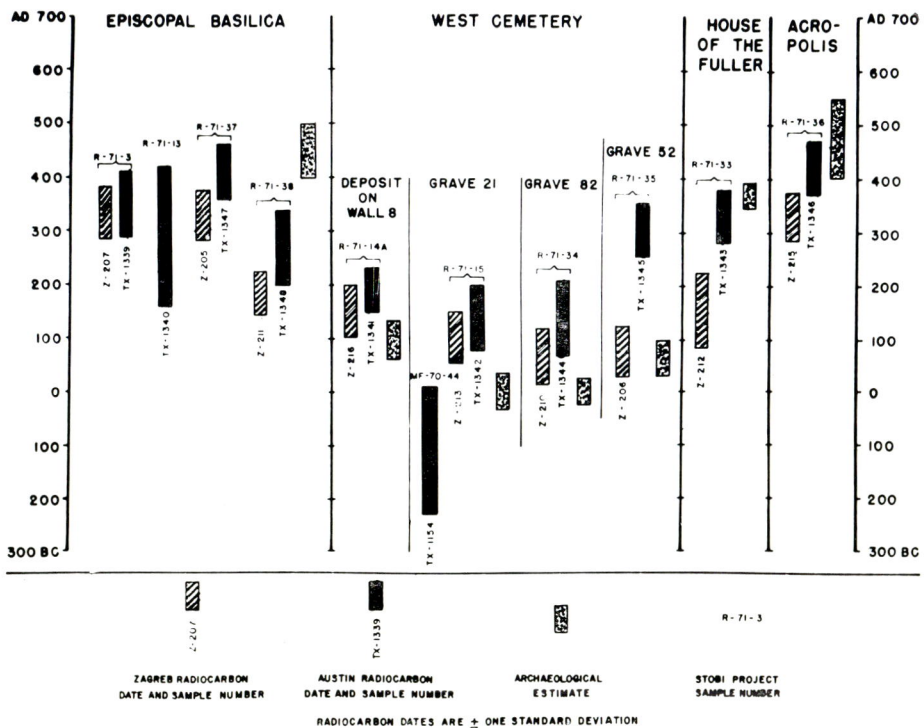

Figure 23. Chart of Radiocarbon dates at Stobi, 1971. Drawing by B. O. Davis.

THE EPISCOPAL BASILICA

R-71-3. EB S Stairway, W Extension; above Steps 2, 3, 4 of S Stairway; later than final destruction of building.
 Z-207: 1617±49; A. D. 284—382
 Tx-1339: 1600±60; A. D. 290—410
R-71-13. EB S Stairway, E Extension 5; W of Wall 9, S of Wall 2, E of Wall 5; below destruction fill, above latest floor; relates to latest use of basilica.
 No Zagreb date.
 Tx-1340: 1660±130; A. D. 160—420
R-71-37. EB S Stairway, N area of E Extension 5; from Wall 5 to and

beyond Wall 13. Burned timber from final layer of destruction fill in this area above latest earth floor.

    Z-205:   1619±46;   A. D. 285—377
    Tx-1347: 1540±50;   A. D. 360—460

R-71-38. EB Baptistery; from deposit above NE and NW parts of mosaic floor encircling piscina.

    Z-211:   1767±43;   A. D. 144—226
    Tx-1348: 1680±70;   A. D. 200—340

THE WEST CEMETERY

R-71-14 A. W Cem, S Trench, N and E parts; from zone resting on Wall 8, with abundant pottery of first and second centuries A. C. Stored damp in polyethylene bag for three weeks, then dried.

    Z-216:   1778±47;   A. D. 105—199
    Tx-1341: 1760±40;   A. D. 150—230

MF-70-44. W Cem, S Trench, Grave 21, fill from west part; vegetal materials from cremation associated with grave goods including terracotta figurines, unguentaria, pottery; ca. 30 B. C. to A. D. 30—40. Collected 1970, with trowel.

    No Zagreb date.
    Tx-1154: 2060±120;   230 B. C. — A. D. 10

R-71-15. Nuts from east part of Grave 21, as above. Collected 1971. Wrapped in tissue, placed in polyethylene bag; tissue removed three weeks later.

    Z-213:   1848±48;   A. D. 54—150
    Tx-1342: 1810±60;   A. D. 80—200

R-71-34. W Cem, fill of Grave 82, dated early in the 1st century A. C. by ceramic associations.

    Z-210:   1882±51;   A. D. 17—119
    Tx-1344: 1810±70;   A. D. 70—210

R-71-35. W Cem, fill of Grave 57, from early in the history of the cemetery, probably 1st century A. C.

    Z-206:   1873±46;   A. D. 31—123
    Tx-1345: 1640±50;   A. D. 260—360

THE HOUSE OF THE FULLER

R-71-33. Charred beam in destruction layer on highest of four floors. Ceramics late 4th century A. C. Collected by hand into tray, moist; transferred to polyethylene bag; left open in laboratory for six weeks.

    Z-212:   1796±69;   A. D. 85—223
    Tx-1343: 1620±50;   A. D. 280—380

THE ACROPOLIS

R-71-36. Arcopolis, Trench 1, from destruction debris in Room 4; probably a roof beam. Should date end of last construction in this part of site, 5th or possibly 6th century A. C.

    Z-215:   1619±46;   A. D. 285—377
    Tx-1346: 1530±50;   A. D. 370—470

THE BRIDGE

R-71-23. Wood from transverse slot ("western slot") in pavement on Pier 1, western abutment pier of former bridge across Crna River. Sample should date bridge construction. No archaeological date for structure; built later than deposition of river silts over ruins of city wall but no earlier than fourth century A. C. Pavement construction appears to be post-Mediaeval. Sample collected with trowel and forceps.

    No Zagreb date.

    Tx-1349: 130±40; A. D. 1780—1860 (this date does not appear on Fig. 23)

DISCUSSION OF THE DATES

In the nine samples that were split and dated by both laboratories, the laboratories are in agreement within 1σ in seven cases, $1.33\ \sigma$ apart in the case of R-17-33, and 2σ apart in R-71-35. Statistically, this is a good record of agreement for such a series.

In the two cases where the difference is greater than 1σ, the laboratories report nothing unusual in the preparation or the counting, and no reason to doubt the assays from the laboratory point of view.

It is, however, to be noted that even though agreement is statistically good, the Zagreb dates consistently tend to be slightly earlier than the Austin dates. As of this writing, the two laboratories have not been able to determine, by correspondence, what factors might cause this consistent trend. Because the differences are in most cases minor they should not affect archaeological results in a large series, but in one or two samples they could cause errors. Plans are being laid for a personal visit between the two laboratories, in the hope of making a more specific comparison of techniques.

DATES FROM THE EPISCOPAL BASILICA

The four samples from the Episcopal Basilica and its Baptistery are from destruction debris of the basilica on its south side, which lies on destruction debris of the Baptistery, which in turn is above at least one coin minted in A. D. 569—70, which lay on the Baptistery floor.

The seven dates on the four samples vary a good deal, but they suggest a fourth century date for the wood used in construction. It must be emphasized, however, that this date does not apply to the destruction of the building, but to the time the wood used in its construction was alive. We have already remarked on the problems associated with this kind of dating, in particular the fact that a radiocarbon date from a beam actually applies to the particular growth rings that are being dated. Unless outside rings are being dated, the radiocarbon assay does not apply to the cutting date of the wood and hence to the date of construction of the edifice. In many cases the errors involved in radiocarbon dating make this problem of no significance, but when one is dealing with slow-growing hardwood beams, such as one would expect in a major structure like the Episcopal Basilica, radiocarbon dates could easily be as much as 100 years earlier than the cutting dates.

It is therefore not inconsistent that the 4th century date suggested by these radiocarbon dates is rather earlier than the 5th century construction date of the basilica based on the evidence of art and architecture.[2] If this difference between radiocarbon and archaeological evidence proves consistent when further evidence of both sorts is available, it may provide a rough correction factor for the dating of such a building. It might be noted that contextual material for the original construction period is still lacking, but new evidence for the periods of remodelling has suggested to the excavators that the basilica may have been built in the very early 5th, or even late 4th century.[3]

---
[2] For references see W—MZ (1971) 400.
[3] Wiseman, *Guide*, Section 19 *fin*.

DATES FROM THE WEST CEMETERY

R-71-14 A, the deposit on Wall 8. Wall 8 was a peribolos, a perimeter wall for Grave 21 (discussed below). The deposit on the wall is later than the wall and the grave; the archaeological evidence allows as much as one hundred years between them. The pottery included in the deposit, and the archaeological evidence from Grave 21, make the late 1st century and early 2nd century a good archaeological estimate for the deposit.

The Zagreb date, A. D. 105—199, agrees with the later part of this estimated range; the Texas date, A. D. 150—230, is slightly later. Thus, the radiocarbon dates favor a more recent date than the archaeological evidence indicates.

In a case such as this, where the archaeological evidence is reasonably abundant and strong and there are few radiocarbon dates (and those on only one sample), the archaeological evidence should weigh most heavily. However, it is not wise to ignore the radiocarbon dates entirely. If possible they should be supplemented by further dates, and in the meantime they serve as a warning that we should be on the alert for factors that may not have been taken into account in the archaeological dating of this feature.

Grave 21 (MF-70-44 and R-71-15). Grave 21, a cremation with associated remains of a funeral feast, was mostly excavated in 1970; the remainder was excavated in 1971. Radiocarbon samples were taken each year, both samples being vegetal materials from the remains of the feast. The burial was at first dated in the mid-first century A. C.,[4] but in the light of subsequent analysis James Wiseman (personal communication) now places it somewhere between 30 B. C. and A. D. 40.

The sample from the 1970 work was dated by the Austin laboratory at 230 B. C. — A. D. 10; the large time range was a result of small sample size. The 1971 sample, split and dated by the two laboratories, produced dates in close agreement with each other, but pointing to the late 1st or early 2nd century A. C., a century later than the archaeological date. This situation is similar to that of the deposit on Wall 8: the archaeological evidence is stronger, but the radiocarbon dates may be taken as a warning that there may be more to be learned.

Grave 82 (R-71-34). Grave 82 is a tile-covered grave within a pit. The sample came from within the grave pit, outside the tiles, and is

---

[4] W—MZ (1971) 406.

interpreted as the remains of a graveside ceremony at the time of interment.[5] Ceramic analysis suggests a date early in the first century A. C., certainly no later. The Zagreb date, A. D. 17—119, is in agreement although the span of time is later.

The Austin date, A. D. 70—210, does not agree with the archaeological evidence unless one takes the 2σ range, which doubles the time span and increases the probability of correctness from 67% to 95%. Persons in the field of radiocarbon dating have no qualms about using the 2σ range, and in fact they feel it is entirely realistic to do so. But archaeologists should not believe that they have solved any chronological problem by using the 2σ range wherever convenient. It must be kept in mind that whether one uses one or two standard deviations, one is simply stating that the age of the sample is, within the indicated probabilities, somewhere--anywhere--within the reported range.

Although it is accurate to say that the radiocarbon dates from Grave 82 do not disagree with the archaeological evidence, they nevertheless do suggest a later date than that provided by the archaeological data. They cannot be used in support of the archaeological date except in a broad way.

Grave 57 (R-71-35). Grave 57 was a shallow-pit cremation without tiles. Ceramic associations, especially those in related deposits, indicate a date of A. D. 150 or earlier. The Zagreb date, A. D. 31—123, agrees well with the archaeological dating, but the Austin date, A. D. 260—360, is in complete disagreement. Neither laboratory reports any problems in the handling of these samples except that the Zagreb laboratory found it necessary to carry out special purification of the sample in the CO_2 stage of chemical preparation. Both laboratories counted this sample twice. The Austin laboratory split its part, prepared the two parts independently, and counted them in different counters, the results being A. D. 280—420 and A. D. 210—350; the reported date is the average of the two counts.

There is, in short, no explanation for the disagreement in dates here. The Austin date is so far at variance with the rest of the data that it should not be considered significant evidence.

This sort of circumstance is not infrequent in radiocarbon dating, and it emphasizes the need to run a series of samples (preferably at least four per context), rather than a single sample, for more meaningful results.

---

[5] See, in this volume, Al B. Wesolowsky, "Burial Customs in the West Cemetery," p. 100, note 5 and p. 135.

THE HOUSE OF THE FULLER

R-71-33. The House of the Fuller (referred to in earlier reports as the North Palace) is a large residential complex, in one part of which was a series of superimposed floors, the latest of the series having been in part a short-lived structure that was destroyed in the late 4th century, according to the evidence of associated pottery and coins. The radiocarbon sample comes from the destruction debris of this structure.

The Zagreb date, A. D. 85—223, is in disagreement with the archaeological evidence, being at least a hundred years earlier. The Austin date, A. D. 280—380, agrees well with the archaeological data. The Zagreb laboratory was only able to count the sample once, but this circumstance does not provide any explanation for the early date, since double counts rarely change a date significantly. The situation is like that of Grave 57, just discussed. We plan to do more dating of the House of the Fuller.

THE ACROPOLIS

R-71-36. A test trench on the highest point of the site revealed a long series of construction episodes. The radiocarbon sample came from a charred beam just below the surface, associated with roof tiles in the latest destruction debris, in which the latest coin is from the fifth year of the reign of Justin II, i. e. A. D. 569/70. The total evidence of coins and pottery indicates a construction date in the 5th, or possibly the 6th, century for the structure.

The Austin date, A. D. 370—470, is in agreement with the archaeological evidence. The Zagreb date, A. D. 285—377, is early (unless one takes the 2σ range). The two dates are statistically in agreement, but the total span of time they provide, from the late 3rd to the late 4th century, is of little help in dating the feature, and principally points out the need for more radiocarbon dates from this context, in order to provide a better check on the archaeological information.

THE BRIDGE

R-71-23. This date (not shown on Fig. 23 because it is more recent than the span of time on the chart) comes from the remains of a bridge across the river Crna at the eastern edge of Stobi. The bridge had long been thought to be a Roman bridge providing one of the principal entrances to the city. Excavation in 1971 revealed that the bridge was built after a major city wall of Stobi had gone into ruin, and after the Crna had deposited several meters of silt on the lower part of the city. The bridge pavement leading up to the top of the floodplain silts is built in a style that is still in use in Macedonia. By the time the field work had been completed, the suspicion was strong that the bridge was Turkish, but no evidence for dating was available except for the remains of a wooden beam in a slot in the pavement, and some fragments of wood from an aperture in the lower part of the western bridge abutment pier.

The Austin laboratory dated the wood from the slot in the pavement, the result being A. D. 1780—1860. The Zagreb laboratory found that there was insufficient carbon remaining in the other sample for dating.

The single date from the nineteenth century can be taken as strong supporting evidence for the recency of the bridge, which is almost certainly Turkish.

DISCUSSION

It is clear that the principal lack in this series of dates is in numbers of samples. There is no need further to belabor the point of the need for series of samples from any one context, rather than a single sample; it is amply illustrated here.

It is also evident that at a classical site such as Stobi, archaeological evidence is often stronger and more specific than radiocarbon dates in determining ages, but that radiocarbon dates can serve as a warning that the archaeological evidence may be incomplete.

The principal use of radiocarbon dates at Stobi is in studying broad, rather than detailed, chronological problems. The dating of the bridge is an excellent example, and other problems also come to mind. When was the site last occupied? Is there a significant difference in time between different parts of the site? Can serious discrepancies in the archaeological data be resolved by the addition of radiocarbon dates to the evidence? These are the types of problems where radiocarbon dating can serve a valuable role in such a site. We plan in the future to apply the technique to a series of such problems, in the interest both of the study of the history of Stobi and of the application of radiocarbon dating in the field of classical archaeology.

СТАРОСНО ОДРЕЂИВАЊЕ УЗОРАКА МЕТОДОМ С-14

Е. М. ДЕЈВИС, Д. СРДОЧ и С. ВАЛАСТРО ЈУНИОР

Током ископавања 1971. године у Стобима, одабрано је једанаест узорака ћумура и дрвета ради одређивања старости методом карбон-14. Девет узорака подељено је на два дела. Један део испитиван је у лабораторији института „Руђер Бошковић" у Загребу, а други у лабораторији Универзитета Тексаса у Остину. Датуми су представљени на графикону, слика 23, где је такође приказан распон сваког старосног одређивања. Резултати анализе двеју лабораторија слажу се у свим осим два случаја, иако су датуми из Загреба нешто старији од датума из Остина.

Датуми узорака из Епископске базилике наговештавају 4. век, што је сто година раније од археолошке процене. Овај раскорак се скоро сигурно јавља због датовања унутрашњих прстенова стабла дрвета, који потичу из времена кад је дрво било младо а не из времена кад је посечено и употребљено за градњу.

Четири гроба из Западног гробља датована су са променљивим резултатима. Археолошки докази су овде одређенији и не препоручује се даља анализа С-14.

Што се тиче других датума, најзначајнији је датум са Моста јер помаже разрешавање главног питања које се тиче старости конструкције за коју се до недавно сматрало да је римска. Карбон-14 метода подупрла је архитектонске доказе да је мост у ствари турски.

Овај мали низ датума наглашава чињеницу да је за добро одређивање старости методом карбон-14 потребно анализирати више узорака из једног контекста да би се добили корисни резултати. Узорци се морају сакупити пажљиво, а археолошко датовање које прати сваки узорак мора бити детаљно и специфично. Мерење старости карбон-14 методом није у ствари датовање све док се не потврди археолошким датовањем пратећег контексног материјала.

THE GEOLOGIC FRAMEWORK OF STOBI*

by

ROBERT. L FOLK

GEOLOGIC SETTING OF THE VARDAR AREA WITHIN THE BALKAN PENINSULA

Stobi (Figs. 24—25; see Plan of Site) lies at the confluence of the Crna and Vardar Rivers in Yugoslavian Macedonia, about 125 km. north-northwest of the point where the Vardar flows into the Aegean Sea near Thessalonica, Greece. The Vardar valley has served as an important communication route for over 2,000 years. In classical times it served as the main road linking the Aegean Sea with the fertile Hungarian plains and the commerce of the Danube.[1] In mediaeval times it was a migration route for Slavic invaders, and later, during the Turkish surge into southeastern Europe, it was a major communication line for the Ottoman Empire. Today the famous trains, the Hellas and Akropolis, cross the northern end of Stobi as they run through the Vardar valley between Athens and Paris. The reason for the existence of this corridor, so important for human history, is a geologic one: the corridor represents a line of geologic "scar tissue," a sunken

---

*This report is based on a visit to Stobi, Yugoslavia, August 3- August 8, 1971. I did no excavation of my own, but inspected the sites already dug, with particular attention to the few existing cuts through material outside the buildings.

[1] Kitzinger, *Survey*, pp. 83—161.

trench marking the juncture between two great, vastly differing blocks of the earth's crust.[2]

The southern Balkans can be roughly divided into two sections: the young Alpine foldbelt in the west, and the old, stable Rhodope massif in the east. The boundary between them follows an almost straight line up the valley of the Vardar and Lepenac Rivers and continues along the Sitnica and Ibar Rivers.

The Alpine foldbelt includes the Dinaric Alps, which join the Italian Alps and thence traverse the length of Yugoslavia, the Albanian ranges, and the Pindus Mountains of western Greece. These mountains have a consistent north to northwest trend parallel to the Adriatic coast, and were intensely folded and thrusted toward the west during middle Tertiary time, about 20—30 million years ago. Earlier, they were the site of a complex series of very mobile and active

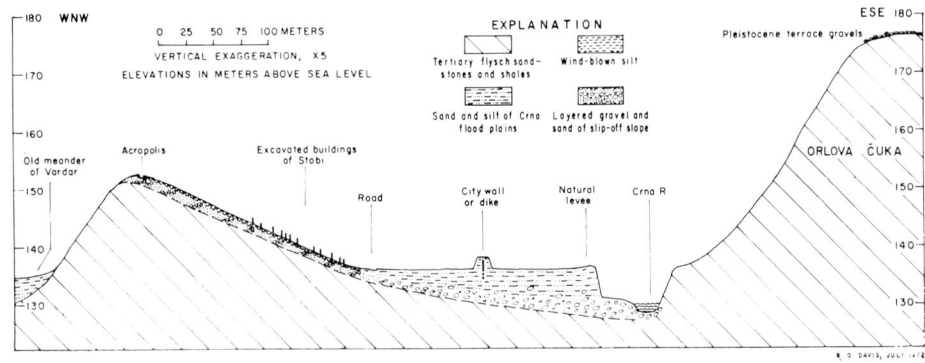

Figure 24. Diagrammatic cross section showing geologic relations at Stobi. Between the steep scarp at the left, an ancient meander scar of the Vardar, and the level flood plain of the Crna is the slip-off slope on which lie the excavated buildings of Stobi. On the right is the hill Orlova Čuka, topped with Pleistocene terrace gravels. The flood plain of the Crna is inundated frequently even today, but the buildings of Stobi have not been flooded in historical times. Drawing by B. O. Davis after a sketch by Robert L. Folk.

geosynclines (marine depositional basins bordered by mountains) also trending north to northwest throughout Mesozoic and Tertiary time, i. e., for the past 200 million years.[3] Tremendous thicknesses of mainly

---

[2] Richard Brinkmann, *Geologic Evolution of Europe*, tr. by J. E. Sanders (New York 1960).

[3] Jean Aubouin, *Geosynclines* (Amsterdam, Elsevier Co. 1965).

Cretaceous limestone are now exposed in most of the mountain belt. Solution of these limestones by rainfall has produced a very rugged topography known as karst[4] in which steep crags and vertical pinnacles of naked carbonate rock separate isolated thin-soiled pocket valleys. Yugoslavia is the classic region for this kind of landscape; indeed, karst is a term of Yugoslavian origin that is now used throughout the world. Because most of the drainage in karst regions is underground through cavern systems, surface streams and rivers are few, so there are no long, through-cutting valleys. The resulting rough, fortresslike topography has proved a great barrier to transportation, and is part of

Figure 25. General view of Stobi, taken from Orlova Čuka looking northwest toward the Dinaric ranges. The Crna River valley in the foreground is the only place where trees grow; the hills are barren. The Crna flood plain and the Inner City Wall lie this side of the small dirt road; above that is the Crna slip-off slope upon which the excavations have been made. The white patch in the right middle distance is the excavation at the Acropolis; beyond lies the valley of the Vardar River, verdant with vineyards, and farther in the distance are terraces of the old lake sediments, and river plains.

[4] Jovan Cvijić, "The Evolution of Lapiés, a Study in Karst Physiography," *Geog. Rev.* 14 (1924) 26—49.

the reason for the thin population there from classical times until today; this rugged country is now occupied sparsely by tough mountaineer peoples, including Bosnians, Montenegrins, and Albanians.[5]

The Rhodope massif forms a triangle whose apices are roughly the Chalcidice peninsula of Greece, Niš (Yugoslavia), and eastern Thrace. The massif mainly consists of very ancient Paleozoic metamorphic and plutonic crystalline rocks, which have remained a stable buttress since Hercynian deformation about 300 million years ago, in contrast to the very recently mobile geosynclinal belt of the Dinaric-Pindus fold-mountains.

The Vardar valley is a linear furrow that occupies the zone between these two contrasting crustal blocks. The Vardar traverses a north-northwest-trending chain of sunken fault basins arranged like beads on a string. In later Tertiary time (Neogene, about 10—20 million years ago) these down-dropped fault-block basins became the sites of isolated lakes, each connected with the next by gorges and rapids. As the gorges were cut down by the ancestral Vardar, the lakes were drained, and their bottom sediments became exposed as flat plains of fertile, fine soil ideal for primitive agriculture (Fig. 25). The alternations are easily visible today to those traveling by train along the Vardar as broad, fertile, flat-floored heavily farmed valleys alternate with narrow, V-shaped rocky canyons. Despite occasional gorges, the down-faulted Vardar valley is the only good line of communication in the region, hence the strategic reason for the placement of Stobi and the later channeling of Slavic infiltrations in midmillenium.

At Stobi the Vardar corridor is relatively wide. The ridges on the skyline to the west (Fig. 25) and southeast (Fig. 26)

Figure 26. View looking southeast across Stobi toward the village of Palikura, which lies on a flat river terrace. Excavations of Stobi are on a slip-off slope of the Crna River, which slopes to the left toward the trees in the Crna valley. Dinaric mountains in the background.

---

[5] George W. Hoffman, *A Geography of Europe* (New York 1969).

represent the Dinaric foldbelt, here made up of a complex series of rocks; mostly Paleozoic schist, marble, and limestone with some granite and volcanics, all intensely deformed. Elevations of peaks in the chain west of Stobi range from 1000—2500 m.

The bedrock at Stobi consists of Upper Eocene gray sandstone and shale about 40—50 million years old (Figs. 24 and 27) now under study by Dimitrijević, Dimitrijević, Rakičević and Karajovanović.[6]

Figure 27. Outcrop of early Tertiary marine sandstone and shales in the roadcut that severs the north edge of Stobi. The uniform thickness of the sandstone beds and the rhythmic sandstone/shale alternation is characteristic of flysch sedimentation. Each sandstone bed is the result of one turbidity current, probably set off by an earthquake or other shock, sending a cloud of sediment rushing into deep oceanic water. At the top of the cliff is a cap of Pleistocene (?) river gravel about 1.0 m. thick, within which one of the city walls is set.

---

[6] M. N. Dimitrijević, M. D. Dimitrijević, T. Rakičević and M. Karajovanović, "Beginning of Turbiditic Sedimentation in the Priabonian near Gradsko, Macedonia," unpubl. ms. presented at VII Congress of Yugoslav Geologists, Zagreb, in 1970.

The beds dip moderately at Stobi itself; but beds are intensely crumpled and some dip nearly vertically east of the road to Negotino, a town about 16 km. to the south. They were mainly folded in mid-Tertiary time, but mountain-making activity is still going on today in the Yugoslav Ranges as witnessed by the great earthquakes at Skopje in 1963 and at Banja Luka in 1969. Stobi itself was badly damaged by an earthquake in A. D. 518. The Eocene rocks at Stobi, characterized by monotonously repeated alternations of uniformly thin, even beds of sandstone with interbeds of shale, are known to geologists as flysch.[7] The sandstone occurs in regular beds 1cm. to 1m. thick, interbedded with gray shale, with straight and very sharp contacts (Fig. 27), the sandstone forming about a third of the total thickness. The sandstone slabs, with their uniform thickness and flat surfaces, make ideal flagstones. There are also a few conglomerate beds as much as a meter thick, showing excellent grading from coarse grains, mainly of limestone fragments, at the base to finer grains at the top of the bed. Almost all of the sandstone slabs have excellent sole marks (i. e., ridges and markings on the bottom of the sandstone beds), consisting mainly of groove casts, but with some animal trails (Fig. 28). Groove casts are made when a swift current drags a pebble, shell, or other object along the bottom, cutting a groove in the soft mud. The groove is later filled in by the overlying sand. The currents that cut the grooves in these rocks ran southwards towards the ancestral Aegean Sea. This textbook assemblage of flysch features indicates that the sandstone-shale interbeds were laid down in an oceanic embayment, bordered by an actively rising mountain mass.

Figure 28. A slab of Tertiary flysch flagstone, used as Roman paving at Stobi. The tiny ridges are groove casts, representing tracks made when these were oceanic sediments by objects dragged along the sea bottom by swiftly moving turbidity currents. Cap gives scale.

---

[7] Roger G. Walker, "Review of Geometry and Facies Organization of Turbidites," *Geol. Assoc. Canada*, Spec. Paper 7 (1970) 219—251. This entire volume deals succinctly with flysch and turbidity currents.

The sea bottom upon which they were deposited sloped steeply and was subject to continual earthquakes. These earthquakes triggered slides of soft sediment which mixed with oceanic waters and sped downslope at high speed, cutting the grooves whose casts we see now, and depositing the beds of graded conglomerate and sandstone. Currents that flow downslope because of the great density of the suspended sediment they carry are known as turbidity currents,[8] and they are present today along many of the world's mountainous coasts. Each sandstone bed represents the product of one such turbidity current--and presumably of one earthquake or similar trigger. Many geologists interpret such features as evidence of deposition in oceanic depths of as much as thousands of feet; however, the author holds the conservative opinion that the water depth need not have been more than a few hundred feet.

On the basis of composition, the Eocene flysch sandstones are classified as submature calclithites; i. e., they are poorly sorted, they vary widely in grain size, and the sand grains and small pebbles are composed largely of fragments of older limestone, probably from the Mesozoic reef carbonates of the ancestral Dinaric ranges. A wide variety of reef-forming fossils are present, including coralline algae and stromatoporoids. Some of these creatures may have been living in contemporary reefs along the rugged shores of the linear seaway, but most of the fossils are reworked from much older carbonate rocks. Thin sections show that, in addition to the carbonate rock fragments, the flysch sandstones contain some basic volcanic-rock fragments and metaquartzite. The interbedded gray shales consist of illitic and montmorillonitic clay with lesser amounts of quartz and calcite.

Overlying these folded Tertiary marine rocks in the vicinity of Negotino is an undisturbed, very soft, massive, pale-yellow sediment made of windblown dust or loess, as noted also by Marković-Marjanović.[9] During Pleistocene time, which began about 2 million and ceased about 11,000 years ago, mountain glaciers were scattered down the spine of Yugoslavia and into Greece as far south as the Peloponnesus.[10] Windblown dust, derived from aeolian action on debris ground up by

---

[8] *Ibid.*

[9] Jelena Marković-Marjanović, "Le Loess en Yougoslavie," *Rept. of VI Int. Congress on Quaternary* 4 (Warsaw 1961) 551—570.

[10] J. K. Charlesworth, *The Quaternary Era* (2 vols.) (London 1957) p. 719 and map, fig. 126.

the continental ice sheet in northern Europe, covered vast areas, including large regions around Budapest, Belgrade, and Bucharest.[11] A smaller pocket of loess derived from local mountain glaciation near Negotino[12] blanketed the Stobi-Negotino area during the Pleistocene and provided source material for the much later dust storms that I believe made Stobi a very unpleasant place to live in during the 5th and 6th centuries and eventually buried the town.

SITE OF STOBI

Stobi is built upon a peninsula that extends like a curving finger between the old meander belt of the Vardar River and the valley of the Crna (Fig. 24). The backbone of this peninsula is formed by the folded Eocene flysch sandstones that crop out in a roadcut that crosses the northern end of Stobi (Fig. 27). The same sandstones are well exposed on Orlova Čuka, the hill across the Crna River from Stobi (Fig. 24) and they underlie the terrace upon which the near-by village of Palikura is built (Fig. 26). Upon this folded, early Tertiary bedrock lies a capping of superficial, weakly consolidated fluvial sediments, mostly gravels with some sand and mud (Fig. 29). These deposits were laid down repeatedly during Pleistocene time (the past 2 million years), when the main channels of the ancestral Vardar and Crna were located at these high elevations. The gravels mainly consist of very resistant quartz pebbles, as well as occasional pieces of

Figure 29. Naturally deposited river gravel beneath the Synagogue at Stobi. Current flowed from left to right, parallel to the present direction of flow of the Crna River. The Synagogue footings were placed in this gravel long after the river had left.

---

[11] *Ibid.*, fig. 101; Jelena Marković-Marjanović, "Loess Sections in the Danube Valley Yugoslavia and their Importance for the Quaternary Stratigraphy of Southeastern Europe," *Proc. VII Int. Congress on Quaternary* 12 (Denver 1968) 261—278.

[12] *Loc. cit. supra,* note 9.

granite, schist, chert and volcanic rocks, generally moderately rounded. At the base of these terrace gravels are occasional large, angular blocks of Tertiary sandstone, pieces that caved into the ancient streams but were not rolled far downstream. A similar assemblage of large, angular sandstone blocks and smaller rounded pebbles can be seen along the modern Crna River bank where it is cutting against the sandstone cliffs.

An entire series of Pleistocene (?) river terrace gravels can be found in the area. At Stobi, the highest and oldest terrace, about 190 m. above sea level--60 m. above the Crna River--caps Orlova Čuka, and consists of thinly scattered rounded quartz gravel. The village of Palikura is on a somewhat lower, younger terrace, flat and particularly well developed (Fig. 26); Stobi lies on a still lower terrace.

The town of Stobi is built on a gentle incline representing mainly a slip-off slope formed by the Crna River as it lowered itself by cutting gradually southward against the resistant Tertiary sandstone of Orlova Čuka (Figs. 25 and 26). This slope consists of three segments (Fig. 24): a narrow terrace at river level, a broad, flat flood plain, and a gentle, smooth, upward slope.

A very narrow terrace lies at about the present elevation of the Crna River (129 m.). E. Mott Davis found World War I cartridge shells buried in 2.0 m. of river sediment of this low terrace, near the bridge of probable Turkish origin.[13] An abrupt bank, about 7 m. high, leads up to the main, flat flood plain terrace at an elevation of 136 m. This level plain is about 200 m. wide and has indistinct natural levees bordering the river (Figs. 24 and 25). Upon this plain are low artificial ridges that mark the line of the Inner City Wall.[14] The grassy surface is littered with roof tiles, occasional river pebbles, and blocks of sandstone apparently once used as building material. This terrace, according to residents of the area, is flooded frequently, most recently in 1951.[15] The terrace sediments consist of silty sand that is finely bedded, micaceous (muscovite and volcanic biotite), and richly feldspathic. Further, in a test trench near the middle of the flood plain there is a layer 10—15 cm.

---

[13] The French-Serbian-British spearhead broke through from the south and captured the key Crna-Vardar triangle in the offensive of September 1918. This broke the back of the Bulgarian-German front facing Thessalonica, and caused the capitulation of Bulgaria less than two weeks later (see *Encyclopedia Britannica*, "Salonika Campaigns 1915—1918").

[14] Wiseman, *Guide*, Section 25.

[15] E. M. Davis, personal communication, 1971.

thick consisting of small river pebbles mixed with rolled and rounded pieces of Roman bricks, roof tiles, and abraded mortar chunks. Thus the floods of the Crna River are now, and presumably were in Roman times, capable of causing deposition of a phenomenal amount of sediment and inflicting much destruction upon any buildings resting upon the flood plain.[16] It should be noted that the semi-arid area around Stobi is ideal for producing extreme floods. Maximum erosion of soil takes place in areas that have about 40 cm. of rainfall annually (about that of Stobi) because there is not enough rain to support soil-retaining vegetation, yet there is enough precipitation to cause destructive erosion. What is more, rainfall in such semi-arid areas generally comes as torrential downpours, rather than as gentle, slow showers, further exaggerating erosion and flooding. Rapid runoff of rain is aided by overgrazing of the hillslopes, and furthermore, the Crna rises in the mountains to the southwest, where it receives additional orographic rainfall from these wetter regions.

Above the level flood plain of the Crna lies the gentle slip-off slope about 225 m. wide, upon which lies most of the excavated part of Stobi (Figs. 24—26). Most of the presently excavated buildings are built at elevations of 136—145 m., i. e., 7-16 m. above the level of the Crna, and are safe from flooding. Like the flood plain, this slope is covered with gravel and sandy silt and is littered with broken roof tiles, sandstone building blocks, and occasional concentrations of river pebbles and cobbles, which probably represent the surface outcrops of gravel beds, now blurred by downslope soil creep.

The highest point of the city, at the top of the Crna slip-off slope (Fig. 24), lies at about 155 m. and overlooks a steep, west-facing scarp. This curving scarp is an ancient meander scar of the Vardar River.

The Synagogue, Civil Basilica, and Fuller's House, as well as the West Cemetery, are all bottomed in Pleistocene gravel deposits. These gravel deposits were laid down at various elevations as the Crna River gradually slipped its channel lower and lower, sliding down the gentle slope to its present course (Fig. 24). The fragment of Roman city wall exposed in the roadcut that goes through the north end of the site penetrates the gravel and rests upon the Tertiary flysch sandstones (Fig. 27).

One problem of geologic archaeology is the distinction between natural river-laid gravels (implying no archaeological data below) and

---

[16] W—MZ (1972) 412—413.

man-deposited gravel consisting of rough heaps from excavation, road paving, and other activities. Most natural gravels (Fig. 29) have fairly distinct bedding, i. e., they are segregated and sorted into finer and coarser grained layers, and they also generally have matrices of fine pebbles or sand. Man-made gravel deposits have less prominent bedding, the pebbles are much more diverse in size, and the matrices are more commonly mud. Most natural gravels have imbricated pebbles, i. e., most of the pebbles dip or slope in one direction: specifically, they dip upstream. Furthermore, at Stobi, some cementation has taken place in the natural gravels due to percolation of rainwater down through the calcareous soil and resulting precipitation of calcite as the rainwater evaporates. Crystals accumulate as coatings on the *undersides* of the pebbles, and these coatings bind sand grains underneath the pebbles. Man-deposited gravels at Stobi do not have this feature; if crystal coatings are present at all, some are on the tops and some are on the bottoms of the pebbles (as in the case of one gravel layer in the West Cemetery), because the pebbles were gathered up and thrown into piles in random orientation.

The top few feet of soil at Stobi, and the material which largely buries the buildings themselves, is a very loose, powdery gray silt; this is wind-blown dust deposited within historic times. Microscopic examination shows that most of the particles are in the 10 to 50 micron size range, with an estimated median of about 20 microns; there is very little clay-size material and very little material coarser than 100 microns. Such well-sorted silts would be abnormal as water-laid deposits, but are typical of loess.[17] The high content of 1—4 micron-size carbonate grains is typical for loess, and these were probably derived ultimately from glacial pulverization of the neighboring carbonate mountain ranges before the dust was blown into Stobi. The loose, powdery nature of the soil is the result of the low clay content.

UTILIZATION OF GEOLOGIC MATERIALS AT STOBI

At least two distinct types of marble are used in the buildings at Stobi. The Theater, many monuments, and parts of other buildings

---

[17] Richard J. Russell, "Lower Mississippi Valley Loess," *Geol. Soc. Amer. Bull.* 55 (1944) 1—40; C. Bertrand Schultz and John C. Frye, "Loess and Related Eolian Deposits of the World," *Proc. VII Int. Congress on Quaternary* 12 (Denver 1968) 369.

consist of a good quality, sugary, crystalline metamorphic marble, white with some gray streaks. Both finer crystalline marble and coarser marble are similar to outcrops in the Pletvar Pass near Prilep, about 35

Figure 30. Excavation in the Baptistery. The main construction blocks visible in the walls are of Tertiary sandstone. Only the ornamental carvings and columns here are of marble. Slate sheets are visible set on edge near the center of the photograph. Much of the dirt fill is interpreted as wind-blown dust.

km. southwest of Stobi.[18] Many of the columns in the religious buildings consist of a pink marble breccia in which the large, angular fragments of

---

[18] James Wiseman, personal communication, 1971.

marble are set in a reddish matrix, and some consist of brecciated red limestone with coral fossils. Marble outcrops similar to this occur at Demir Kapija 30 km. southeast of Stobi.[19]

In addition to marble, the Paleozoic ranges also contain large amounts of slate, and slabs of both slate and marble were used to face the wall of the piscina in the Baptistery (Fig. 30); good quality slate occurs near Pletvar Pass. Purplish "imitation porphyry" columns were made of a fine-grained purple sandstone outcropping south along the Vardar.

The material used most in construction was the Tertiary flysch sandstone. This formed the bulk of the buildings, the marble being used chiefly for ornamental purposes. The sandstone provides parallel-faced blocks of hard, yet easily trimmable sandstone, ideal for producing building blocks of almost any shape or size. The sandstone is an attractive, warm, brownish gray on exposed surfaces, and is resistant to weathering. Embedded in soft shale, the thin sandstone layers a few centimeters thick (each representing the deposit of one turbidity current) made ideal flagstone, easy to quarry in thin, even sheets as much as a meter wide (Figs. 27 and 28). Thus, it was extensively utilized in making pavements and floors at Stobi. The Romans and Greeks may have esthetically appreciated the groove casts on the surfaces of the flagstone, as most of the stones used in pavements have these marks facing up (Fig. 28), but they could not have understood their origin. The sandstone was also used extensively by the Turks during their occupation of Macedonia. The Turkish Tower in Negotino is made of the same sandstone, as is the ruined Turkish bridge across the Crna at Stobi. Tertiary sandstone is also used today in the houses and out-buildings of Negotino, and as paving for some of the side streets.

The gray clay interbedded with Tertiary sandstone is of proper illitic composition to make good brick, tile, and pottery. The massive reddish bricks of the Hellenistic constructions at Stobi are made of red clay that contained a high percentage of straw and other vegetable debris. These bricks are crudely made and quite soft; similar red clay is used to make brick along the Vardar valley toward Demir Kapija. The Roman roof tiles do not contain straw, are harder, much better made, and have been fired at a high temperature.

Pleistocene (?) gravel was used apparently as fill, and occasional large boulders were incorporated into buildings. Several gigantic

---

[19] *Ibid.*

boulders of reddish quartzite were probably hauled in for ornamental purposes. Since river sand was utilized as aggregate for mortar, it is quite possible that these lime mortars might be datable by radiocarbon analysis, thus pinning down the construction date of the buildings. When limestone is burned to make lime, the carbon dioxide is driven off, but when the lime is slaked with water for use as mortar, carbon dioxide from the atmosphere combines with it as it sets up to form crystals of calcite that bind the bricks. The radiocarbon clock is thus set. Sand used as aggregate at Stobi has very little limestone in it, so there should be no dilution by the "dead carbon" that hampers mortar dating in England.[20] Preliminary work by S. Valastro has shown that this technique is indeed workable, and one date from the mortar of the narthex floor of the Synagogue Basilica came out as 270 A. D. ±180 years.

The white ash from wood fires at Stobi has been examined by X-ray and optical microscope and found to consist of 10—40 micron rhombohedral crystals of calcite, as it does in the United States.[21] In external form the rhombohedra are of single crystals of calcite or calcium oxalate (this is the way the mineral occurs in wood of oak, elm, and some other trees), but heating converts them to an aggregate of one micron crystals. During or after burning, the calcium oxide recombines with carbon dioxide in the smoke or air to become calcite. Thus radiocarbon dating of the ashes should provide good dates for conflagrations, much more reliable than charcoal dating, which gives the time when a specific tree was alive, but not when it was burned. For example, a building might have been built with timbers of diverse ages--some even re-used or hundreds of years old--so a radiocarbon date on the charcoal is meaningless as to the date of *destruction*. The ashes, however, should give a precise, pinpoint date, since all the carbon would be dated from the time of holocaust; the date obtained would be a "mean" date from all the materials that were burned.

A few specimens of rare, brilliantly colored minerals have been found in association with slag near the ancient city wall where it is crossed by the Turkish bridge. These were probably specimens brought in by Roman "prospectors" to the foundry for possible utilization in provincial metal technology. One specimen was tentatively identified as

---

[20] M. S. Baxter and A. Walton, "Radiocarbon Dating of Mortars," *Nature* 225 (1970) 937—938.

[21] R. L. Folk, ms. in preparation.

crocoite, a brilliant orange lead chromate mineral. At present, lead, chromium, zinc, and iron are mined in the mountains within a 40 km. radius of Stobi.[22]

A curious occurrence is a small lens of pure bentonite, 15 cm. wide and 1 cm. thick, found in the Synagogue Basilica area. Someone--perhaps the fuller?--must have carried a lump of bentonite into the building and left it in the corner where it became buried. Bentonite is a green, waxy, non-gritty clay that forms through the chemical alteration of volcanic ash. It is used in folk medicine, as soap, and as a clarifier of oils, but its main use is in the fulling of wool or the removal of grease from cloth. Fuller's earth is really a type of bentonite.

THE DEATH OF STOBI: A GEOLOGIC ARGUMENT

Most ancient cities have been effaced by one of the four Aristotelian elements: Earth (quake), Water (flood), Fire, or Air. It is my opinion that a major cause of the death and nonresurrection of Stobi was the last element, Air. I would suggest that about a century of excessively dry climate in Macedonia, accompanied by severe dust storms, had made agriculture very difficult and living conditions unpleasant. Worsening drought, combined with decreasing commercial and political importance as imperial power waned, and the impact of repeated barbarian raids with attendant destruction, led to gradual abandonment of the city. Stobi never came to life again because of continuation of the unfavorable climatic regime. Wind then administered the final *coup de grace* by inflicting a silent entombment in wind-blown dust.

C l i m a t i c   c h a n g e. Macedonia is now a very dry area, yet people do manage to live there. What evidence is there to show that it was even drier during the time Stobi died? The evidence of climatic *change* at the site itself is essentially nonexistent. The number of excavations through surrounding sediments undisturbed by man has so far been very limited; most of the excavations have been in artificial fills inside ruined buildings. Dirt fill inside houses is of very limited value in detecting climatic change, especially during the short period of human occupation--less than a millenium--now uncovered at Stobi, and any zones that might have developed there would have been mixed

---

[22] Petar Mardezić and Zvonimir Dugački, *Geografski Atlas Jugoslavije* (Zagreb 1961).

up by human disturbance. Furthermore, soil zonation is detected by observation of chemical effects on the soil minerals; but these chemical effects are the results of periods of heavy weathering, i. e., warm and particularly humid periods. The available data indicate that the region around Stobi has been permanently semi-arid since the retreat of the glaciers 11,000 years ago, thus there has been no time of heavy weathering which would have left a mark, for example, a zone of red soil, indicative of heavier oxidation caused by more rainfall. Except at the West Cemetery, no weathering profiles could be seen in the excavations into undisturbed soil. The soils are all of about the same ashy-gray color with a pale-orange tint. To obtain a quantitative measure of soil color, the Munsell soil color chart was used.[23] The highest and oldest soil at Stobi apparently is that at the West Cemetery, where a sterile soil 7.5 cm. above the top of the gravel bed measures 10 YR 7/2.5 (light gray; weak, very light yellow orange).[24] This soil contains small streaks and pea-sized accumulations of soft, powdery white caliche indicating some soil zonation (rainfall dissolves calcium carbonate from the uppermost layers of soil and reprecipitates it at lower depths as caliche). This process is common in all semi-arid areas: West Texas, for example.

The matrix mud in lower and younger Pleistocene gravel at the Synagogue is slightly paler, 10YR 6/2.5 (light brownish-gray; weak light yellow-brown). The youngest soil, that on the floodplain, is of still weaker color, 10 YR 6.5/1 (light gray; very weak light yellow-brown).

If significant weathering had taken place, we should expect more intense red or orange colors, especially since the sands contain such good sources of iron as biotite and volcanic rock fragments. The pale-grayish color of all sediments and soils and the presence of fresh feldspar indicate that a similar semi-arid climate has existed in the area from the deposition of the Pleistocene river gravel on the high terraces until the present day. As indicated by the quantitative color data above, there is an increase in strength of yellow-orange tint with increasing age, but the change is extremely slight. There is a red soil layer in the West Cemetery, but this layer is an artificial one, as the color comes

---

[23] Robert L. Folk, "Toward Greater Precision in Rock-Color Terminology," *Bull. Geol. Soc. America* 80 (1969) 725—728.

[24] First designations are those of the Munsell soil color chart; second designation, in parentheses, is a more detailed system of Folk, *supra*, note 23.

from disintegration of fragments and dust of soft, red bricks resembling the Hellenistic type. The fact that fine clay-size carbonate from windblown dust is still present in the surface soil layers also indicates that the rainfall was not sufficient to produce any zonation in the soil.

Thus, from the soils exposed at Stobi we see evidence of a dry climate that persisted for at least several thousand years, with no interspersed wet periods. A brief summary of evidence for this dry period from the rest of Europe will permit us better to decipher the climatic history of Stobi.

One of the favorite subjects for speculation is the evidence for change of climate in Europe during postglacial, and especially historic, times, and the effect of that change on the collapse of civilizations and on mass migrations.[25] The subject is fraught with much hypothesis, guesswork, and biased opinion. Nevertheless, it is now agreed that Europe went through a "Little Ice Age" from A. D. 1500—1700[26] and an unusually warm period from A. D. 1000—1200. Lamb[27] also cites evidence to show that a severe cold period affected the region from the Adriatic Sea to the Bosporus between A. D. 600 and 900, accompanied by increased aridity, and Schwarzbach[28] notes an unusually arid period between A. D. 500 and 700. Link[29] postulates 400-year climatic cycles caused by solar activity and has astronomical evidence for maximum dryness at about A. D. 600. Brooks[30] asserts that Greece was also driest in the 600's. Even at the present time the strip from Titov Veles and Stobi down the Vardar valley lies in a marked rainshadow zone between lofty mountains, the hottest and driest part of Yugoslavia.[31] Gradsko, 3 km. north of Stobi, receives only 42 cm. of

---

[25] Ellsworth Huntington, "The Burial of Olympia," *Geogr. Jour.* 36 (1910) 657—686; C. E. P. Brooks, *Climate Through the Ages*, 2nd ed. (New York 1949); H. H. Lamb, *The Changing Climate* (London 1966).

[26] H. H. Lamb, "The Early Medieval Warm Epoch and its Sequel," *Paleogeogr., Paleoclim., Paleoec.* 1 (1965) 13—37.

[27] *Idem*, "The Climatic Background to the Birth of Civilization," *Adv. of Sci.* 25 (1968) 103—120.

[28] Martin Schwarzbach, "The Climatic History of Europe and North America," in A. E. M. Nairn, ed., *Descriptive Paleoclimatology* (New York 1961) 284; idem, *Climates of the Past-an Introduction to Paleoclimatology*, tr. by Richard O. Muir (Princeton 1963) 203.

[29] František Link, "Změny Klimatu a Sluneční Činnosti v Posledních Čtyřech Tisíciletích" (Changes of Climate and Solar Activity during the past Four Thousand Years), *Československé Akad. Věd, Řada M. P. V., Ročnik* 66, *Sešit* 2 (1956).

[30] *Op. cit.* in note 25, p. 315.

[31] *Op. cit.* in note 22, p. 63.

rainfall annually[32] and has high summer temperatures (July mean 80° F, 27° C), indicating a severely dry climate, much like that of semidesert southeastern New Mexico. Although large trees occupy the river valleys, the hills are barren and treeless with thorny shrubs, very scanty grass, and much bare gray-brown clay soil which, it if had a normal amount of rainfall, should support plentiful vegetation. Most rain at Stobi is in the form of torrential downpours, which cause erosion and floods and do little to support plant growth. According to local people it seldom rains at Stobi, although rain often can be seen falling in the distance. Stobi is so extremely dry today that it is not difficult to believe that the city was finally abandoned during the even drier late 6th century and not refounded in the 7th, a century that was the driest in all recorded European and Asiatic history.[33]

Huntington[34] describes the drying and denuding of Greece that culminated about A. D. 600, and points out increased flooding and burial of archaeological sites in fluvial silts at this time. He describes a similar time of aridity, and similar effects on mankind, in western Asia at this period.

According to Vita-Finzi[35] there has been widespread alluviation (due to excessive flooding) of river valleys in the entire Mediterranean area since Classical times. Thus, many ancient riverine cities have been buried, and large deltas have been built from the mud swept down to the sea; specifically the Vardar River (called Axios in Greece) has built a large delta plain west of Thessalonica, moving the shoreline out about 5 km. and adding about 160 square km. of new land since Classical times.[36] This very high rate of deposition was a consequence of two factors. First, the rainfall amount was optimum for greatest erosion, and second, abundant soft shale was present in the drainage basin, particularly along the Vardar valley. In general, the erosion rate on hill slopes and flooding and alluvial deposition in stream valleys all increase as vegetation dies off during a time of change from moderate to dry climate. I believe that most of the sediment of the Crna flood-

---

[32] Later data from 1930—1960 furnished by Dr. Jakob Pamić gives 41 cm. per year.

[33] Ellsworth Huntington and Stephen S. Visher, *Climatic Changes, Their Nature and Causes* (New Haven 1922) 73.

[34] *Loc. cit.* in note 25.

[35] Claudio Vita-Finzi, *The Mediterranean Valleys: Geological Changes in Historical Times* (Cambridge Univ. Press 1969).

[36] William R. Shepherd, *Historical Atlas* (Pikeville, Md. 1956) 11.

plain terrace accumulated by severe flooding during the first half of the millenium as the climate desiccated. Later floods and wind-blown dustfall added the "icing" to the cake.

D u s t f a l l. An important factor in the accumulation and preservation of soil is the fallout of atmospheric dust. The younger sediments visible in yellowish bluffs on the road just north of Negotino are Pleistocene loess deposits. With such little vegetation cover these could have provided a gigantic source of recent dust storms and contributed to the burial of the city. This is why much of the soil in the higher parts of Stobi is dust-size material; it filtered into buildings (Fig. 30), covered the ground, and was interspersed with the gravel by rainwash. Buildings and streets acted as baffles, accumulating more dust than did the surrounding bare ground, and impeding erosion of the dust.

Has the quantity of dustfall been great enough to bury the ruins of Stobi? Kukal and Saadalah[37] have described dust storms in Iraq as a factor in the burial of archaeological sites. They obtained a dustfall rate (not considering any later erosion) of 2.1 cm. per year. Of course the Stobi area is not as dry as Iraq, but dust storms are reported as very common today[38] although no quantitative measurements have been made. If, in the 1,400 years since abandonment of Stobi, the dustfall rate had been as great as in Iraq, 27 m. of windblown dust could have accumulated. At Stobi the streets and buildings are buried in approximately 1 m. of windblown dust, which would require a dustfall rate only one-thirtieth of that in Iraq. Péwé[39] shows dust accumulation rates in Alaska of 1.0—2.0 m. per thousand years in most areas, a rate close to that postulated for Stobi; and Page Twiss[40] believes that dust-accumulation rates in the Great Plains are now 0.5—3.0 m. per millenium. Hence the hypothesis that the main agent of burial of Stobi was windblown dust is quantitatively viable. There is no other way to explain the burial on the hill*tops* of Stobi of the West Cemetery and Acropolis, which are far out of the reach of river floods and are not subject to burial by soil creep.

---

[37] Zdeněk Kukal and Adnan Saadallah, "Složení a rychlost usazovaní sedimentů prachových bouří v Iráku" (Composition and rate of deposition of the recent dust storm sediments in Iraq), *Časopis pro Min. a Geol.* (Praha), roč. 15 (1970) 227—234.

[38] Todor Gruev, personal communication, 1971.

[39] Troy L. Péwé, "Loess Deposits of Alaska," *Proc. XXIII Int. Geol. Congress* 8 (Praha, Proc. Sect. 1968) 297—309.

[40] Page Twiss, personal communication, 1971.

SUMMARY

The geologic history of the area begins in early Tertiary time when a deep and narrow oceanic embayment, receiving heavy sedimentation and undergoing active thrusting and folding, extended between rugged mountain ranges from the Aegean Sea toward the northwest. In mid-Tertiary time the area was uplifted and folded as the sea retreated to the south. Block-faulting occurred, and the ancestral Vardar corridor became a chain of lakes occupying a down-dropped trench between the Dinaric ranges on the west and the Rhodope massif on the east. Gradually the lakes were drained, leaving local basins with fertile soils. Human occupation may have begun at about this time. The Vardar and Crna Rivers gradually cut their way downward, leaving gravel terraces behind. During Pleistocene time, glaciers formed in the mountains to the west, and windblown dust from glacial debris occasionally covered the area. About 2,500 years ago, the area became a part of the classical world as Macedonians, Greeks, and Romans civilized the Vardar valley, and Stobi became a provincial center of the Roman, and later the Byzantine, Empire. About A. D. 500, as the eastern Roman Empire went into political and military decline, several centuries of colder and much drier weather afflicted southern Europe. As the surrounding vegetation died, the area around Stobi became subject to choking dust storms, and the worsening climate made agriculture increasingly difficult. Stobi's political and commercial importance collapsed with the decline of imperial trade routes. Runoff from the increasingly naked hills led to repeated violent flooding along the Crna and Vardar valleys, frequently inundating the lower parts of the town and the only good arable land. Perhaps impelled by the increasingly severe and desiccating climate, as dramatically stated by Huntington,[41] bands of raiding Slavs and nomadic horsemen from the east came storming along the downfaulted Vardar corridor to attack the civilized towns. By the 700's Macedonia had passed from the Greek world into Slavic hands. Thus, for a variety of reasons, Stobi, in mid-millenium, gradually became an increasingly undesirable place to live; there was no longer enough rain for agriculture, the climate was severely cold, dry, and very dusty, the city was often flooded or raided, and it was no longer a commercial crossroad. People probably moved away to wetter regions to the north or west, to the mountains for better

---

[41] *Supra* note 19; *loc. cit.* in note 25.

protection, or to the coastal zone, gradually abandoning Stobi to its silently accumulating blanket of windblown dust.

Acknowledgments

I would like to acknowledge the Geology Foundation, The University of Texas, for providing part of the expenses of the trip to Yugoslavia. The manuscript has been improved by the comments of J. Wiseman, A. Wesolowsky, and E. M. and B. O. Davis.

ГЕОЛОШКИ ОКВИРИ СТОБА

РОБЕРТ ФОЛК

Геолошка историја ове области почиње у раном терцијару када се дубок и узан залив океана пружао између набораних планинских венаца од Егејског мора према северозападу. Долазило је до великог таложења материјала, активних потреса и набирања. Током средњег терцијара простор је подигнут и набран а море се повукло ка југу. Долази до пропадања терена и некадашњи пролаз Вардара постаје ланац језера која су заузимала котлине између динарског венца на западу и родопског масива на истоку. Поступно, језера су пресушила остављајући иза себе басене са плодним земљиштем. Људско насељавање долине Вардара могло је да почне у то време. Вардар и Црна река временом пресецају своја корита остављајући иза себе терасе шљунка. За време плеистоцена, у планинама на западу формирали су се глечери а ветром ношена прашина из глацијалних одрона земљишта повремено би прекривала овај простор. Пре два и по миленијума, ова област постаје део класичног света пошто Македонци, Грци и Римљани цивилизују долину Вардара; Стоби постају провинцијски центар прво римске а касније и византијске империје. Од 500. године н. е., у време када је Источно римско царство доживљавало политичко и војно опадање, клима Јужне Европе се мења; наступа неколико векова хладније и много сувље климе. Пошто је вегетација у околини града уништена, Стоби трпе загушљиве пешчане олује и све лошија и лошија клима чини земљорадњу знатно тежом. Политичка и економска важност Стоба нестаје са опадањем царских трговачких путева. Бујице, са већ увелико огољених брда, доводе до честих поплава дуж долина Вардара и Црне реке, често плавећи доње делове града и једину обрадиву земљу. Можда су гоњене све оштријом и сувљом климом, како је то драматично изјавио Хантингтон, гомиле Словена и номадских јахача, расположене за пљачку, дошле са истока пустошећи цивилизоване градове дуж долине Вардара. Македонија је 700их година прешла из грчких у словенске руке. Тако су због разних разлога, Стоби, средином миленијума, постали прилично незгодно место за живот: нема више кише довољно за земљорадњу, клима постаје врло хладна, сува и са веома много песка. Град је често био пљачкан и плављен, а и престаје да буде трговачка раскрсница. Људи су се вероватно селили у области са више кише на северу или западу, на планине ради боље заштите, или ка приобалним крајевима, потпуно напуштајући град који је временом прекривен нечујно наталоженим покривачем ветром донесеног песка.

THE WEST CEMETERY

EXCAVATIONS IN 1965

by

IVAN MIKULČIĆ

In comparison to the urban architecture, which has already been investigated on a large scale, the cemeteries of Stobi have hardly been touched. We do not yet know either their approximate extension or their number. Until recently, ancient graves were uncovered only occasionally and were incidentally recorded in the literature.

In 1918, when the large Cemetery Basilica was uncovered in front of the Porta Heraclea, some 60 late Roman graves[1] were excavated within it and its precincts. Except for several vaulted graves, the burials were all in broad, quadrangular cists built of dressed slabs and intended for several consecutive burials. They were dated in general terms only, as was the building itself, to the late 4th and 5th centuries.

The presence of the graves and the church indicated the existence of a rather large cemetery around the south and west accesses to the city. The dimensions of the plateau over which those ancient high-

---

[1] H. Dragendorff, "Archäologische und kunstwissenschaftliche Arbeit während des Weltkrieges in Mazedonien," *Zeitschrift für bildende Kunst* 54 (1919) 259—270. Ć. Truhelka, "Grobljanska bazilika u Stobi," *Glasnik* 3 (1927) 78—81. R. F. Hoddinott, *Early Byzantine Churches in Macedonia and Southern Serbia* (London 1963) 167—168. For the location, see Plan of Site, no. 28.

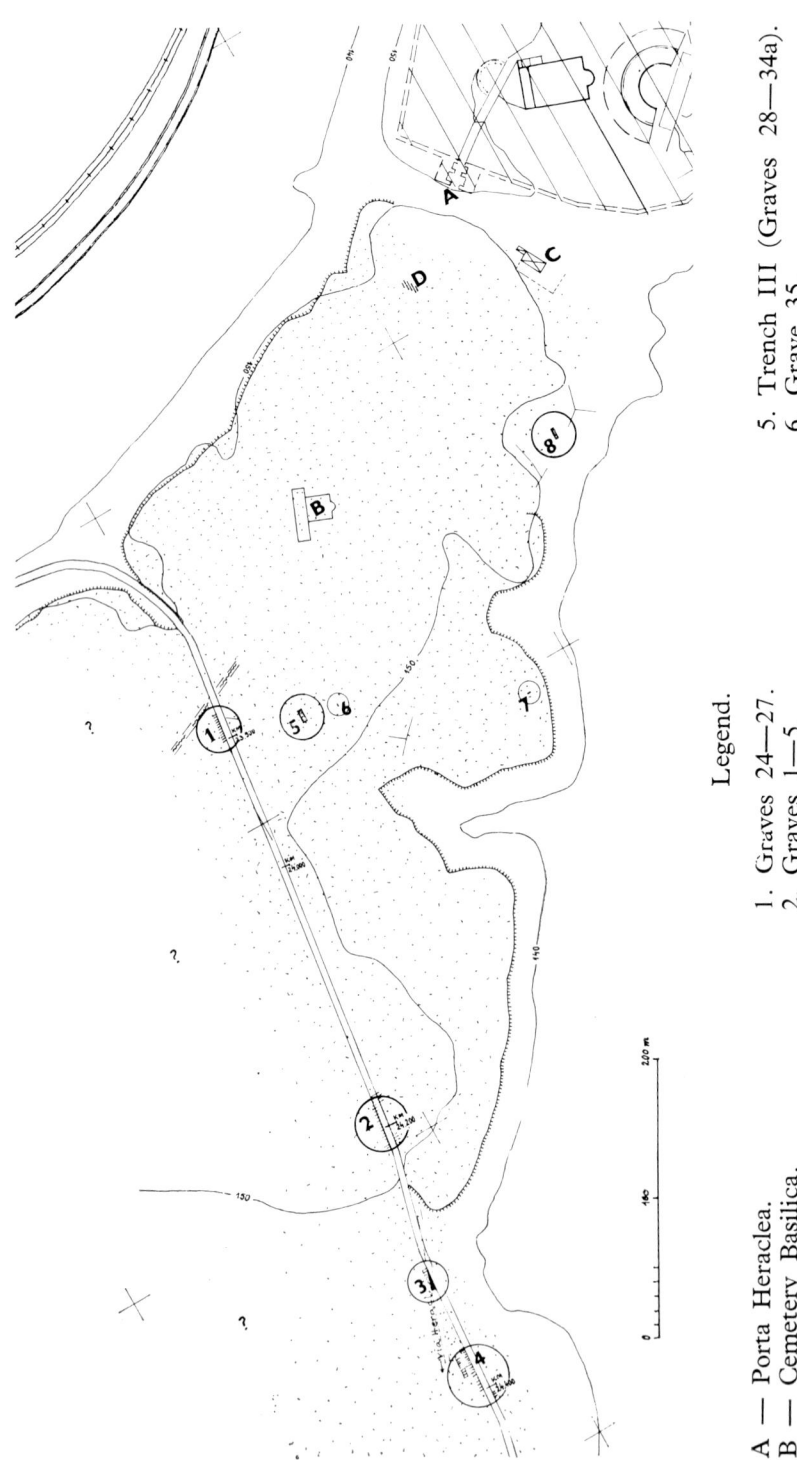

Figure 31. The West Cemetery, showing the situation of the excavated graves (1965) and the approximate dimensions of the cemetery.

A — Porta Heraclea.
B — Cemetery Basilica.
C — Old Excavation House.
D — Graves excavated in 1970—1971.

Legend.

1. Graves 24—27.
2. Graves 1—5.
3. Trench II (ancient road).
4. Trench I (Graves 6—23).
5. Trench III (Graves 28—34a).
6. Grave 35.
7. Grave 36.
8. Trench IV.

ways had been traced seem also to indicate that the main cemetery of the city was situated there.

On the other side of the city, east of the confluence of the Erigon and the Axius, the road to Thessalonica lay between the steep front of Orlova Čuka and the right bank of the Vardar. The present thoroughfare has also been constructed there and is oriented in the same direction. An early Christian basilica, surrounded by graves, was partially uncovered in that area in 1940, at a distance of ca. 400 meters from the city wall.[2] The constricted space, however, indicates that the cemetery must be rather small.[3]

The West Cemetery of the city, where the new Stobi Project has been at work since 1970,[4] was the object of some small-scale salvage excavations in 1965.[5] The necessity of that measure arose during the reconstruction of the wagon road Gradsko-Palikura (parallel to the road Babuna-Negotino), when some 30 graves were accidentally discovered, and for the most part destroyed, in the road section 23.850—24.430 km. Those graves were situated over the whole width of the plateau that lies between the alluvial valleys of the Erigon and the Axius.[6]

The road section is oriented N-S, except for slight deviations. The graves were exposed in lateral road ditches, especially in scarps, in

---

[2] J. Petrović, "U Stobima danas," *Glasnik Sarajevo* 54 (1942) 472, 488. Of the golden jewelry mentioned by the author, an earring and a finger ring (4th century A. C.) are in the Archaeological Museum of Skopje. Cf. also K. Petrov, "Kon otvorenoto prašanje na 6. bazilika vo Stobi," *Zbornik na filozofskiot fakultet* 22 (Skopje 1970) 313. During work on the railway in the vicinity in 1970 several Roman graves were excavated west of the above mentioned basilica; this discovery confirmed for the second time the existence of that Northeast Cemetery.

[3] Graves have also been found on the plateau of Orlova Čuka, 200—400 m. south of the basilica, perhaps within the broader limits of that Northeast Cemetery. The digging in 1970 of an irrigation canal along the western border of the plateau resulted in the discovery of 16 graves dating from the early and late Roman Empire.

[4] W-MZ (1971) 403—406; W-MZ (1972) 413—417; Al B. Wesolowsky, "Burial Customs in the West Cemetery," in this volume.

[5] The excavations were conducted by the Archaeological Museum of Skopje from August 18 — September 1, 1965. Cf. I. Mikulčić and V. Dautovska, "Stobi — antička nekropola," *Arheološki Pregled* 7 (1965) 126—128, pls. XLIV, XLIX.

[6] During the summer, 1971, the fields surrounding the Cemetery Basilica were again deeply plowed and a number of graves, mostly late Roman, were inadvertently disturbed. This unfortunate occurrence confirmed the extension of the cemetery, north of the Cemetery Basilica, to the northern edge of the plateau.

places where the road cuts slightly into the embankment. Many graves were so damaged that archaeological study of them seemed scarcely justified. It was, however, possible to get at least an idea of grave forms, of their construction, density and, in some cases, of the types of burial customs.

The destroyed graves were rather widely scattered along the road; their dispersal could give a wrong impression about the density and the disposition of the graves along that line. Four additional trenches, therefore, were dug at a more or less short distance from the road. Better preserved graves were uncovered in those trenches, and at one point the pavement of an ancient road was recognized, as well as the line of an aqueduct that ran along the road (Fig. 31).

GRAVES ALONG THE NEW ROAD

The graves formed three main groups along the above-mentioned road section of 580 meters' length. They are:

1) Part of the road from 23.880 to 23.900 km. Four graves were visible in the west ditch of the road (Nos. 24—27). Though they were almost totally destroyed, they were cleaned and examined. Their construction and the indicated burial customs suggest the late Roman period.

2) Part of the road from 24.175 to 24.215 km. Nine graves were visible in both road ditches and in the scarps; they were spacious chambers with walls of dressed stone slabs. The cover of only one grave was preserved. Five less damaged graves (Nos. 1—5) were cleaned and investigated. They had been dug relatively deeply into the ground; the level of the cover lay 0.70—1.10 m. below the present surface of the terrain. They contained several burials each and probably should be dated to the end of the ancient period (Fig. 33).

3) Part of the road from 24.367 to 24.407 km. (Fig. 32). Five graves were cut through in the west ditch and two more in the east ditch. All of them were investigated. They were either early Roman cremation burials (Nos. 6, 9, 12), or late Roman inhumation burials (Nos. 7, 8, 10, 11).

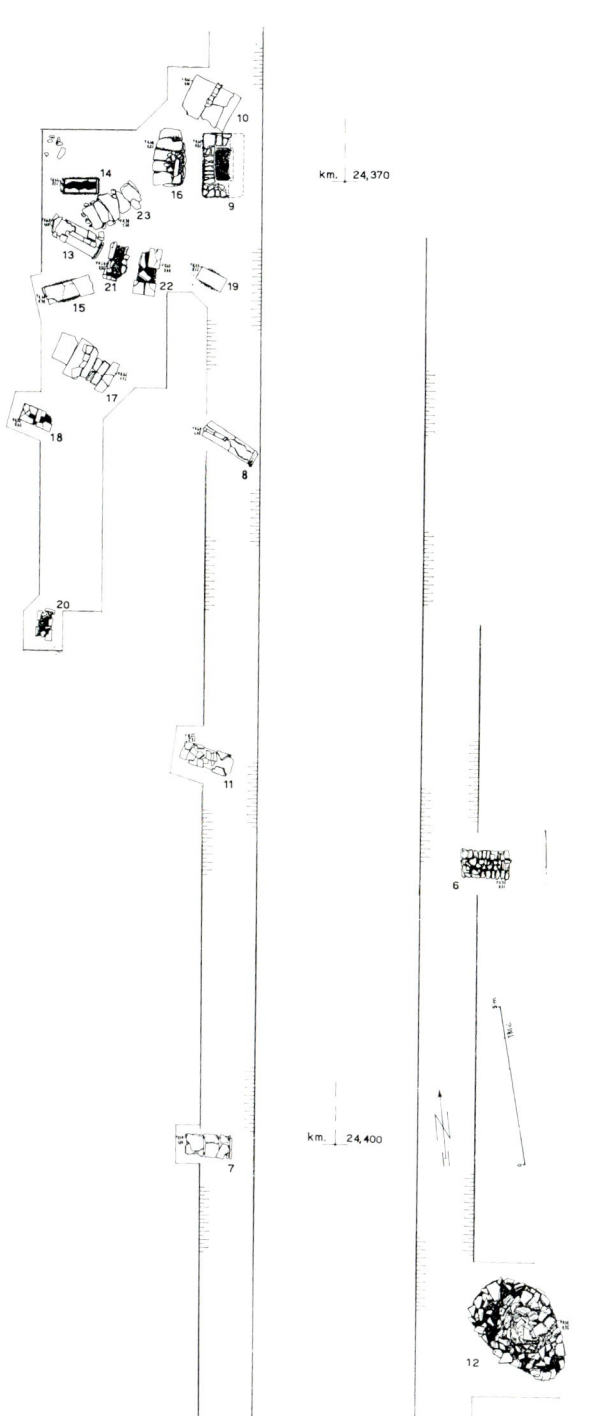

Figure 32. Graves 6—23 (road section 24.367—24.407 km. and Trench I).

GRAVES AND OTHER FINDS IN TRENCHES

Trench I. The trench was laid out along the road portion between 24.370 and 24.385 km., parallel to the west road ditch, and at a distance of 3.50 m. from it. The northern half of the trench, whose initial dimensions were 15 m. x 2 m., was later extended eastwards up to the east road ditch, so that it joined the area of the investigated Graves 8—10 (Fig. 32).

Trench I was dug in order to determine, in a minor section, the density of graves, their disposition and eventually their stratigraphy, since early Roman graves had been uncovered there for the first time along with late Roman graves. Eight more cremation graves were uncovered (Nos. 14—16, 18—22) at 0.25 to 0.40 m. below the surface, as well as three inhumations (Nos. 13, 17, 23), whose covers lay at a depth of only 0.65—0.90 m. below the surface.

Although those graves belong to a rather long period of time (1st-4th centuries), they formed a dense group in the northern part of the trench; the southern part, on the contrary, was empty.

Trench II. This trench was dug lengthwise against the western drainage ditch of the road between 24.320 and 24.330 km. Its dimensions are 10 m. by 4 m. and the orientation N-S. In the west scarp of the road, at a depth of 0.25—0.40 m. below the surface and extending over a length of several meters, a stone construction and a pile of stones were discovered. Further excavations showed that the stones formed the pavement of a road, probably ancient. Only the west edge of the pavement was recognizable; it lay at an angle to the line of the new road. In the northern part of the trench the line of pavement disappears into the scarp of the ditch in the direction of the new road; in the southern part of the trench, a part of the pavement 2.0 m. wide was recovered.

Towards the middle of the road, the stone pavement is firmer and better preserved; the larger and smaller stones are more densely packed. The stones are further apart at the edge, and at some points they are completely loose; there is no curb. Mingled with stones are some fragments of ancient tegulae, bricks and tiles. A few fragments of late Roman pottery were also found.

In the immediate vicinity of the excavated portion of the ancient road, an aqueduct line had been cut through during the construction of the new road. It consisted of terracotta pipes (interior diameter:

0.16 m.), cemented at the joints with white lime mortar. The aqueduct line was parallel to that of the ancient road pavement.

The aqueduct ran towards the Cemetery Basilica, i. e., the area in front of the Porta Heraclea. Roughly defined, it came from the west suburbs of the present village of Rosoman. It is a logical line of the aqueduct that supplied Stobi with water from springs in the vicinity of Sirkovo.

Trench III. At the time the new road was being built and graves laid bare along its line (summer 1965), Zemljoradnička Zadruga (Agricultural Cooperative) of Rosoman undertook the deep plowing of a piece of land extending to the Cemetery Basilica in the north. The fields between the newly built road to the west and the edge of the plateau along the Erigon to the east, were full of grave tegulae and stone slabs that had been pulled out by the plows. The highest concentration of that material was visible in the northern part of that area. There, at a distance of 120—130 m. SSW from the Cemetery Basilica, Trench III (10.0 m. x 3.0 m.) was laid out with a N-S orientation (Fig. 34).

The excavation revealed 8 graves, of which 2 were cremation burials (Nos. 28 and 34 a), and the rest (Nos. 29—34) inhumations. The graves were found at the depth of 0.15— 0.25 m. below the surface.

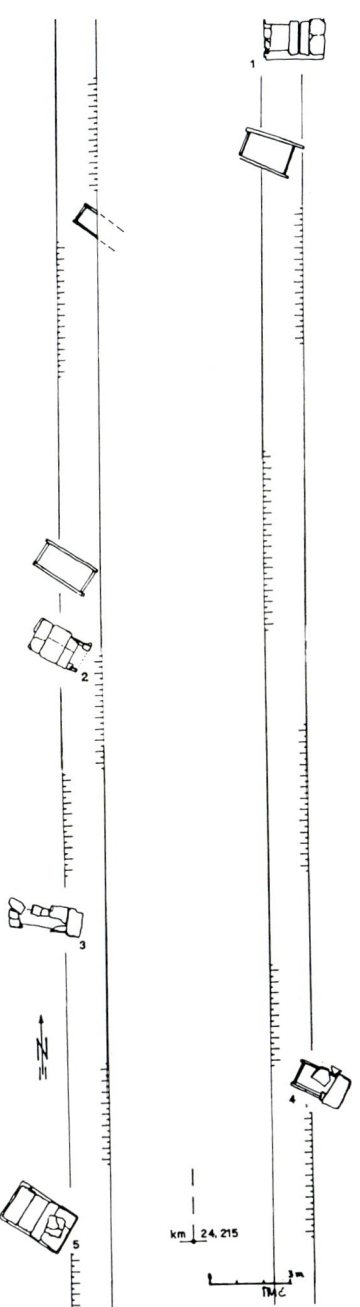

Figure 33. Graves 1—5 (road section 24.175—24.215 km.).

Some 25 meters east of that trench, the plows had destroyed an early cremation burial and had churned up to the surface much of the burnt material and some burial offerings. That grave (No. 35) was also investigated. At a distance of 165 m. southeast of Trench III, at the very edge of a plateau that slopes steeply into the alluvial valley of the Erigon, grave constructions consisting of large tiles are partly protruding above the surface of the field. One grave (No. 36) was excavated.

Trench IV. Trench IV was dug along the same edge of the plateau lying above the valley of the Erigon, but much further to the north than the graves mentioned above (at a distance of 112—120 m. SSW from the old Excavation House, in front of the south City Wall). Its dimensions are 8.0 m. x 2.0 m. and the orientation N-S. The trench was dug in order to determine the NE limits of the necropolis, i. e., the boundary line between the city and the cemetery (Fig. 31).

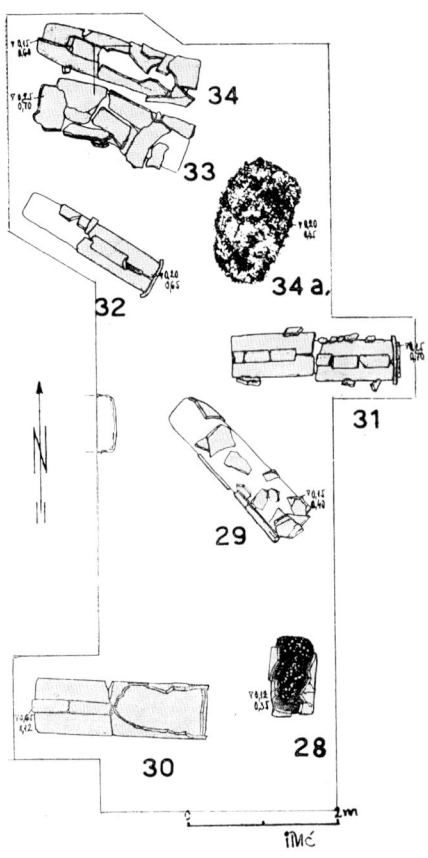

Figure 34. Graves 28—34a (Trench III).

A habitation horizon was recognized in the southern part of the trench, beginning at a depth of 0.15—0.20 m. below the surface, and wall foundations reach a depth of 0.55 m. Parts of four walls forming a small irregularly-shaped room were cleared. The walls are oriented NE-SW and NW-SE; they were built of stones cemented with mud.

Besides numerous animal bones, the finds included only ceramic cooking wares of the late 4th-5th centuries (and later?).

In the northern half of the trench, at a depth of 0.20 m., was a deposit of yellow earth representing decayed, unburnt bricks and containing a few pottery fragments. At a level of 0.75 m. below the surface, a dark earthen deposit was encountered which included a few fragments of late Roman hearth pottery, perhaps of the 4th century. Below that deposit, at a depth of 0.98 m. and 1.05 m. respectively, two open hearths were uncovered whose bases were bordered with stones. They were full

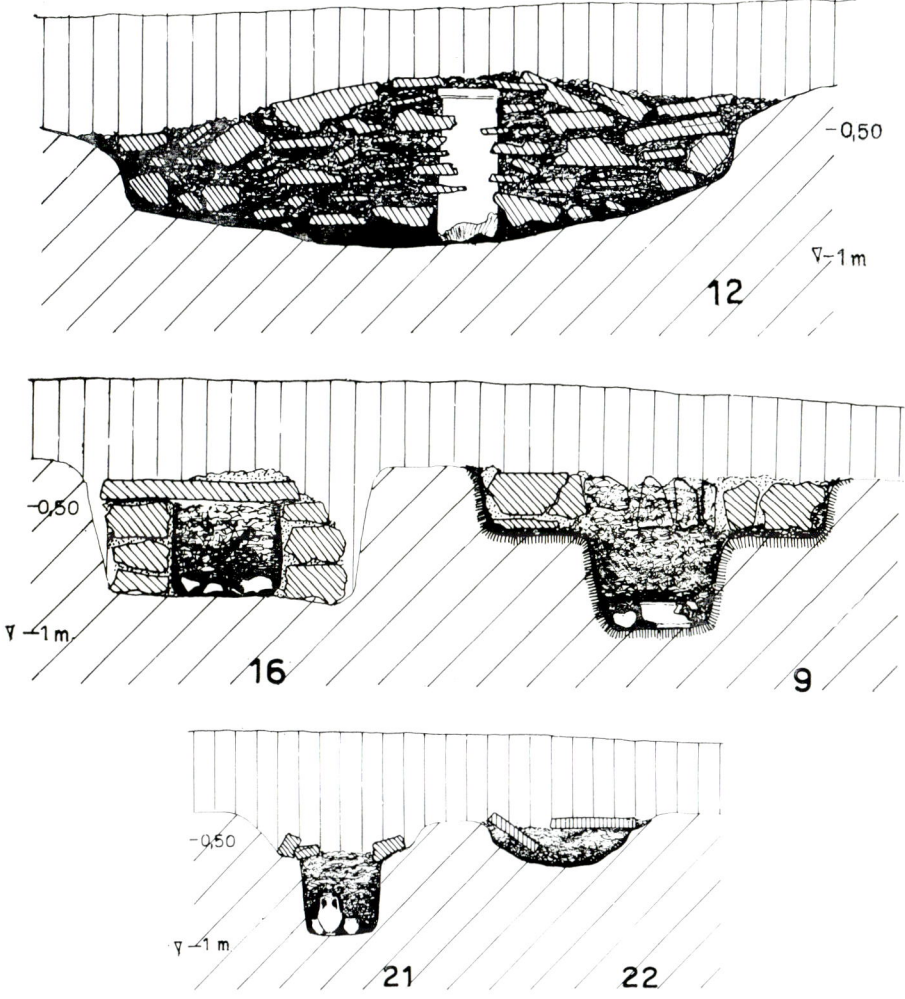

Figure 35. Cross-sections through early Roman Graves 12, 16, 9, 21, and 22.

of ashes and included numerous animal bones. The hearths lay on virgin soil, which is a light gray-yellow, hard clay, partly petrified.

Trench IV indicates that another settlement (a suburb?) existed outside the south City Wall at some period of late antiquity.

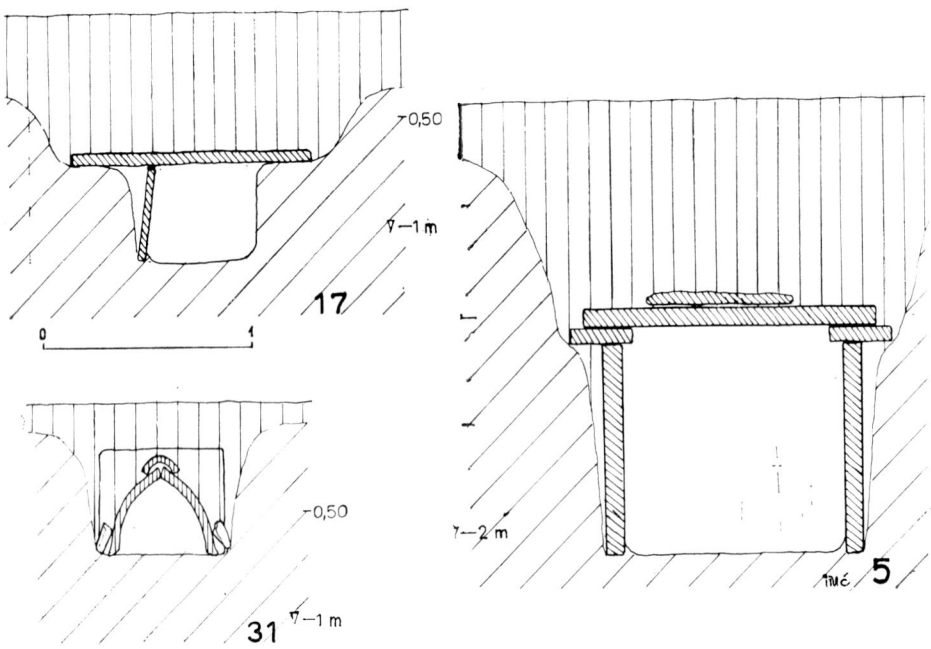

Figure 36. Cross-sections through late Roman Graves 17, 31, and 5.

★ ★ ★ ★

The excavated graves are to be grouped into two principal categories: cremation and inhumation burials.[7]

GRAVES WITH CREMATION BURIALS

Fifteen graves of this category were excavated. Nine of them included burial offerings, which enable us to date them to a period beginning with the late 1st century B. C., and lasting to the first half of the 3rd century A. C. They are described below.

---

[7] There is a striking difference in duration between certain grave forms discussed herein and the group of graves excavated more recently near the Porta Heraclea. For the latter see the references in footnote 4 above.

Grave 35. Orientation N-S. Dimensions ca. 1.60 m. x 0.70 m. Buried between 0.15 m. and 0.55 m. below the surface. A simple pit in the ground had been filled with cremation remains: plenty of soot and ashes, carbonized wood, fragments of burnt human bones. The plow brought to the surface the major part of the contents of the pit, including burial offerings, of which we do not know the exact number. The burial gifts recovered were as follows.

1) Alabastron of black glass with burnt white ornaments (feather-like motif), enamelling technique. Deformed in the fire and incomplete (Fig. 37).

2) Amphoriskos of ivory. Deformed in the fire (lower part missing). P. H. 0.065 m. (Fig. 38).

Figure 37. No. 1. Alexandrian glass alabastron from Grave 35.

Figure 38. No. 2. Ivory amphoriskos from Grave 35.

Figure 39. No. 3. Terracotta figurine fragment from Grave 35.

3) Terracotta figurine. P. H. 0.063 m. Gray clay. Fragmented in the fire, representation indistinct. The conic base of the figurine is open at the bottom (Fig. 39).

4) Fusiform unguentarium. H. 0.193 m. Ocher-gray clay. Brown slip, diluted, on neck. Exceptionally long foot, slightly curved rim (Fig. 40).

5) Fusiform unguentarium. P. H. 0.076 m. Only the upper part preserved. Yellow-brown clay, brown slip on neck (Fig. 41).

6) Fusiform unguentarium. P. H. 0.053 m. Only the lower part preserved. Yellow-brown clay. Type identical to Nos. 4 and 5 above but of a much smaller size (Fig. 42).

7) Lamp fragments partially disintegrated in the fire. Gray-brown clay, diluted lustrous brown slip. Late Hellenistic type.

8) Fragments of a small patera damaged in the fire. Reddish-gray clay. Fine work. Red lustrous slip.

9) Fragments of a small patera damaged in the fire. Light-brown clay. Brown lustrous slip.

10—11) Fragments of two small ceramic vessels damaged in the fire.

12) Fragments of a large amphora, type undetermined. Dark-yellow clay.

13) Bronze finger ring. D. 0.021 m.

14) Fragment of an iron object, perhaps the broad blade of a knife.

Figure 40—42. Nos. 4—6. Terracotta fusiform unguentaria from Grave 35.

Grave 34a. Orientation N-S. Buried between 0.20 m. and 0.45 m. below the surface. Dimensions 1.60 m. × 0.95 m. Oval, shallow pit, filled to the top with dark earth containing much soot and ashes, as well as several stones. Small fragments of partly burnt bones are scattered at the bottom.

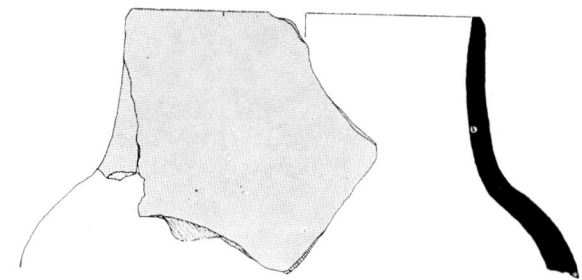

Figure 43. No. 15. Handmade bowl from Grave 34a.

The burial gifts were broken and mixed with the ashes.

15) Fragments of a large, ceramic vessel. Clay color ranging from dark gray to black. Coarse, handmade, with strokes polished on the exterior. A spherical bowl with cylindrical neck. Width of body ca. 0.155 m. (Fig. 43).

16) Fragments of a small pot. Gray clay. Rather good local work.

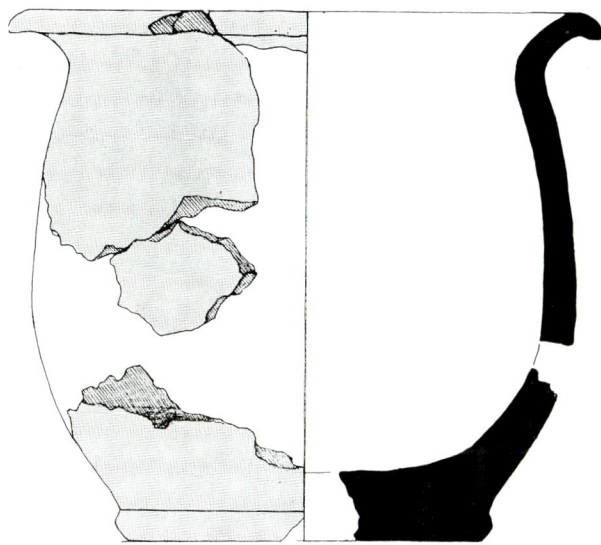

Figure 44. No. 17. Bowl from Grave 12.

Grave 12. Orientation NW-SE. Dimensions 3.70m. × 2.50 m. Buried between 0.30 m. and 0.95 m. below the surface. A simple, shallow pit of oval form; the edges were marked with large pebbles. The pit was filled with fragments of flat stone and of several tegulae. The thickness of the deposit in the center of the pit was 0.60 m. At the bottom of the pit, in its center, the upper part of a broken ancient column was erected (gray-green sandstone, simple work; D. 0.26 m. H. 0.57 m.). West of the column, a circular, earthen surface (D. 0.60 m.) appeared that was covered with fragments of burnt human bones, much ash, and parts of carbonized wood. The fragments of the following four ceramic vessels were intermingled in the soot of that deposit.

17) Fragments of a bowl. Clay color ranging from dark gray to black; admixture of quartzite. Roughly modelled, hand-made, exterior polished. Bottom large and flat, rim sharply curved outside. H. 0.075 m. (Fig. 44).

18) Fragments of a shallow dish. Coarse clay; color ranging from dark-gray to black. Roughly modelled by hand, exterior polished. Body almost horizontally extruded, vertical rim, exterior decorated with shallow, obliquely set grooves (turban dish).

19) Fragments of a small pot. Gray-brown clay, thin walls. Wheelmade. Spherical body and vertical rim.

20) Fragments of another similar small pot. Ocher clay. Orange-red, lustrous slip.

Grave 21. Orientation N-S. Dimensions 0.80m. × 0.40 m. Buried between 0.50 and 0.95 m. below the surface. Rectangular pit, filled with the cremation remains (plenty of ash; burnt human bones at the bottom). Rubble stones forming an incomplete chain, had been put around the upper part of the pit after the burial.

The following burial offerings were found at the bottom of the grave.

21) Roman coin. Aes. D. 0.022 m. Tiberius.

22) One-handled jug. Ocher-brown clay. Brown-red, lustrous slip over upper half. H. 0.191 m.; spherical body, small ring foot; small bell-shaped rim (Fig. 45).

23) Two-handled amphora. H. 0.194 m. Grey-ocher clay, diluted brown, lustrous slip over upper half. Ring foot slightly widened; mouth profiled (Fig. 46).

24) Bowl. H. 0.066 m. Fragmented. Ocher clay, fine work, red slip over upper half. Conical foot cut to form flat bottom. Out-turned rim; ribbon handle (Fig. 47).

(25) Bowl. H. 0.094 m. Fragmented. Dark clay, brown slip over upper two-thirds of vessel. Form similar to that of No. 24. Body nearly spherical (Fig. 48).

Figure 45. No. 22. One-handled jug from Grave 21.

Grave 6 (Fig. 58). Orientation E-W. Dimensions 1.40m. × 0.75 m. Buried between 0.35 m. and 0.75 m. below the surface; quadrangular pit. The upper part is lined with small stones arranged in a rectangular chain. The pit was covered with field stones. The deposit at the bottom included ashes, burnt bones of the deceased, and the following burial offerings.

Figure 46. No. 23. Amphora from Grave 21.

Figure 47. No. 24. Bowl from Grave 21.

Figure 48. No. 25. Bowl from Grave 21.

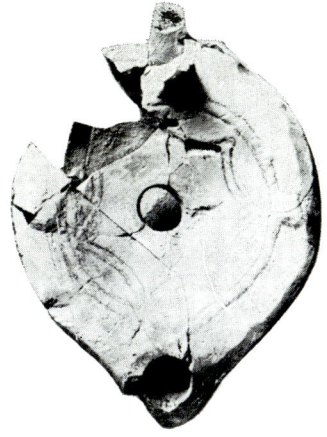

Figure 49. No. 31. Terracotta lamp from Grave 15.

26) Fragments of a small pot. Ocher clay, fine work, red-brown. Incomplete form.

27) Fragments of a small amphora. Ocher-yellow clay.

Grave 22. Orientation N-S. Dimensions 1.05 m. × 0.50 m. Buried between 0.40 m. and 0.60 m. below the surface. A simple, quadrangular pit, covered with flat, horizontally laid tiles. It contained a small quantity of soot and ash and the burnt bones of the deceased (perhaps a child) dispersed at the bottom. The following offerings were arranged in the center of the bottom.

28) Roman coin. Aes. D. 0.024 m. Marcus Aurelius.

29) Small pot. Fragmented in the fire and incomplete. Ocher-brown clay, thin, red-brown slip. Flat circular foot. Upper part unknown.

Grave 15. Orientation WSW-ENE. Buried between 0.38 m. and 0.70 m. below the surface. A simple, oval pit, covered with a large stone slab (1.55 m. by 0.65 m.).

The pit was filled with dark earth, a small quantity of ash; a few burnt bones of the deceased scattered at the bottom, and the following burial offerings.

30) Fragment of a beaker. Damaged in the fire; gray clay, probably local.

31) Moldmade terracotta lamp. It was found at the southeast end of the cover, outside the grave. L. 0.101 m. H. 0.027 m. Fragmented, red clay, unpainted. Disc bears a seven-angled figure of double lines. Framing band. Panels on rim (Fig. 49).

Grave 9. Orientation N-S. Dimensions 2.00 m. × 1.35 m. Buried between 0.35 m. and 1.15 m. below the surface. The quadrangular pit had vertical walls and two levels. The upper pit was 0.25 m. deep. The grave pit (0.98 m. × 0.56 m.; 0.35 m. deep) had been dug into the middle of the levelled bottom. The walls of the two pits were deeply burnt; the layer of red-burnt earth is 0.04—0.06 m. thick. A cover was placed above the upper pit. The cover consisted of a layer of rubble stones, cemented with poor lime mortar, set first into a rectangular frame; the interior was then filled with the same type of stones. One third of the upper pit and the major part of the cover were destroyed in the course of the road construction.

At the bottom of the lower pit a fairly large quantity of ash and carbonized wood was concentrated, together with the burnt bones of the deceased and the following burial offerings.

32) Terracotta moldmade lamp. Fragmentary; L. 0.082 m. Gray clay, dark-brown lustrous slip. A well-modelled child's head, hairless, with a chubby face and mild expression. The mouth was used as an opening for the wick. The filling

hole is on top and surrounded by a molded strip. The handle begins at the eyebrows and ends at the filling hole. The bottom is circular, concave, and includes a molded rosette (Fig. 50).

33) Semi-spherical bowl. D. 0.22 m. H. 0.095 m. Fragmentary. Brown-red clay with lustrous brown slip unevenly applied (outside and inside are both painted). Small, low, ring foot. High vertical rim (Fig. 51).

34) Decorative bone needle, smooth and without ornaments. Broken tip. L. 0.084 m.

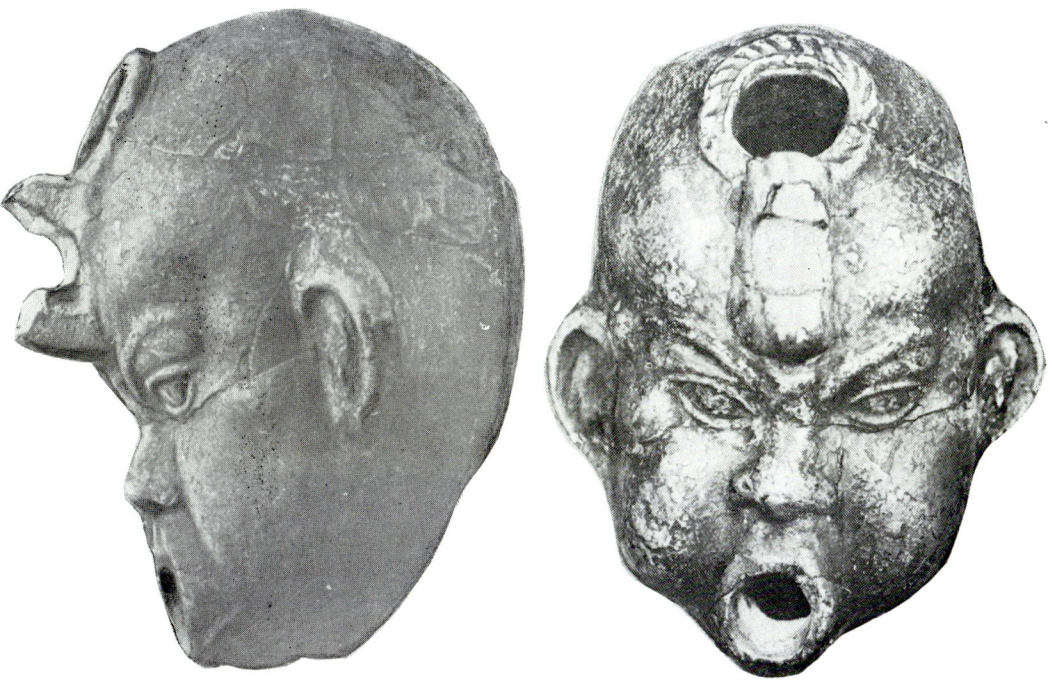

Figure 50. No. 32. Plastic lamp from Grave 9.

35) Unguentarium. Glass, melted in the fire and incomplete. There were also 5 iron nails, very small, probably for shoes.

Grave 16 (Fig. 60). Orientation N-S. Buried between 0.36 and 0.85 m. below the surface. A quadrangular pit with walls of rubble stones cemented with lime mortar. The pit walls were evenly coated with a smooth mortar. Dimensions 1.50 m. × 0.43 m. × 0.40 m. Covered with five stone slabs cemented with the same type of mortar.

At the bottom of the grave, which was of compact, white clay, there was a deposit of soot and a large quantity of ashes in which the burnt bones of the deceased were dispersed. The burial offerings, which lay at the north end, included the following.

36) A very small jug, fine work. Pale-red clay; diluted, lustrous brown slip. The vessel had been partially disintegrated in the fire and the major part of it is missing.

37) A pile of very small iron nails for shoes; head semi-spherical, body short and slim.

Figure 51. No. 33. Bowl from Grave 9.

The remaining five graves of that type did not contain any finds and cannot be even approximately dated. Graves 18—20 were in small, shallow pits covered with stone plates or tegulae. The cover of Grave 28 consisted of two tiles forming a roof. Grave 14 had a roof of the same sort, while the walls of its pit were burnt red.

* * *

The funeral offerings found in the graves described above, with two exceptions, were poor both in quantity and quality. They are the graves of the humbler inhabitants of Stobi. This allegation is supported in addition by the fact that they are 400 meters distant from the city wall and 900 meters from the Porta Heraclea. The exceptions are two of the oldest graves that were excavated, i. e., Graves 12 and 35.

Grave 35 contained some luxurious burial gifts. Unfortunately, only a small part of the grave's contents are preserved. The alabastron belongs to a characteristic group of Alexandrian enamelled glass. Judging by its form, it is probably Syrian in origin.[8] The vessel is characteristic of the period 3rd—1st centuries B. C. Grave 35, however, could hardly be dated earlier than to Augustan times. The serious political and economic crises in this region during the late Hellenistic era have already been recognized.[9] A stagnation remained until Augustan times, when an extraordinary economic and cultural revival started a new era of prosperity and a fundamental reconstruction of North Macedonian cities. This radical change has already been confirmed by a series of archaeological finds, and now, as a result of the most recent excavations, seems also attested at Stobi.[10] The existence of graves at such a distance from the city, and the large expanse of the cemetery at Stobi, are themselves indicators of the conversion of a small Hellenistic community into a large town.

The origin of the ivory amphoriskos, also found in Grave 35, is doubtless to be attributed to the same circles as the glass vessel just discussed. No analogous artifact has yet been found at other near-by sites. The ceramic unguentaria, with their slender and prolonged shape, represent the final stage of development of that Hellenistic type,[11] before it was replaced with the simpler bulbous form.

Grave 12 differs from the others in its dimensions. The importance of the deceased is stressed by, among other things, a column fragment brought from the ruins of some building and erected like a shaft in the middle of the grave. On the other hand, the grave construction itself is very simple and of a common type. Even among quite modest funeral gifts, one is astonished to find the fragments of two, roughly handmade vessels. They are certainly representative of simple autochthonous hearth pottery.

The process of Hellenizing the pottery in the North Macedonian region started rather early and was finished by the end of the late Archaic period.[12] In the course of the succeeding centuries, handmade pottery

---

[8] B. Filarska, *Szkla Starozytne* (Warszawa 1952) 72.

[9] I. Mikulčić, *Pelagonija u svetlosti arheoloških nalaza* (Beograd 1966) 84—85.

[10] Wiseman, *Guide*, "Historical Sketch."

[11] Mikulčić, *op. cit.* in note 9, pp. 51—52.

[12] *Ibid.*, pp. 30, 53. I. Mikulčić, "Ilirskoarhajski grobovi iz okoline Štipa," *Starinar* XIII—XIV (1962—1963) 205—206.

was uncommon in that region. The gray pottery of the Hellenistic period, intended mainly for household use, was also wheelmade. All the more strange, therefore, is the appearance of rough, handmade pottery in our Graves 12 and 34a (as well as in Graves 3 and 5 in the south court of the House of Peristerias at Stobi, dated to the 2nd—1st centuries B. C.[13]). The continuity of such a simple technique for rough kitchen wares, from pre-historic to Roman times, is certainly understandable, but the presence of such vessels in graves at Stobi is remarkable.

Early Roman pottery of fine quality is represented in Graves 6, 12, 21 (early 1st century), 22 (late 2nd century), 9 and 16 (the first half of the 3rd century). A red, red-brown or brown lustrous slip, often diluted, had been unevenly applied and it covered almost regularly only the upper half of vessels. The manner of painting, of shaping, and the colors of slips used are reminiscent of the technique and patterns of the contemporary Aegean civilization.[14]

The lamp (No. 32) from Grave 9, in the form of a child's head, is identical in both details and size to a lamp from the Athenian Agora of the first half of the 3rd century A. C.[15] Our lamp was either imported or made from a Greek mold. It is worth mentioning that a fragment of an identical lamp was uncovered in the Civil Basilica, Stobi, during the excavation campaign of 1956.[16]

The lamp (No. 31) from Grave 15 is of a very simplified make and had probably been manufactured in a local workshop. Judging by its form, the lamp should be dated to the transition from the 2nd to the 3rd century A. C.[17]

* * * *

The constructions of graves are more interesting than the finds they yielded. The basic form is an oval-quadrangular pit with irregular, oblique walls, shallowly dug in the ground and filled with the cremation

---

[13] I. Mikulčić, "Stobi. Peristerija. Kasno helenistički grobovi," *Arheološki pregled* 8 (1966) 113—114. For the location, see Plan of Site, no. 10.

[14] H. Robinson, *The Athenian Agora*, V: *Pottery of the Roman Period* (Princeton 1959) G. 103, Pl. 7, 42; G. 76, Pl. 4.

[15] Cl. Grandjouan, *The Athenian Agora* VI: *Terracottas and Plastic Lamps of the Roman Period* (Princeton 1961) p. 73, No. 915, Pl. 24.

[16] (Unpublished) The lamp is in the Archaeological Museum of Skopje, Inv. No. 495. For the location of the Civil Basilica, see Plan of Site, no. 2.

[17] T. Szentléleky, *Ancient Lamps* (Budapest 1969) 112—114.

remains. The orientations N-S and W-E are approximately equally represented.

The earliest graves were differently covered: Graves 34a and 35 have no cover, while the periphery of the big Grave 12 was marked by a wreath of large gravel, and the grave itself was filled to the top with stones. All the other graves were of small dimensions and covered either with rubble laid in the form of wreaths, forming frames above the grave pits (Nos. 6, 20, 21), or with horizontally-laid stone slabs or tegulae (Nos. 15, 18, 19, 22). The tegulae of Grave 18 are shown in Fig. 59. They belong to a period running from the early 1st to the early 3rd century A. C. In Graves 14 and 28, the cover consists of two tegulae forming a roof. That burial custom of a later epoch will be commented on below.

The graves of the group just cited, doubtless, belong to the autochthonous residents of Stobi. We have already pointed out their peripheral position, i. e., their distance from the city, and the modest character of the funeral offerings they contained. That simple grave form has its direct antecedents at Stobi, the graves uncovered below the House of Peristerias (2nd-1st centuries B. C.; see above). The pits of those graves are of the same type, but larger and more deeply dug; besides, they have no cover. Our early Graves 12, 34 a, and 35 are the most similar to them. Another analogy should be noted: the early Roman graves at Heraclea Lyncestis in front of the south city gate.[18]

In Grave 14, the walls of the pit were red-burnt, the remains of the faggot having been put into the grave in incandescent state; otherwise, the grave form is the same. Demir Kapija is the nearest geographical point where similar graves have been excavated. Six such graves were uncovered there in an early Roman cemetery (2nd and early 3rd centuries) along the right bank of the Bošava River.[19]

D. Srejović has recently described the burial ceremonies of early Roman times within the territory of present Yugoslavia.[20] He singles out the west region of that territory, the coastal zone of the Adriatic

---

[18] On the occasion of the regulation of the brook Siva Voda, in summer 1961, a group of early Roman cremation graves was uncovered along the south bank of the brook and in front of the southern gate of the city. The author investigated two burials which contained modest offerings. Regarding the position of the graves, see Mikulčić, *Pelagonija*, Pl. XXVIII, Fig. 39.

[19] D. Vučković-Todorović, "Antička Demir Kapija," *Starinar* XII (1961) 240.

[20] D. Srejović, "Rimske nekropole Ranog carstva u Jugoslaviji," *Starinar* XIII—XIV (1962-1963, 1965) 49—88.

littoral and the Danubian frontier region, where the process of Romanization was very intense and the largest settlements were inhabited by the Italians. Italic burial customs are met within those regions. On the other hand, there remains a large territory in the highlands (the north and east parts of Dalmatia, the inland of Pannonia Inferior and the whole of Moesia Superior outside the Limes zone) where there are graves dug into the ground without urns. Formally, territorially, and chronologically, they constitute a separate whole. They are strange to Italic settlers, and were used for the burial of autochthonous inhabitants.[21] The most archaic among them are the graves with singed sides (walls).

The graves at Stobi, cited above, belong also to that type. The region of North Macedonia is, therefore, at least in that respect, part of the territory just delimited. Besides, the graves at Stobi show that the ancient funeral custom of cremation was in use at Stobi, without interruption, until the middle of the 3rd century, whereas it was largely abandoned already about the middle of the 2nd century in Italy and in all Romanized province centers. The conservative adherence to the ancient custom is also confirmed by the simplicity of grave pits that underwent no change during the whole period of their existence.

Grave 9 is a double-pit with burnt walls, a specific variant of the general type cited above. Such graves are encountered in a restricted area that includes the province of Moesia Superior (Scupi,[22] Ulpiana, Viminacium-Žuto Brdo, M. Kopašnica,[23] Ratiaria[24]), and, sporadically, western Thrace.[25] The appearance of multi-storied graves in the Illyrian Domavia (northeastern part of the province of Dalmatia) was due to the opening of silver mines and the influx of inhabitants from the surrounding regions at the end of the 1st and in the course of the 2nd century A. C.[26]

---

[21] *Ibid.*, p. 81.
[22] I. Mikulčić, "Scupi. Istočna nekropola i jugo istočni bedem grada," *Arheološki pregled* 12 (1970/1971) 134—141; *idem.* "Scupi. Istočna nekropola, radovi u 1971," *Arheološki pregled* 13 (1971/1972).
[23] D. Srejović, *Starinar* XIII—XIV (1962—1963, 1965) 69, 71.
[24] D. Džonova in *Arheologija* IV, 4 (Sofija 1962) 3, 30, 32.
[25] D. Nikolov and H. Bujukliev in *Arheologija* IX, 3 (Sofija 1967) 10; G. Tabakova and L. Getov in *Arheologija* XI, 4 (Sofija 1969) 29, 31, Fig. 3. Other sites where such grave constructions of "Thracian" type were noticed are quoted by L. Getov in *Arheologija* XI, 1 (Sofija 1969) 42, 44, 45.
[26] M. Baum and D. Srejović, *Članci i građa za kulturnu istoriju istočne Bosne* III (Tuzla 1959) 23—54; IV (1960) 3—31; and VI (1965) 7—31.

The explanation of the origin of such graves far in the northern part of Pannonia (Intercisa)[27] is still uncertain. Their use was most probably due to the colonization of that region by soldiers and civilians emigrating from southeast provinces.

The oldest graves of that specific type have been found in the east necropolis of Scupi. They are the graves of autochthonous pilgrims, traceable from Augustan times; they had developed there directly from a similar form coming down from pre-Augustan times.

I believe that form came into use at Stobi through the neighboring Scupi. Geographically it is the nearest point, but there are other evidences of direct contacts between the two cities at that time. E. g., S. Caelidius Secundus, a native of Stobi, became a "decurio coloniae Scupensis."[28] The potter Σεκούνδος Στοβαῖος stamped his lamps, of which one has been uncovered in the necropolis of Scupi.[29] On the other hand, the name Σκουπῖνα[30] is registered among the natives in the surroundings of Stobi.

GRAVES WITH INHUMATION BURIALS

According to burial technique, three principal forms of these graves are to be distinguished.
1) Graves covered with large tegulae forming sloping surfaces in the form of a roof.
2) Quadrangular narrow pits covered with horizontally-laid stone slabs.
3) Spacious chambers of finely worked stone slabs, destined to harbor several consecutive burials.

1) GRAVE CONSTRUCTIONS WITH TEGULAE FORMING TWO SLOPING SURFACES.

Ten graves of this form have been excavated; only three of them (Graves 8, 11 and 36) contained burial gifts.

---

[27] K. Sági, *Intercisa* I (Budapest 1956/57) 112 ff.

[28] *CIL* III, 8203 (2nd century A. C.).

[29] Graves of foreigners within the East Necropolis, Grave No. 123 (early 3rd century A. C.); unpublished.

[30] N. Vulić, *Spomenik* 71 (1931) No. 123, from Vataša near Kavadarci; early 3rd century A. C.

Grave 11. Orientation E-W. Dimensions 1.75 m. × 0.65 m.; buried between 0.55 m. and 0.95 m. below the surface. The construction includes four tegulae, fragmented, probably in repeated handling during consecutive burials.

The grave contained three skeletons, stretched on the back, with hands on the hips. Two of them (L. 1.53 m. and 1.58 m.) had the head to the east, and the third (L. 1.46 m.) to the west. The latest buried skeleton, which was in the middle, is best preserved. Near its head was a jug, the only burial gift found in that grave.

38) Jug. H. 0.212 m.; red-burnt micaceous clay; diluted, red lustrous slip, unevenly applied (only the upper half is painted). Very shallow grooves around the body and the neck; slightly concave foot with a molded button in the center; out-turned rim (Fig. 52).

Grave No. 8. Orientation NW-SE. Dimensions 2.20m. × 0.55/0.43m. Buried between 0.60 m. and 1.08 m. below the surface. The construction consists of four tegulae (0.85 m. × 0.45 m.); the upper ridge is protected by two imbrices (0.70 m. × 0.17 m. × 0.16 m.). The front sides were closed with fragments of tegulae.

The skeleton of a rather short person, very badly preserved, was stretched on the back with legs to the east. The left hand lay alongside the hip.

There was only a single burial offering in the grave, in the vicinity of the ilium.

Figure 52. No. 38. One-handled jug from Grave 11.

39) Roman coin. Aes. D. 0.023 m. Licinius.

Grave 36. Orientation NW-SE. Dimensions 2.10m. × 0.58m. Buried between 0.00 m. and 0.35 m. below the surface. The construction consists of 4 fragmented tegulae.

The skeleton was that of an adult (L. 1.52 m.). It was stretched on the back with the head to the NW. Heaps of soot and ash were underneath the skull; the slightly bent arms rested on the hips. The following ornaments were on the right forearm and around the neck of the deceased (a female).

40) Bracelet of bronze wire, of quadrangular section. D. 0.062 m. The wire ends were twisted crosswise, thinned, and bound into two loops (Fig. 53).

41) Torques of a rather thick iron wire. D. 0.126 m. The ends were twisted crosswise like those of the above-mentioned bracelet. Reduced to small fragments (Fig. 54).

Figure 53. No. 40. Bracelet from Grave 36.
Figure 54. No. 41. Necklace from Grave 36.

Graves 13, 24, 25, 27, 30, 31, and 32 did not contain any gifts. They all are of similar construction and oriented E-W; Grave 31 is illustrated in Fig. 61. Graves 27 and 30 contained two burials each. The skeletons were poorly preserved.

The jug (No. 38) from Grave 11 is the most ancient find in that group. Its characteristics date it to the middle or second half of the 4th century A.C.[31]

Grave 8, which contained a coin of Licinius (remarkably well preserved; evidently only briefly in circulation), is most probably to be dated to the 3rd or 4th decade of the 4th century. Grave 36 is of the same date. A direct analogy, a female grave with an identical bracelet and torques, is represented by Grave 5 in the necropolis of Keralo Živojno near Bitola.[32] The grave contained 14 coins (Constantius I, Constantinus I, Maximinus Daja, Licinius, Crispus), and could be precisely dated to the 3rd or 4th decade of the 4th century.

Eight similar bracelets, which have been found at Scupi, have been dated as a group to the first half and the middle of the 4th century.[33] With the exception of the two examples cited, the metallic necklaces (torques) are unknown within a fairly large surrounding region.

The construction of the graves is that of the well-known late Roman type that was in use in the major part of the Empire by the late 3rd and 4th centuries. It is also found in a large number of cemeteries of the North Macedonian region, in fact in all areas where large tegulae were manufactured. In regions to which those tegulae could not be transported, they were replaced by graves of a simpler type, constructed of stone slabs roughly arranged in a narrow pit or a narrow chamber, dug in the ground and covered with slabs. In any case, the tegulae constructions with two sloping surfaces were already used in early Roman graves with cremation burials. Later on, they were also used for inhumation burials.

As parallels within the period of time in which those graves were built at Stobi, I will cite two important adjacent centers: Scupi, with its already mentioned East Necropolis, which still existed at that time, and the cemeteries at Varoš-Prilep (Bakalica, Padarnica, Tašačica).[34] Such a grave construction for inhumation burials does not appear at those sites until the transition from the 3rd to the 4th century, and it goes out of use before the last quarter of the 4th century.

---

[31] Cf. H. Robinson, *The Athenian Agora*, V, L. 9, Pl. 16; M. 164, M. 172, Pl. 25.

[32] The Museum of Bitola, v. k. 2994, 2996. The excavations of the cemetery were conducted by that museum in 1956; the results are as yet unpublished.

[33] East Necropolis, Graves 90a, 135, 163; all as yet unpublished. Previous reports on those excavations were cited above in note 22.

[34] B. Babić, "Bakalica, Tašačica — Prilep," *Arheološki pregled* 3 (1961) 97—100.

2) QUADRANGULAR NARROW PITS COVERED WITH HORIZONTALLY LAID STONE SLABS.

Eight graves of this type have been excavated; two of them included burial gifts.

Grave 10. Orientation NW-SE. Dimensions 1.60 m. × 0.80 m. Buried between 0.45 m. and 0.95 m. below the surface. A simple rectangular pit covered with 3 large stone slabs. The gap between two slabs was covered with a row of imbrices, probably after the additional burial.

The grave contained two skeletons of adults lying on the back with an indistinct position of arms. The first burial, whose head is to the west, was much disturbed. The head of the second burial was to the east.

The following burial gifts, which belonged to the first deceased, a woman, were found.

42) Part of bronze earrings, fragmentary. Consists of a wire ring with a loop to which a pendant was attached. A flattened glass bead was inserted in the pendant (Fig. 55).

43) Eight beads of dark glass paste, strung in a necklace. Very tiny and decayed.

Figure 55. No. 42. Bronze earrings from Grave 10.

Grave 17 (Fig. 62). Orientation WNW-ESE. Dimensions 1.75 m. by 0.53 m. Buried between 0.65 m. and 1.15 m. below the surface. The south and east walls of the pit were faced with broken slabs. The cover consisted of 6 such slabs laid horizontally.

The bones of the first burial were heaped at the east end of the grave. The skeleton of the second burial (a rather young woman) was partially flexed with its legs drawn up to the left (Fig. 63). The head was to the west, the left arm stretched along the body with right arm on the ilium (L. 1.53 m.). Earrings were found in the region of the ears and a ring on the middle finger of her right hand.

44) A pair of silver earrings, identical. Each consists of a ring with a locket and a noose to which a long pendant is attached. The latter has five identical bead like thickenings in a row, divided by grooves. Total length 0.059 m. D. of ring 0.024 m. (Fig. 56).

45) A finger ring of poor silver. D. 0.019 m. Made of a narrow strip, bent to form a ring, with a head added in the form of a square plate. The upper surface of the latter is ornamented with an indistinct figure set within a frame formed by a series of dots (Fig. 57).

Figure 56. No. 44. Silver earrings from Grave 17.

Figure 57. No. 45. Silver finger ring from Grave 17.

The other graves are of similar construction, except for Grave 7 (a child's grave), in which the four walls of the pit were lined with stone slabs, while the bottom was paved with small, square bricks.

Figure 58. Grave 6 before removal of stones.

The earrings from the graves just described belong to the late Roman type of earrings with pendants that were frequent at that epoch, especially in eastern provinces. Representative examples in gold are known from the following sites: Stobi (Northeast Cemetery),[35] Pešterica

Figure 59. Grave 18 showing horizontally-laid tegulae.

Figure 60. Grave 16 after excavation.

---

[35] Archaeological Museum, Skopje; finds before World War II; see note 2.

near Prilep,[36] Dobri Dol near Skopje;[37] typologically, the most similar to our finds are gold examples from Ulpiana[38] and a bronze pair from Grave 51 at Scupi. Those finds belong to the middle and to the second half of the 4th century.

The finger ring (No. 45) from Grave 17 also has characteristics of the 4th century.[39]

The author's opinion regarding the construction of this group of graves has been offered above. They are for the most part contemporary with tile graves, but outlive them by far; they were in use by the end of the 4th century. It is actually the most common type of late Roman graves in the North Macedonian region.

3) SPACIOUS STONE CHAMBERS (CISTS).

This form doubtlessly developed from the previous type towards the end of antiquity; it was adapted for family burials in one tomb. From a group of 8 such graves that were uncovered in the road section between 24.175 and 24.215 km., only four graves have been completely excavated (Nos. 1, 2, 4, 5). All of them had been built in the

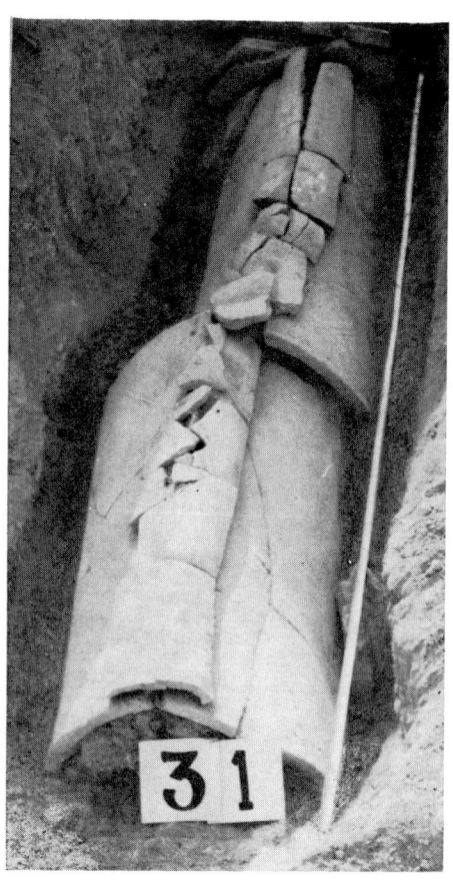

Figure 61. Tile Grave 31.

[36] B. Babić, "Pešterica — Oreovec — Prilep," *Arheološki pregled* 7 (1965) 133.

[37] D. Vučković—Todorović, "Rimski dvojni grob iz Dobrog Dola," *Starinar* VII—VIII (1959) 259.

[38] E. Čerškov, *Rimljani na Kosovu* (Beograd 1969) fig. 15.

[39] F. Henkel, *Die Römischen Fingerringe der Rheinländer und der benachb. Gebiete* (Berlin 1913) S. 16, Nos. 98, 99, Taf. VI (almost identical to our find; late 4th and beginning of the 5th century); also p. 98, Nos. 1062—1064, 1070, 1071, Taf. XLII (type A. IV-s: rings without stone, with a flattened bezel separately made).

same manner of monolithic slabs of soft sandstone, carefully dressed and polished. The corner joints had been cemented with clay so that the tombs give the impression of monolithic sarcophagi.

Their capacity is impressive: 1.90—2.30 m. long, they are 0.96—1.05 m. wide and 1.00—1.25 m. deep. The cover consists of several

Figure 62. Grave 17 before opening.

long, dressed slabs, laid perpendicularly to the grave's axis. In order to remove more easily the cover slabs for additional burials and prevent wearing out the upper edges of wall slabs, a new element had been introduced in the construction of graves: a frame of horizontally-set slab strips that covered the edges of the grave lining. The slabs of the cover slid easily on that frame.

The four graves had all been opened and robbed in antiquity (the other graves of that group, which were not excavated, had suffered a similar fate; their covers had for the most part been taken away).The bones of skeletons were disturbed and piled at one end. The remains of at least 2—3 skeletons were found in each of the four graves. There were no traces of burial offerings.

This group of graves is identical to the graves found below the Cemetery Basilica. It is for the time being the only argument in support of the dating of those graves. They may be dated roughly to the late 4th—5th centuries.

The number of excavated graves is not sufficient to provide even an approximate answer to questions such as: What was the extent of the necropolis, the direction in which it was spreading, the time of its creation, and that of its abandonment? However, taking into account the distribution of points that have been examined, as well as the superficial indications found in the surroundings, I would make the following suggestions.

Figure 63. Skeleton of young woman in Grave 17 from the east.

1) Beginning in Augustan times and in the course of the early Roman era, the graves extended to a distance of at least 900 meters beyond the Porta Heraclea. The points which confirm that conclusion (line: Trench I—Trench III—Cemetery Basilica) are roughly congruent with the line of the ancient road to Heraclea, of which part was uncovered in Trench II. The belt of early Roman graves along that road does not seem to have been very broad.

2) In late Roman times, the southwest necropolis (West Cemetery) covered quite a spacious area of at least 15—16 hectares.

3) In late antiquity (5th century?), the area of the necropolis is very much reduced. That can be deduced from the architecture in Trench IV as well as from the entirely limited position of the latest graves that have been excavated.

ЗАПАДНА НЕКРОПОЛА

ИСКОПАВАЊА У 1965. ГОДИНИ

ИВАН МИКУЛЧИЋ

У времену од 18. VIII до 1. IX 1965 г. Археолошки музеј у Скопљу извео је мање заштитно ископавање на југозападној некрополи Стоба[3]. Ово је било наметнуто радовима на реконструкцији локалног пута Градско - Паликура, који је на деоници км. 23,850—24,430 пресекао и разорио већи број гробова. И дубоко преоране парцеле Пољопривредног добра из Росомана, што леже на великом делу ове некрополе, масом гробног конструктивног материјала извученог на површину наговестили су обим некрополе, конструкције гробова и њихово груписање у појединим секторима.

Поред ископавања оштећених гробова уз поменуту деоницу пута, отворене су и 4 сонде (види сл. 31). Испитано је укупно 37 гробова, који испуњавају време од епохе Августа до Касне антике.

Од гробова са кремацијом откопано је укупно 15. Основни тип претстављају плитке овалне јаме малих димензија и неоформљених страница сл. 35). Сумарно су покривене водоравно положеним каменим плочама, комадима тегула, опекама или ситнијим каменом који углавном формира правоугаони венац над јамом.

Најстарији гробови (бр. 12, 34 а, 35) су већих димензија и са елементима који упућују на предавгустовско време (сасвим блиске аналогије имају у гробовима испод Перистеријине куће у Стобима, II-I век ст. е. [10]. Гробови 12 и 34 а. су дали делове грубих посуда, рађених слободном руком (сл. 43, 44). У гробу 35 дарови су били богатији, иако тешко оштећени у ватри, распаднути и некомплетни (3 вретенаста унгуентариа, александриски алабастрон од двобојног стакла, амфориск од белокости, лампа, теракотна статуета, више посудица, бронзан прстен и распаднуто железо сечиво сл. 37—42).

Преостали гробови су сиромашни даровима. Керамика носи сва обележја истовремених производа у егејском свету (сл. 45—51). Најмлађи гроб ове групе, бр. 9, датиран је лампом у рани III век) (сл. 51)[12]. Овај гроб има правилну етажну конструкцију, са јако опаљеним (нагорелим) зидовима. Ове специфичне конструкције се срећу углавном на подручју које је обухватала провинција Горња Мезија[19-21]. Иначе, основни тип откопаних гробова најближи је таквим гробовима из унутрашњости слабо романизованог Средњег Балкана[18], а индицира њихову припадност скромнијим слојевима аутохтоног становништва.

Од гробова са инхумацијом уочена су 3 типа. Двосливне конструкције, грађене од великих гробних тегула, заступљене су са 10 откопаних гробова. Од ових само 3 су имали дарове: гроб 11 — керамички крчаг (сл. 52; друга половина III века)[27], гроб 8 — монету императора Лицинија и гроб 36 — наруквицу од бронзе са двојно везаним крајевима и железни торквес — огрлицу (сл. 53, 54; друга четвртина IV века).[28—29]

Следећих 8 гробова претстављају просте раке укопане у земљу, покривене водоравно положеним плочама. У 4 случаја, једна или обе бочне стране су обложене комадима камених плоча да се земља не би обрушила. Гроб 7 је потпуно оформљена камена циста, са подом од мањих опека. Гроб 33 датиран је новцем Констанција II и Валентинијана I; гроб 17 - наушницама и прстеном од сребра (сл. 56, 57), гроб 10 делом наушнице истог типа (сл. 55) — сви из друге половине IV века и са краја истог.

Гробови бр. 1—4 су веома простране цисте, савршено склопљене од лепо обрађених монолитних плоча и делују као саркофази (сл. 36). Садржавали су по неколико скелета. Ови су редовно били испретурани од провалника још у антици. Ове породичне гробнице идентичне су таквој групи гробница испод и око Гробљанске цркве, откопаних током I светског рата[1]. Можемо их датирати само оквирно: под крај IV и у V век.

Закључићемо следећим опаскама: већ од времена Августа некропола се простире дуж пута ка југу (ка котлини Пелагоније) у дужини од најмање 900 m испред југозападне капије града. У сонди II откривена је и деоница поменутог пута са каменом калдрмом, као и античка водоводна жила уз пут. Архитектонски остаци у сонди IV потврђују постојање скромног подграђа изван јужних градских зидина, у једном краћем периоду касне антике (углавном V век).

BURIAL CUSTOMS IN THE WEST CEMETERY

by

AL B. WESOLOWSKY

INTRODUCTION

Excavations in the West Cemetery of Stobi were conducted during the 1970 and 1971 seasons, ultimately opening up a trench measuring 9.00 m. × 10.75 m. The area of excavation was approximately bounded by Stobi grid areas S 81-87 and W 135-140. The original trench was laid out prior to the extension of the site grid area system to these excavations. Thus, the trench lines do not coincide exactly with the site grid area system.[1]

Generally, the excavations reached a depth of some 2.35 m., from the modern surface at 150.75 m. down to 148.40 m. Tests through sterile Quaternary gravels encountered a weathered Tertiary sandstone at an

---

[1] Earlier reports on these excavations were published by James Wiseman and Djordje Mano-Zissi in *AJA* 75 (1971) 395—411, and *AJA* 76 (1972) 407—424, cited hereafter as W-MZ (1971) and W-MZ (1972) respectively. The Stobi grid is explained in W-MZ (1972) 407. For the location, see Plan of Site, no. 22.

Ivan Mikulčić, elsewhere in this volume, reports on earlier excavations of Roman graves along a modern road to the W of the Cemetery Basilica. Doubtless these graves, as well as those of the West Cemetery, were those of inhabitants of Stobi.

elevation of 147.13m.[2] This last is some 3.62 m. below the modern ground surface.

The excavations located a total of 93 graves which were numbered sequentially as they were found. Four graves were located in excavations outside the West Cemetery and will not be considered here except to mention that Graves 7 and 9 were found in a test to the NW of the Cemetery Basilica and Graves 87 and 97 were encountered in the East Parodos of the Theater. Of the 93 graves found in the West Cemetery, 9 were not completely excavated since they extended into one trench face or another for the greater part of their length.

The use of the area as a cemetery extends from early in the time of Augustus up through part of the 4th century after Christ. Five periods have been recognized in this sequence on the basis of stratigraphy and the dates of the individual graves as indicated by context ceramics and grave offerings. A variety of grave constructions, referred to as "grave forms," have been recognized and these are described in the body of this paper.

This paper is not a complete report on the archaeology of the West Cemetery. At this point in our investigations at Stobi we are concerned with dating the periods of use of the cemetery, the definition of grave forms, and the description of individual graves. Work on the analysis of the skeletal remains is incomplete. Also, more study must be done on the grave offerings before they can be articulated with the archaeology of the cemetery. Detailed descriptions of the grave offerings would have made an intolerable addition to the length of this report.

GRAVE FORMS

Ideally, any system of organization of archaeological data should have as its goal the replication of cultural reality. A well-understood chronology is essential towards such an end as well as information presented in ancient texts. However, since archaeologists are forced to deal primarily with non-perishable cultural manifestations, it is inevitable that disputes will arise concerning the cultural appropriateness of such systems of organization. This is particularly true of attempts to order data from cemeteries where stratification is complex, samples are small,

---

[2] The interpretation of the geological setting of the West Cemetery was provided by Dr. Robert Folk during his stay at Stobi in 1971.

and we are ignorant of a host of culturally important funeral rites. Within these limitations it remains for the archaeologist to define his attributes and to generate probability statements about associations among attributes. Associations that are recognized will eventually figure in the identification of types.

The use of the term "form" rather than "type" of grave is deliberate. The archaeological type concept as discussed by Irving Rouse,[3] Alex D. Krieger,[4] and others refers to artifacts and other cultural manifestations sharing a number of attributes and which are distributed within certain temporal and spatial limits. To apply this potentially rigorous notion to a sample of only 93 graves dating through four centuries would give an unwarranted formality to this paper. Some of the attributes of these graves exist throughout the span of the sequence, and some of the grave forms share most of their attributes. The problem of trying to weigh attributes would likely lead us to the formulation of several "types," each of which might be represented only by a single grave.

The sample of graves from Stobi, of course, represents a portion of a sequence from a single site. Even if we were to identify the temporal parameters of an attribute, the problem of spatial distribution would remain. Since these graves represent an aspect of life during the Roman period, any ordering of data should reflect the mores of a cultural unit more generally distributed than merely the settlement at Stobi.

What, then, can be considered the minimum dimensions of spatial distribution for "types" which are present not only at Stobi but likely within the Central Balkans as well? Although interesting, this question is not germane to this paper. Rather, we seek to recognize and identify attributes which will be of eventual use in the formulation of a typology of Roman graves in (at least) Macedonia. Any forms of graves recognized at Stobi should be testable against additional information from future excavations.

Grave forms are first divided on the basis of the treatment of the corpse, whether it had been inhumed in the flesh or had been cremated. Other attributes were the presence or absence of tiles or other constructions covering the grave and the arrangement of the tiles. Thus, each variant in the attribute of grave construction is itself an attribute.

---

[3] *Prehistory in Haiti: A Study in Method*, Yale University Publications in Anthropology, No. 21 (New Haven 1939).

[4] "The Typological Concept," *American Antiquity* 9 (1944) 271—288.

1. The treatment of the corpse.
   A. Inhumation (Figs. 64, 66—68).
   B. Cremation[5] (Figs. 64, 65, 70, 71, 73, 76).

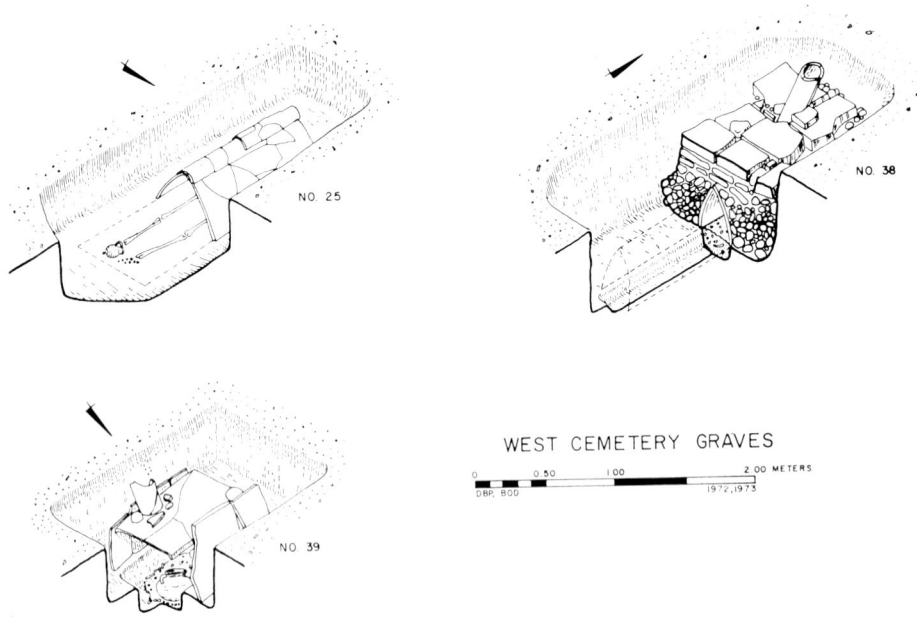

Figure 64. Examples of arched tile inhumation (No. 25), arched tile double pit cremation with rock cairn and libation spout (No. 38), and a boxed tile double pit cremation with libation spout (No. 39).

---

[5] In a number of the cremations there was evidence that a fire had been built in the pit of the grave at some point in the funeral ceremonies. In such cases, the walls and bottom of the pit would be scorched. Also there would be carbonized wood in such quantity that it could not have been gathered up inadvertently with the cremated bones at the site of the cremation and subsequentially deposited in the grave pit. In no instance, however, was there a sufficient quantity of ash and carbonized wood to indicate that the corpse had been cremated in the grave. W-MZ (1972) 414, comment on these circumstances and suggest that there may have been a reburning of the cremated remains at the time of interment or that the fire may have served to consecrate the grave site. These suggestions, as they point out, are not mutually exclusive. In the present report there is a distinction between the "cremation fire", in which the corpse was cremated, and the "grave fire" which was built in the grave pit.

J. M. C. Toynbee, *Death and Burial in the Roman World* (London 1971) 49, states that in the Roman World, "For obvious reasons no cremations were allowed to take place within the city's precincts." Since our excavations at Stobi have concentrated on the city proper, it is not too surprising that we have yet to identify a locale where cremations took place. See "Summary" infra.

2. The construction of the grave.
   A. Tiles absent.
      The remains, whether cremated or inhumed, were placed in a pit which was then backfilled (Figs. 65—67, 70, 71). In two cases cremated remains were placed in a vessel set into a shallow pit in the ground (Fig. 71).

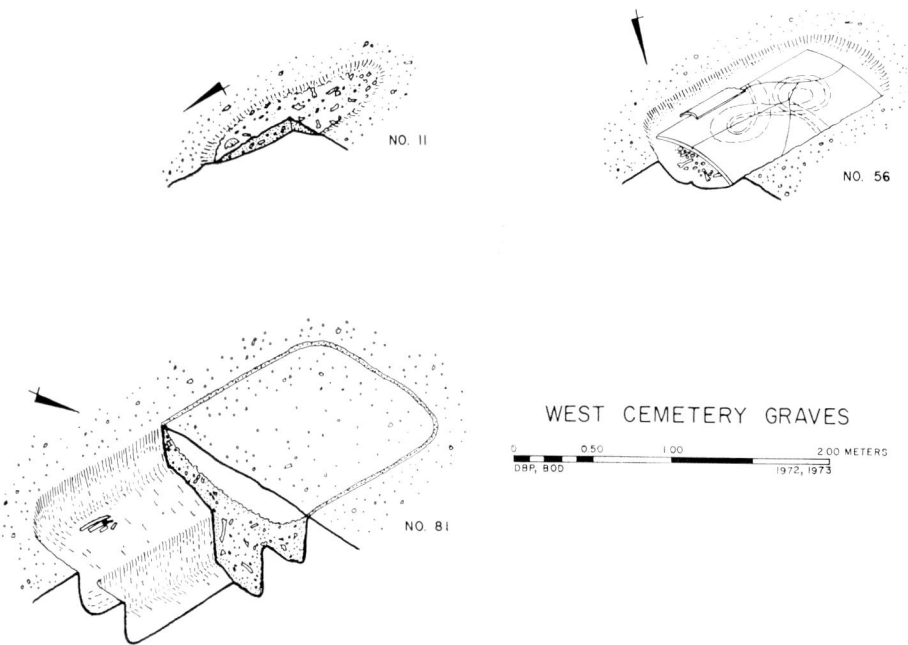

Figure 65. Examples of shallow pit cremation (No. 11), flat tile cremation (No. 56), and a double pit cremation with ash border (No. 81).

   B. Tiles present.
      Tiles used in grave construction were predominately Laconian pan tiles. In a few cases these were supplemented by Laconian cover tiles or Corinthian pan tiles.
      (1) *Arched tiles* (Figs. 64, 69, 72). After the corpse or cremated bones were interred in a rectangular pit, Laconian pan tiles were arranged along the sides of the pit and formed a tent-like arch over the remains. Occasionally, Laconian cover tiles were set atop the apex of the arch.

At the ends of the pan tiles the grave was often closed off with stones or fragments of tiles.[6]

(2) *Flat tiles* (Fig. 65). The corpse or cremated bones were placed in a pit, and one or more Laconian pan tiles were laid flat over the pit.

(3) *Boxed tiles* (Figs. 64, 75). Within a rectangular grave pit, a combination of Laconian and Corinthian pan tiles was arranged to form a rectangular box. Only cremations were found with boxed tile graves.

Any of the three forms of graves with tiles could have additional features.

(a) A stone cairn could be built atop the tiles, but none of these rose above the elevation of the top of the grave pit (Figs. 64, No. 38; 77).

(b) A libation spout, usually constructed of two Laconian cover tiles with their long edges together, could be built into the grave (Figs. 64, Nos. 38—39; 75, 77). Such spouts would have one end above the top of the grave pit and the other end going down into the grave.

(c) The cremated remains could be placed into a container which would then be placed in the pit before the tiles were arranged (Figs. 64, No. 39; 73, 76).[7]

(d) A low boundary wall (peribolos) could be built around the grave (Fig. 78).

(e) A number of graves (all cremations except Grave 20 of Period I) had "double pits" (Fig. 64, Nos. 38, 39; Fig. 65, No. 81). These were composed of an "outer pit" which was excavated from the ground surface, and an "inner pit" which was dug from the floor of the "outer pit". Both pits would be rectangular and both would have the same orientation. The depth of the inner pit would be measured from the floor of the outer pit to the floor of the inner pit.

The preceding outline of attributes could be extended indefinitely if we were to include the size of the grave pit, the amount and kinds of grave offerings, and so forth. We will, for the moment, limit ourselves to the treatment of the corpse and the construction of the grave, discrete attributes which ought to be readily apparent.

---

[6] W-MZ (1971) Fig. 11.
[7] W-MZ (1971) Fig. 13.

CEMETERY PERIODS

From the information acquired during the 1970 and 1971 excavations five periods can be recognized in the use of the cemetery. The dates of individual graves are based on a review of context ceramics from the deposit into which the grave was dug, the deposit overlying the top of the grave pit, and the materials within the grave pit. The last category includes grave offerings as well as context ceramics from the fill of the grave.

The relative stratification of the surfaces from which grave pits were dug weighed heavily in the assignation of graves to periods. The periods, then, were assigned dates based on the range of dates provided by context materials and grave offerings. The satisfactory correspondence of these two operationally semi-independent methods of dating has provided a sequence of periods through which we can observe changes in funeral customs.

The sample size of graves from any one period ranges between 11 (Periods III and V) and 36 (Period II). Trials of dividing the graves among sub-periods on the basis of relative stratigraphy within the phases resulted in such reduced samples that the probability of sampling error increased dramatically. In addition, these sub-periods did not add appreciably to our understanding of changes in funeral customs.

PERIOD I. Early Augustan; 20 graves.

The separation of Period I from Period II is based primarily on stratigraphic grounds. All the graves in Period I, for at least part of their depth, intrude into a weathered floodplain soil. This soil is a natural deposit resting upon a compact gravel which is a Quaternary bed of either the Crna or Vardar River. All of the grave pits were covered by a late 1st century B. C. to early 1st century A. C. deposit into which the graves of Period II were cut. The date of the graves in both Periods I and II is Augustan, but the stratification indicates an earlier and a later grouping.

PERIOD II. Later Augustan; 36 graves.

As described above, Periods I and II are separated on the basis of observed stratification. The graves of Period II cut into a late 1st century B. C. through early 1st century A. C. deposit, and are overlain by a deposit of the 1st century A. C. through the early 2nd century A. C.

PERIOD III. Late 1st century A. C. through the 1st half of the 2nd century A. C.; 11 graves.

This assemblage of graves cut through deposits of the last three quarters of the 1st century A. C. through perhaps the first half of the 2nd century A. C. The surface from which the latest graves in Period III were dug is overlain by a relatively thick (*ca.* 1.00 m.) deposit dating perhaps as early as the late 2nd century A. C. through the 3rd century A. C. In addition, several graves are beneath an artificially deposited layer of gravel which must have been intended to serve as a visible funeral marker for this group.

PERIOD IV. 3rd century A. C.; 15 graves.

The pits for the graves in Period IV were dug from within an extensive deposit of the 3rd century A. C. This deposit could have resulted from land filling operations intended to raise the surface of the cemetery, or possibly dumping incidental to some program of construction within the city proper.

PERIOD V. 4th century A. C.; 11 graves.

Period V was the last phase of the use of the area as a cemetery. The tops of its graves were dug into deposits of the 4th century A. C. Some of the uppermost of these deposits contained pottery datable as late as the 5th century A. C., but because of the amount of 5th century disturbance in the area, I am reluctant to date any graves to later than the end of the 4th century A. C. Clearly the area went out of use as a cemetery during the late 4th to early 5th centuries A. C. A number of carelessly constructed rubble walls later than the last graves were found during both seasons of excavation. None of these walls was preserved to a height exceeding 0.30 m. and the tops of most were only a few centimeters below the present ground surface. None of these short stretches of wall was adequately preserved to provide any identification of the structures they represented.[8]

---

[8] Originally, Period V was thought to date no later than the early 4th century A. C. (W-MZ [1972] note 50). Since then, further studies of the coins found near Grave 22 (see *infra* Period V) suggests that Period V may be as late as the third quarter of the 4th century A. C. However, the association of the skeleton and the coins is not a certainty.

Figure 66. Adult inhumation (Grave 17), from northwest.

PERIOD I. EARLY AUGUSTAN.

Period I, with its 20 graves, is the earliest evidence of human activity within the area of the West Cemetery. As mentioned earlier, these graves cut at least partly into a weathered floodplain soil, and they are dated to Early Augustan times.

Inhumations (Four humans, and one *Equus* sp.).

Grave 20 was the only adult inhumation in Period I. The double pit grave was oriented NW-SE with the head to the SE. The outer pit measured 1.80 m. × 1.18 m. × 0.20 m. deep. The inner pit was the same length as the outer, but was only 0.68 m. wide × 0.80 m. deep. There were no tiles. The skeleton was extended on its back with the arms straight along the sides with the hands pronated and resting alongside the pelvis. The inner pit was dug entirely through a very compact Quaternary gravel, representing a considerable expenditure of energy. In another portion of the trench a test in this gravel proved exhausting work for seasoned pickmen.

Graves 89, 90, and 96 were shallow pit inhumations of infants, none of whom was older than a year at the time of death. The pits were only *ca.* 0.15 m. deep. Like Graves 16, 53, 63, and 78 of Period II, the shallow pits and the lack of grave offerings give an impression of casual interment.

Grave 89 was oriented N-S, in a pit measuring 0.86 m. × 0.50 m. The bones were so badly disturbed that the orientation of the corpse could not be determined.

Grave 90 (Fig. 67) was oriented NE-SW within a pit measuring 0.78 m. × 0.27 m. The head was to the SW and the skeleton was extended on its back with the elbows and knees slightly flexed.

Grave 96 was simply a disarticulated, disturbed skeleton and the orientation and dimensions of the grave could not be determined.

Grave 79 was a simple pit cremation of an adult (see Cremations without Tiles below) and associated with it in an adjacent pit was an inhumation of an adult *Equus* sp.[9] The animal had been decapitated prior to interment; the skull was in the appropriate anatomical position but a gap of some 0.10 m. separated the uppermost cervical vertebrae from the skull. The forelegs were extended to the posterior while the hind legs were extended anteriorially. The legs crossed at the knee and hock, with the knees passing between the hocks. The skeleton was oriented E-W with the head to the E. The pit measured 1.90 m. × 1.08 m. × 0.50 m. A pre-Augustan Greek coin (coin 71-374) was found with the skeleton.

---

[9] W-MZ (1972) Fig. 23.

Cremations without Tiles (Five).

Grave 72 had been disturbed in antiquity. It was preserved only as a scattering of ash and a few cremated human bone fragments over an area about 0.40 m. in diameter. No grave offerings were recovered.

Grave 79 was a shallow pit cremation at the W end of the *Equus* sp. inhumation described above. The pit for the cremation was immediately outside the larger and deeper pit for the inhumation, and was oriented E-W. It measured 0.70 m. × 0.44 m. × 0.08 m. deep. A bronze fibula (MF-71-251 A,B) was recovered from among the bones and ashes, as well as an iron blade (MF-71-199, possibly a spear point) and an iron harness ring (MF-71-203).

Grave 81 was one of a group with Graves 82, 83, 84, and 86. All of these were dug from the same surface and, in each case, the perimeter of the grave was visible as a thin line of ash and carbon from 0.01 m. to 0.02 m. wide. This line results from the ash and carbon within the grave pit having slumped slightly in the center of the pit. The ash and carbon were then at a slightly higher elevation at the periphery of the pit as compared to the center of the pit. It is likely that these lines served as visible grave markers (Fig. 65, No. 81).[10] Grave 81 was oriented E-W, the outer pit measuring 1.88 m. × 0.94 m. × 0.24 m. deep. The inner pit was in the center of the floor of the outer pit, and it measured 1.37 m. × 0.31 m. × 0.29 m. deep (measured from the floor of the outer pit to the floor of the inner pit). Cremated bone, pieces of carbonized wood, and charred whole nuts tentatively identified as *Juglans* (walnut) were scattered throughout both pits. In the SE corner of the outer pit were two iron strigils (MF-71-159, 160) and an iron "arm band" (MF-71-161).

Grave 85, an ash-bordered grave, was oriented NE-SW and measured 1.05 m. × 0.40 m. × 0.06 m. deep. There were no grave offerings.

Grave 86 was oriented NE-SW and measured 1.97 m. × 0.40 m. × 0.29 m. deep. This was another of the graves with an ash border. Grave offerings included at least six glass unguentaria (none of which was inventoried), all of which had collapsed from exposure to heat. Partly melted glass unguentaria were recovered from several other graves in the cemetery. If such vessels had been included as offerings

---

[10] Graves 83 and 84 were not excavated.

with the corpse in the cremation fire or in the grave fire they would surely have been melted beyond recognition. They were most likely introduced into the grave fire as it died to coals.[11]

Figure 67. Infant inhumation (Grave 90), from northeast.

Cremations with Flat Tiles (Four).

Graves 80, 82, 91, and 94 were all adult cremations in shallow pits covered at least partly with a flat-lying Laconian pan tile.

---

[11] Grave 92 (a shallow pit cremation) and Grave 93 (a stone cairn of which only part of a corner was exposed) were not excavated.

Grave 80 was oriented N-S and its pit measured 1.35 m. ×0.75 m. ×0.06 m. deep. Grave offerings included three ceramic vessels (C-71-129, 130, 155), a fragmentary glass unguentarium (not inventoried), and coin 71-398 (pre-Augustan Greek). The presence of several small iron nails and four larger iron nails indicated that a wooden artifact[12] had been burnt either in the cremation fire or in the grave fire. This could have been a coffin or litter for the corpse, or a smaller casket with some burial offering.

Grave 82, partly disturbed in antiquity, was another of the carbon-lined pits. Oriented NE-SW, the pit measured 2.00 m. ×0.65 m. ×0.18 m. deep. There were no grave offerings.

Grave 91 was only partly exposed since its greater portion extended into the trench face. Its orientation appears to have been NW-SE.

Grave 94, partly disturbed in antiquity, was oriented N-S in a pit measuring 1.30 m. ×0.50 m. ×0.18 m. deep. Grave offerings included eight piriform ceramic unguentaria (C-71-156 through 163).

Cremations with Arched Tiles (Three).

Graves 71, 88, and 95 were the arched tile graves in Period I. Graves 88 and 95 were partly collapsed and Grave 95 was supplemented by a low stone peribolos.

Grave 71 was oriented NE-SW in a pit measuring 1.25 m. ×0.95 m. × 0.51 m. deep. Its Laconian pan tiles were supplemented by Laconian cover tiles placed along the apex of the arch. In addition, rectangular bricks were placed along the outside of the bottom edge of the pan tiles. Fragments of Laconian pan tiles closed the ends of the grave. Inside the grave there were two bricks stacked atop one another at either end. Grave offerings included three slender glass unguentaria (G-71-32, 33, 34). As in Grave 80 there were several small iron nails scattered among the cremated bones and carbonized wood.

Grave 88 was oriented E-W with a pit measuring 1.45 m. ×0.75 m. ×0.22 m. deep. The upper portion of the side tiles had collapsed in antiquity but the grave appeared to have been otherwise undisturbed. Grave offerings included a hemispherical ceramic cup (C-71-154), a

---

[12] It is a possibility that these nails, as well as nails found in other cremations, came from footwear that was burned with the deceased. On the other hand, no nails were found with any inhumation.

ceramic unguentarium (C-71-166), and a small iron blade (MF-71-197).

Grave 95, like Grave 88, was a partly collapsed arched tile cremation but was supplemented by a low stone peribolos. The grave pit measured 1.27 m. × 0.95 m. × 0.15 m. deep, and was located in the approximate center of the peribolos. Like the peribolos, the long axis of the grave was oriented NE-SW.

The peribolos was constructed of two courses of flat field stones and was only partly exposed since approximately one-third of it went into the N trench face. The short axis of the boundary measured 2.26 m., not including a short "spur" 0.50 m. long which was an extension of the short axis wall. As exposed, the long axis measures 3.20 m. and if we assume symmetry around the grave pit the wall should not be much longer. The grave contained eight bulbous ceramic unguentaria (C-71-167 to 171, 173, 174, 176), two piriform ceramic unguentaria (C-71-172, 175), five bulbous glass unguentaria (G-71-54, 56—58, 61), one globular glass unguentarium (G-71-55), one squat glass unguentarium (G-71-59), one slender glass unguentarium (G-71-60), a mold-blown glass amphoriskos (G-71-53), and a slender, pointed glass "needle" or hairpin (G-71-52).

PERIOD II. LATER AUGUSTAN.

As mentioned earlier, Period II is separated from Period I on the basis of stratigraphy rather than on datable materials. Both Periods I and II are of Augustan date, but there is no question that the graves of Period II are later. The pits of the graves of Period II cut into deposits of the late 1st century B. C. through the early 1st century A. C.; and these pits are overlain by deposits dated to the 1st century A. C. through the early 2nd century A. C. The 36 graves of Period II constitute the largest sample of any of the five periods recognized in the West Cemetery.

Inhumations (Five).

Graves 16, 53, 63, and 78 were all shallow-pit inhumations of infants, none of whom was more than a year of age at the time of death. These four graves were quite similar to Graves 89, 90, and 96 of Period I, and likewise give an impression of casual, almost careless interment.

Graves 16 and 63 were, in antiquity, disturbed to the extent that burial position or grave size could not be determined with certainty. Grave 16, however, was probably oriented N-S with the head to the N. The bones were resting a few centimeters above the covering tile of Grave 80 of Period I. Since the few bones present of Grave 16 were articulated, it is certain that Grave 16 was not disturbed by Grave 80.

Figure 68. A 4th century grave (Grave 24) cut through by Wall 6. View from west.

Grave 53 was also oriented N-S, but with the head to the S. A flat field stone measuring 0.13 m. ×0.24 m. ×0.04 m. had been placed upon the trunk and upper legs of the skeleton with the stone's long axis at right angles to the long axis of the corpse. The body was extended on its back with the arms straight along the sides. The legs were very slightly bowed. The grave pit was not preserved, or else it had been so shallow that we were unable to distinguish grave fill from the surrounding matrix. The good preservation of the skeleton and its complete articulation indicate that the bones, at least, were not disturbed.

The pit for Grave 78 measured 0.59 m. ×0.34 m. ×0.15 m. deep and was oriented N-S with the head to the N. The corpse had been interred face-down, the only such example in the West Cemetery excavations. The right humerus was parallel to the trunk and the forearm was hyperflexed until the radius and ulna were almost directly underneath the upper arm. The right hand was pronated on the bottom of the grave pit. The left arm was likewise hyperflexed. The right leg was straight, but the left was slightly flexed. There were no grave offerings.

Grave 17 (Fig. 66) was the only adult inhumation discovered in Period II. The grave, measuring 1.91 m. × 0.60 m. × 0.40 m. deep was a simple pit with no covering tiles. The pit was oriented NW-SE with the head to the SE. The fairly well-preserved skeleton was extended on its back. The right humerus was straight alongside the torso with the forearm flexed slightly across the abdomen with the hand pronated on the abdomen. The left humerus was likewise straight alongside the trunk but the forearm was hyperflexed such that the pronated hand was resting slightly to the left of the manibrium. The legs were straight. No offerings were found with this grave.

Figure 69. Grave 28 (foreground, an arched tile cremation) was cut through by Grave 25 (arched tile inhumation). View from southwest.

Cremations without Tiles (Fifteen).

Graves 11, 14, 15, 18, 19, 21, 49, 51, 57, 59, 64, 67, 68, 73, and 75 were all shallow-pit cremations with no covering tiles. They are similar to Graves 72, 85, 86, and 93 of Period I.[13]

Figure 70. Grave 11, an adult cremation in a shallow pit. View from west.

Grave 11 (Fig. 70) measured 1.15 m. × 0.50 m. × 0.04 m. deep with the long axis oriented N-S. The only grave offering recovered was coin 70-99 (pre-Augustan Greek) found among the bones and ash.

---

[13] The preserved depth of the pits for these graves in Period II ranges from 0.01 m. (Grave 75) to 0.25 m. (Grave 49). The mean preserved depth of these 15 graves is 0.10 m. It is certain that the shallowness of about half the graves is a function of preservation rather than originally shallow pits. Graves 11, 14, 59, 64, 67, 68, 73, and 75 had pits ranging in depth from 0.01 m. to 0.07 m. Alternatively, if the pits were indeed so shallow originally, they could have been supplemented by small mounds of earth above them. Some of these graves, however, had such few bone fragments that they must have been disturbed in antiquity.

The horizontal size of some of these graves is also likely a function of preservation. The area occupied by a single grave ranged from about 0.20 m. in diameter (Grave 67, likely disturbed) to 1.90 m. x 0.85 m. (Grave 21, the perimeter of which could be traced with confidence).

Grave 14 (Fig. 71) measured 1.10 m. ×0.30 m. ×0.07 m. deep and was oriented N-S. Coin 70-101 (Greek Imperial, 1st-2nd centuries A. C.) was found among the cremated bones.

Grave 15 measured 0.80 m. ×0.40 m. ×0.13 m. deep and was oriented N-S. Coin 71-166 (38 A. D.—41 A. D.) was recovered from this grave.

Grave 18 was roughly circular, measuring 0.90 m. in diameter ×0.13 m. deep. Along with coin 71-35 (illegible) there were 18 ceramic unguentaria (C-70-63 through 80) included as grave offerings.

Grave 19 was also circular, 0.50 m. in diameter ×0.22 m. deep. There were no grave offerings.

Grave 21 was oriented E-W, measuring 1.90 m. ×0.85 m. ×0.23 m. deep. Only a few scraps of bone were found among the grave offerings, which may indicate a very thorough cremation. Over the bottom of the pit a fire had been made which resulted in a layer of ash, carbonized wood, peach and olive pits, and nuts identified as walnut. This burned layer measured 1.40 m. E-W ×0.60 m. N-S (thereby occupying almost the entire floor of the grave pit) ×0.02 to 0.03 m. thick. Doubtless the food remains represent a meal at the site of the grave as part of the funeral customs, perhaps with the deceased intended as the recipient. Grave 81 from Period I, it will be recalled, also contained a quantity of *Juglans* sp. nuts, many of which were unbroken though carbonized. Grave 21 also contained unbroken nuts. Although the presence of the peach pits in Grave 21 is equivocal, the unbroken nuts must have been intended for the deceased.

Atop the burned layer were found the scraps of burnt human bones and a host of grave offerings. Some of the ceramic offerings were scorched and the majority of the glass offerings were distorted from heat. It is likely that the grave offerings were introduced into the grave as the fire was dying. Had the offerings been placed in as brisk a fire as the layer of carbonized vegetal materials indicates, we might have expected a more complete destruction of the gifts.

At the E end of the grave was a concentration of seven ceramic and three glass unguentaria (C-70-48, 49, 50, 57, 59, 60; C-71-95; and G-70-23, 24, 35), a glass rod with a looped end (G-70-14), a small beaker (C-70-58), and a small pot (C-70-160). These were scattered about in no apparent organization. At the W end of the grave was a collection of terracotta figurines in a small heap,[14] again with no discern-

---

[14] W-MZ (1971) Figs. 16, 17, 18, and 19.

ible orientation. There were four figurines representing Telesphorus (MF-70-32, 33, 34, 35), two of Europa riding a bull (MF-70-36, 37), two of a youth on horseback (MF-70-39, 40), and two of riderless bulls (MF-70-42, 43).

Grave 21 also had a peribolos wall (Wall 8), but this was preserved only on the SE side of the grave. The crosswall is preserved completely, measuring 2.06 m. between two extensions of the sidewalls. These extensions form spurs projecting some 0.50 m. beyond the crosswall. A spur is all that remains of the SW sidewall. The NE sidewall including the spur is preserved for a length of 3.20 m. All the walls are 0.50 m. wide and are 0.20 m. high. Since the tops of the walls, made of flat field stones, have a smooth and finished appearance this peribolos must have served as a low boundary wall rather than a physical barrier. Grave 21 was located in the approximate center of the area enclosed by Wall 8, but we cannot be certain that the wall ever formed a complete enclosure. We are almost certain, on the other hand, that the peribolos walls of Graves 60 and 95 formed complete enclosures.

Grave 49 was circular, about 0.35 m. in diameter ×0.12 m. deep. Grave offerings included an iron finger ring (MF-71-98) and a fragment of a smoothed stone, possibly a whetstone (MF-71-103).

Grave 51 was oriented NE-SW and measured 1.70 m.×0.65 m. ×0.12 m. deep. It was first exposed as a thin (0.02 m. wide) line of ash and carbon outlining the grave pit. This line is analogous to the pit outlines for Graves 81 through 86 in Period I. Grave offerings included a small round-mouth jug (C-71-40) and coin 71-194 (23 B. C. — 14 A. D.).

Grave 57 was oriented E-W and measured 1.45 m.×0.62 m. ×0.13 m. deep. The only grave offering was a small ceramic bowl (C-71-35).

Grave 59 was a thin scattering of carbon and bones in a circular depression approximately 0.40 m. in diameter ×0.04 m. deep. Along with a quantity of carbonized nuts (*Juglans* sp.?) there was a fragment of a bronze finger ring and a fragment of a glass unguentarium.

Grave 64 was about 0.31 m. in diameter ×0.02 m. deep. No grave offerings were recovered.

Grave 67 was a small circular pit 0.20 m. in diameter ×0.05 m. deep filled with carbonized wood and cremated bones. A small two-handled ceramic cup (C-71-51) was found with this grave.

Grave 68 was a circular pit some 0.74 m. in diameter ×0.07 m. deep. Among the ash and cremated bones was an apparently unburnt femur of an *Equus* sp. The meat on this bone may have been a burial offering.

Grave 73 was another circular pit 0.94 m. in diameter ×0.04 m. deep. No grave offerings were recovered, although two iron nails were found among the cremated bones.

Grave 75 measured 1.10 m. ×0.50 m. ×0.01 m. deep and was oriented NE-SW. No grave offerings were recovered from this thin scattering of bone and ash.

Cremation within a Vessel (One).

Grave 13 (Fig. 71) is the only grave from Period II contained within a vessel with no other form of covering. The vessel (C-70-62) had been set into a pit of which only the bottom 0.20 m. was preserved. Part of the top of the vessel had been broken away in antiquity, indicating that the upper part of the grave may have been disturbed as well. Among the cremated bones in the vessel were four glass unguentaria (G-70-17, 19, 20, and 25) and a Sidonian mold-blown bottle (G-70-18).

Cremations with Flat Tiles (Five).

Graves 12, 66, 70, 74, and 77 were all classed as flat tile cremations although 12 and 77 were variant in their construction.

The Laconian pan tiles of Grave 12 were neither arched nor completely flat, but were arranged in a rectilinear fashion with Laconian cover tiles lining the edges.[15] The grave was oriented NE-SW within a pit measuring 2.52 m. × 1.21 m. ×0.14 m. deep. The tiles alone covered an area 1.98 m. ×0.57 m. Underneath the tiles was a second, shallower pit measuring 1.40 m. ×0.55 m. ×0.07 m. deep. There was a thick ceramic "casserole dish" (C-70-61) at the NE end of the grave. The dish contained cremated bones and two slender glass unguentaria (G-70-15, 16). More cremated human bones were scattered down the length of the inner grave pit.

Grave 66 was a disturbed flat-tile cremation within a pit measuring 1.70 m. × 1.20 m. ×0.15 m. deep and oriented N-S. The only grave offering recovered was a bronze finger ring (MF-71-217).

---

[15] W-MZ (1971) Figs. 12, 13.

Figure 71. Grave 13 (foreground), a cremation in a vessel; and Grave 14 (background), a shallow pit cremation. View from west.

Grave 70 was an ash-rimmed pit similar to Grave 52 of this same period, except that Grave 70 had flat-lying fragments of Laconian pan tiles covering the interior of the grave. The pit was oriented E-W and measured 1.50 m. ×0.64 m. ×0.15 m. deep. The only grave offering recovered was coin 71-319 (illegible).

Grave 74 had a single flat-lying fragment of a Laconian pan tile placed over a scattering of bone and ashes. The pit was oriented E-W and measured 1.98 m. ×0.63 m. ×0.17 m. deep. Grave offerings included coin 71-232 (Greek, pre-Augustan), a small cup with barbotine decorations (C-71-69) and a squat glass unguentarium (G-71-35).

Grave 77 had two flat-lying Laconian pan tiles in a pit measuring 1.46 m. ×0.81 m. ×0.28 m. deep, and oriented E-W. The tiles were almost completely covered by a carelessly constructed cairn of cobble-sized field stones. Fragments of seven terracotta figurines (TF-71-4 through 10) were found atop the stones, among the stones, and beneath the tiles. Joins among the figurines from all three locales indicate that they must have been broken intentionally and the fragments placed in the successive layers of the grave. The figurines represented Aphrodite,[16] Europa riding a bull, and seated women.

Cremations with Arched Tiles (Nine).

There were nine arched tile cremation graves in Period II: Graves 50, 52, 58, 60, 61, 62, 65, 69, and 76. Grave 60 was placed within a peribolos similar to that of Graves 21 and 95, and Grave 52 was later built within the same perimeter atop Grave 60. Excepting Grave 76 with its collection of terracotta figurines, the remaining graves are typical of arched tile graves.

Grave 50 is unusual since it had a pair of fragmentary Laconian pan tiles set on end, rather than on their long sides, covering the bones. The circular grave pit had a diameter of 0.52 m. and was 0.42 m. deep. Six iron nails (one of which was inventoried as MF-71-64) and a slender glass unguentarium (G-71-11) were found among the cremated bones.

Grave 52, as mentioned above, was placed within the perimeter of Grave 60 (see below) and was squarely atop Grave 60. Oriented NW-SE, the pit for Grave 52 measured 1.45 m. × 0.97 m. × 0.40 m. deep. A jug (C-71-125) was found outside the grave atop the tiles, while two slender glass unguentaria (G-71-28, 29) and a squat glass unguentarium (G-71-30) were recovered from within the grave. Near the unguentaria was a mold of some sort of perishable container within which the cremated bones had been placed.

The mold was in the form of a small "column" of very compact earth and cremated human bone, situated in the very center of the grave. The mold was oval in plan and measured 0.30 m. long × 0.12 m. in maximum diameter × 0.20 m. tall. This evidence for a perishable container for bones is unique for these excavations. No trace of the material of which the container was made was preserved, but it may have been a small wooden casket or a basket made of leather or wicker.

Grave 58 was not excavated since almost all of its length extended into the E trench face. Immediately outside the grave a terracotta lamp

---

[16] W-MZ (1972) Fig. 30. TF-71-9 is from Grave 76, not from Grave 77. TF-71-36 is from Grave 76.

(L-71-15) and a small globular jug (C-71-37) were found. It is certain that both of these artifacts were associated with this grave.

Grave 60 was built within a low peribolos built of field stones and an occasional brick, and oriented NW-SE (Fig. 78). Although two corners of the peribolos remained within the trench faces, four sides were exposed enough so that the long axis was ascertained to be 2.36 m. and the short axis to be 2.10 m. The peribolos was only 0.10 to 0.15 m. high and could have served only as a boundary rather than a real barrier.

Figure 72. Grave 76 (a disturbed arched tile grave over a vessel containing an adolescent cremation), exterior. View from south.

The peribolos served as the top edge of an outer pit while Laconian pan tiles covered an inner pit. The distance from the top of the peribolos to the bottom of the outer pit was 0.60 m. The inner pit was only 0.10 m. deep. At the SW end of the outer pit, outside the grave tiles, were fragments of two amphoras (one was inventoried as C-71-127). Inside the tiles were a coin (71-316, illegible pre-Augustan Greek) and a single glass unguentarium (G-71-97).

Figure 73. Grave 76, interior. Note the base of a funeral urn on the right, the edge of a roof tile to the left of the urn, and the glass unguentarium in the material above the roof tile. View from northeast.

Grave 61 appears to have been disturbed in antiquity. It was oriented E-W within a pit measuring 1.37 m. × 0.82 m. × 0.22 m. deep. Among the cremated bones were coins 71-317 (illegible 1st—2nd centuries A.C.) and 71-318 (illegible pre-Augustan Greek).

Grave 62 was an arched tile grave, but so much of it extended into the trench face that we were unable to excavate it. We do not know whether it covers a cremation or an inhumation.

Grave 65 was only partly preserved, but it appears to have been an arched tile grave oriented N-S. A neck from a large vessel (the fragment was inventoried as C-71-202) served as a libation spout at the S end. The preserved dimensions of the pit measured 1.00 m. × 0.50 m. × 0.27 m. deep. No grave offerings were found.

Grave 69 appears also to have been disturbed in antiquity. The grave pit measured 0.90 m. × 0.57 m. × 0.27 m. deep, and was oriented E-W. No grave offerings were recovered.

Figure 74. Grave 76, interior. Part of the figurine deposit beneath the roof tile. View from northeast.

Grave 76 was a disturbed arched tile grave with a fragment of a Corinthian pan tile forming a "floor" underneath the arched tiles (Figs. 72-73). Resting on the Corinthian tile were cremated bones and carbonized wood surrounding a slender glass unguentarium (G-71-98). Underneath the Corinthian tile was a compact mass of terracotta figurines and ceramic unguentaria (Fig. 74).

The grave was oriented NW-SE, and the pit was 0.83 m. ×0.50 m. ×0.48 m. deep. The Corinthian tile was at the SE end of the pit, while in the NW portion of the grave there was the bottom of a vessel some 0.30 m. in diameter. This large pot contained the cremated remains of an adolescent.

There were over 50 figurines, representing Aphrodite in various poses, a youth playing a lyre, a youth and a dog, seated women, and standing figures of men and women.[17] With the figurines were seven bulbous ceramic unguentaria (C-71-96, 109-114). Grave 76 had more grave offerings than any other grave excavated in the 1970-1971 seasons.

Cremation with Boxed Tiles (One).

Grave 55 was the only boxed tile grave in Period II, but, like Grave 65, had a libation spout. The grave was oriented E-W within a pit measuring 1.35 m. ×0.90 m. ×0.22 m. deep. The sides of the grave were constructed of field stones and tiles and the roof was a single Corinthian pan tile. Two Laconian cover tiles with their long edges together formed a libation spout at the E end. A small ceramic vessel (C-71-74) was found in fragments both inside and outside the tiles of the grave. Apparently the vessel was broken during the burial rites.

PERIOD III. LATE 1ST CENTURY A. C. THROUGH THE 1ST HALF OF THE 2ND CENTURY A. C.

The eleven graves of Period III cut through the deposits overlying the graves of Period II, and are in turn overlain by an extensive deposit of the 3rd century A. C. A group of six graves in the SE corner of the excavations were overlain by an artificial deposit of gravel which probably served as a visible grave marker. There were no inhumations in Period III.

Cremation in Vessel (One).

Grave 45 was the only instance in Period III of a burial contained solely within a vessel. The cremated bones were within an ovoid-body, coarseware amphora (C-71-201) which had been partly broken in

---

[17] W-MZ (1972) Figs. 31—36.

antiquity. The amphora was lying on its side with the neck to the NW. No convincing sign of any grave pit could be discerned, probably because of earlier disturbance.

Cremations without Tiles (One).

Grave 43 was the only example of a shallow pit cremation with no covering tiles in Period III. The pit was oriented N-S and measured 1.80 m. × 0.80 m. × 0.13 m. deep. No burial gifts were recovered from this grave.

Flat-Tile Cremations (Two).

Grave 46 had two Laconian pan tiles lying flat in a pit measuring 1.63 m. × 0.80 m. × 0.13 m. deep. The grave was oriented NW-SE. The NW end of the grave was covered with flat field stones and tile fragments forming a carelessly built cairn. A fragment of a Laconian cover tile stuck up from the central portion of the grave and likely represented a libation spout. Along with the cremated bones was a considerable amount of carbonized wood. Grave offerings included a terracotta lamp (L-71-9), two bone pins (MF-71-83, 84), and two bone needles (MF-71-85, 86). The lamp was scorched and the bone implements likewise showed signs of having been burnt in the grave fire. A quantity of small nails scattered throughout the grave pit suggested that some wooden artifact had been burned in the cremation fire.

Grave 56 (Fig. 65) had a single flat-lying Laconian pan tile in a pit oriented NE-SW. The pit measured 1.20 m. × 0.70 m. × 0.17 m. deep. The only grave offering was a small round-mouthed ceramic jug (C-71-34).

Stone Cairn

One stone cairn, designated as Grave 42 was only slightly exposed in the course of the excavations. It extended too far into the trench face to be dug. It is similar in construction to the upper part of Grave 38, so it is possible that it contains arched tiles over a cremation.

The Libation Spout Burials (Five with spouts, one without).

"The Libation Spout Burials"[18] refers to a group of graves immediately beneath a compact spread of gravel in the SE corner of the

---

[18] W-MZ (1972) 414.

excavations. The gravel deposit is identified as of human origin on the basis of details of pebble deposition and carbonate precipitation pointed out by Dr. Folk. In plan, the exposed portion of the gravel lens is approximately ¹/₄ of a circle, suggesting that the remaining ³/₄ of the feature, if it is indeed a circle, may lie in the unexcavated ground to the S and E of the trench. The deposit averaged 0.30 m. thick and the context ceramics from within it date to the 1st century A. C.

The graves immediately underneath the gravel (Graves 38, 39, 40, 44, 47 and 48) were all dug from the surface upon which the gravel rested. This indicates some contemporaneity of the graves and, furthermore, suggests that the graves and gravel are associated. Graves 38, 39, 44 and 48 all had libation spouts, but none of them extended up through the gravel. Perhaps the spouts were never intended to protrude above the gravel; or, if they originally did so, they may have been broken off in the course of time. If the former was the case, the gravel must have been deposited to seal off the graves sometime after the completion of funeral rites.

Grave 38 (Figs. 64, 77) was a double pit cremation with arched tiles over the inner pit and a carefully built cairn of field stones covering the tiles. A libation spout made of two Laconian cover tiles with their long edges together went from inside the NE end of the grave to outside the cairn. The outer grave pit measured 2.26 m. × 0.96 m. × 0.56 m. deep. The covering tiles (one Corinthian and three Laconian pan tiles were used) were resting on the bottom of the outer pit and enclosed the inner pit which measured 1.49 m. × 0.42 m. × 0.32 m. deep.

The lower 0.35 m. of the outer pit (between the walls of the pit and the covering tiles) was packed with cobble-sized stones. Above the tops of the covering tiles there were three more or less regularly laid courses of flat field stones of varying sizes. The top of the uppermost course was slightly below the top of the grave pit. Atop the cairn, at the SW end of the grave, were two broken bowls (C-71-11 and 17).

The inner grave pit yielded fragments of carbonized wood and burnt human bone, 36 small nails (one of which was inventoried as MF-71-109), and the base of a terracotta lamp (L-71-17). The lamp base was thoroughly scorched, and although the fill from beneath the tiles was passed through a 0.002 m. hardware cloth no other fragments were found. The lamp base must have been burned in the original funeral fire and fragmented from the heat. Only this portion of the base was collected with the bones (and perhaps the nails) for deposition in the grave.

Grave 39 (Figs. 64, 75-76) was a double-pit boxed tile grave oriented NE-SW. The outer pit measured 1.51 m. × 1.01 m. × 0.46 m. deep; and the inner pit was 0.80 m. × 0.60 m. × 0.20 m. deep. The side tiles were Laconian pan tiles while a Corinthian pan tile was used for the top. At the NE end of the covering tiles a single Laconian cover tile formed a libation spout.

The inner pit contained a quantity of ash and carbonized wood, as well as a round-mouth bowl (C-71-32)[19] filled with the cremated remains of an adult. More bones from the same cremation were scattered throughout the inner pit. Other grave offerings included a small bowl (C-71-38) and a lamp (L-71-4).[20]

Figure 75. Grave 39 (a boxed tile cremation with libation spout), exterior. View from northwest.

Grave 40 was a partly collapsed arched tile grave oriented N-S in a pit measuring 1.30 m. × 1.00 m. × 0.60 m. deep. The grave was at right angles to the adjacent Grave 44. A fragment of a Laconian cover

---

[19] W-MZ (1972) Fig. 20.
[20] W-MZ (1972) Fig. 21.

tile libation spout stood upright from this grave, but it is possible it could have served Grave 44, or even both graves. The only grave offering recovered was coin 71-133 (23 B. C.—14 A. D.).

Figure 76. Grave 39, interior. View from northwest.

Grave 44 was a flat tile grave oriented E-W within a pit measuring 1.40 m. × 0.68 m. × 0.79 m. deep. A terracotta lamp (L-71-10) was found immediately outside the tiles. Both inside and outside the tiles were fragments of a glass cup (G-71-6). Coin 71-134,[21] a Greek issue of Vitellius (A. D. 69), was recovered from among the cremated bones.

Grave 47 had no libation spout but it was immediately underneath the gravel and its pit had been dug from the same surface as the others in this group. Its stratigraphic position certainly assigns it to the Libation Spout group. Grave 47 was an arched tile grave situated between the pits for Graves 38 and 39, and was oriented N-S in a pit measuring 1.12 m. × 0.67 m. × 0.58 m. deep. No grave offerings were

---

[21] W-MZ (1972) Fig. 22.

recovered but 47 small iron nails (one of which was inventoried as MF-71-93) were scattered among the bones.

Grave 48 was an arched tile grave with a carelessly composed layer of field stones atop the tiles. The pit was 1.70 m. × 1.13 m. × ×0.29 m. deep and was oriented N-S. A libation spout made of two Laconian cover tiles extended from under the N end of the tiles covering the grave and protruded above the cairn. Grave offerings included a terracotta lamp (L-71-8), an iron strigil (MF-71-158), a small terracotta altar (MF-71-233), and coin 71-195 (1st century A. C. illegible). Of the 42 iron nails scattered among the bones and ashes, one was inventoried as MF-71-58.

Figure 77. Grave 38, exterior. Note libation spout in foreground. View from north.

PERIOD IV. 3RD CENTURY A. C.

Between Periods III and IV there is a hiatus in the use of the cemetery. The context ceramics and the datable grave offerings place the graves of Period IV no earlier than the 3rd century A. C. Since the latest graves of Period III date no later than the first half of the 2nd century A. C., there is a period of perhaps three generations during which no new graves were placed in the area investigated.

During the 3rd century A. C. a thick deposit with considerable quantities of pottery and some brick fragments accumulated over the area. This meter-thick deposit could represent landfill intended to raise the surface level of the cemetery for additional graves. Alternatively, it could have resulted from casual dumping during a phase of construction activities within the city proper.

While this deposit was accumulating, 15 graves were placed in the area of our excavations. There were three cremations, eight inhumations, and four graves that we were unable to excavate.

Arched Tile Cremations (Three).

Grave 28 was an arched tile, double pit cremation partly cut through by Grave 25, an arched tile inhumation (Fig. 69). The grave pit was oriented N-S and had been at least 1.80 m. long (Grave 25 destroyed the N end of the pit) ×0.96 m.×0.42 m. deep. The inner pit was 1.00 m.×0.30 m.×0.12 m. deep. Grave offerings included an illegible bronze coin (71-49), a small globular jug (C-71-9), a hemispherical bowl (C-71-11) and a small bronze disc and handle (MF-71-30), possibly a mirror.

Grave 31 also had arched tiles and a double pit oriented N-S. The outer pit measured 1.84 m.×1.16 m.×0.52 m. deep. The inner pit was 1.25 m.×0.46 m.×0.11 m. deep. The only grave offering was an illegible 1st century A. C. coin (71-81).

Grave 37 was a partly disturbed arched tile cremation oriented E-W within a pit measuring 1.54 m.×0.42 m.×0.33 m. deep. Among the cremated bones five iron nails were found (of which two were inventoried as MF-71-57 a, b).

Inhumations with Arched Tiles (Six).

Grave 1[22] had arched Laconian pan tiles in a pit oriented E-W and measuring 1.21 m.×0.48 m.×0.31 m. deep. The skeleton was that of a juvenile, and was extended on its back with the skull to the W. The arms were straight along the sides with the hands pronated on the ground alongside the pelvis. Coin 70-23 (A. D. 238—244) was in the right hand.

---

[22] W-MZ (1971) Fig. 11.

Grave 6 was oriented NE-SW with the head at the SW end. The pit measured 1.46 m. × 0.69 m. × 0.55 m. deep. The skeleton was extended on its back with the arms straight along the sides. No grave offerings were recovered.

Grave 8 was an arched Laconian tile grave of an adult oriented E-W within a pit measuring 2.00 m. × 0.75 m. × 0.55 m. deep. The skeleton had its skull to the E and was extended on its back in such a very linear, constricted fashion that it must have been tightly wound in a shroud.[23] A small bronze figurine of Mercury (MF-71-22) and a hollow hemispherical bronze attachment (MF-71-23) were found at the feet. A bronze ring (MF-71-21) was on the 4th finger of the left hand.

Grave 10 was an arched tile inhumation oriented NW-SE with the head to the NW. The pit measured 1.96 m. × 0.71 m. × 0.41 m. deep. This grave cut partly through the uppermost part of the pit for Grave 17 of Period II. The skeleton was extended and the head rested on a field stone "pillow." The bones were so poorly preserved that the position of the arms could not be ascertained, but the right arm appears to have been slightly flexed across the abdomen and the left arm straight along the side. No grave goods were recovered.

Grave 29 was a badly disturbed arched tile interment of a juvenile. The grave and most of its contents had been destroyed in antiquity, but enough of the tiles were in place to determine that the grave was oriented E-W. Cranial fragments were found at the W end of the grave and some articulated ribs showed that this was the original position of the corpse. No grave offerings were recovered.

Grave 36 was an arched tile inhumation with flat field stones closing off the ends of the grave. The pit was oriented E-W, with the head to the W, and measured 1.98 m. × 0.72 m. × 0.35 m. deep. The extended adult skeleton had both hands pronated on the ilia. A thin bronze bracelet (MF-71-87) was on the left forearm, and a bone pin (MF-71-82) rested on the floor of the grave pit near the top of the skull.

Grave 33 was an arched tile grave but could not be excavated since most of it went into the trench face.

Inhumations with Flat Tiles (Two).

Grave 30 had two flat-lying Laconian pan tiles over a pit oriented E-W and measuring 1.20 m. × 0.35 m. × 0.25 m. deep. The skull was at

---

[23] W-MZ (1972) Fig. 16.

the W end. The adult skeleton was semi-extended and appeared to have been "crammed" into a short, narrow pit. The humeri were straight along the ribcage but the shoulders were "rolled" anteriorly to fit the upper torso into the pit. The right forearm was flexed across the abdomen, while the left was flexed across the chest. The knees were flexed slightly. No grave goods were recovered.

Grave 35 was an extended adult inhumation covered by flat-lying Laconian pan tiles. The pit measured 1.60 m. × 0.78 m. × 0.08 m. deep, and was oriented SE-NW with the cranium to the NW. The right forearm was flexed and pronated with the hand resting in the center of the lower chest. The left forearm was slightly flexed and the pronated hand rested atop the left ilium. The grave had been disturbed in antiquity and the lower legs were not preserved. No grave goods were recovered.

Graves 32 and 34 (flat tiles) and Grave 41 (probably flat tiles) were not excavated since their greater parts were in the trench faces.

PERIOD V. 4TH CENTURY A. C.

Period V is the last period of the use of this area as a cemetery, and many of the graves were disturbed by subsequent building activities, possibly in the last decades of the 4th century A. C. but more likely during the 5th century A. C. Shortly after the end of Period V a series of insubstantial rubble walls and a stone hearth were constructed in the area of excavations. Since these walls were so poorly preserved (none more than 0.20 m. to 0.30 m. high nor more than 2.00 m. long) we cannot be certain what sort of structure is represented. It could not, however, have been a very important one. Eleven inhumations were recovered from Period V, of which seven were disturbed. Since we do not know whether the disturbed graves all had tiles or not, the graves of this period will be described in numerical order.

Grave 2 was almost completely destroyed by Wall 2, but enough of the skeleton remained to identify it as an adult oriented E-W with the head to the W.

Grave 3 was a badly disturbed, arched tile adult inhumation. Most of the grave pit had been destroyed in antiquity, but the tops of the preserved tiles showed that the grave had been at least 0.16 m. deep. The grave was oriented E-W with the head to the W. The skeleton was articulated only from the level of the hips on down. The right hand was pronated on the floor of the grave pit alongside the pelvis, so the right arm must have been straight along the side. The position of the left arm is not known. No grave offerings were recovered.

Grave 4 was an inhumation of an infant in a pit measuring 1.05 m. ×0.80 m.×0.74 m. deep. The grave was oriented NE-SW with the head to the SW. The skeleton was extended but so poorly preserved that we cannot be certain of the position of the arms. A number of glass beads (G-70-22) were recovered from the neck area.

Grave 5 was a flat tile grave containing the extended inhumation of a juvenile. The pit was oriented SW-NE and measured 0.81 m.×0.36 m.×0.16 m. deep. The skull was at the SW end of the grave and the arms were straight along the sides. No grave offerings were recovered.

Grave 22 was preserved only from the lower chest upwards, including both arms. A near-by large fragment of a Laconian pan tile may have been a covering tile. The adult skeleton was lying on its left side with the arms flexed up to the chest. This could have been a flexed burial. The corpse had been oriented NW-SE, with the head to the NW and the face to the NE.

Two coins were found within 0.10 m. of the bones and may have been grave offerings. Coin 71-15 dates to A. D. 375—378 and coin 71-16 is an illegible 4th century A. C. issue.

Grave 23 was an adult inhumation represented only by the left arm and clavicle, and a few ribs. The grave would have been oriented approximately N-S, with the head to the S.

Grave 24 was an extended adult inhumation cut through at right angles by a rubble wall (Wall 6), leaving no evidence of the grave pit (Fig. 68). The skeleton was destroyed between the manibrium and the knees. The skeleton was oriented N-S with the head to the N. The right forearm was hyperflexed with the hand resting on the right shoulder. The left arm was not preserved.

Grave 25 had arched tiles over an extended adult skeleton (Figs. 64, 69). The pit was oriented SE-NW and measured 2.40 m.×0.94 m. ×0.45 m. deep. The skull was at the NW end of the grave and both arms were straight along the sides. A small pot (C-71-10) was found at the feet. Five coins were found in the fill underneath the tiles, and three of these could be dated: A. D. 375—378 (coin 71-68), A. D. 351—354 (coin 71-69), and A. D. 364—378 (coin 71-70).

Grave 26 was an extended adult inhumation in a shallow pit covered by two flat-lying Laconian pan tiles. The pit ran E-W and measured 1.20 m.×0.48 m.×0.12 m. deep. The skull was at the W end. The right arm was straight along the side, while the left arm was flexed slightly to place the pronated hand on the abdomen. No grave offerings were recovered.

Grave 27 was the only double interment found in the 1970—1971 excavations. The pit is not preserved at all, but the proximity of the skeletons, their parallel orientation, and the observation that both of them were resting on the same surface indicates that these were not two separate interments. The skeletons were oriented NW-SE, with skulls to the NW. Both are extended on their backs with the arms straight along the sides.

Grave 54 was an adult inhumation represented only by a single femur. The remainder of the skeleton must have been destroyed by Wall 2. Since no articulation was present nothing can be said about the orientation of the grave.

OBSERVATIONS

The study of the archaeology of the West Cemetery of Stobi has begun;[24] but as pointed out in the Introduction the analysis of the skeletal remains and the grave offerings remain to be completed. Only after these studies are done will we begin to have adequate information with which to examine the interactions among burial customs, mortality trends, and the activities of the living within the city proper. This last would include not only the wider Roman world of which Stobi was a part, but also evidences of indigenous practices modified by Roman culture.

Nonetheless, there are certain aspects of the West Cemetery which deserve some comment now.

1. The range of variation in the elaborateness of graves, particularly within a single period.[25]

2. The funeral banquet.

3. The grave fire.

4. Cremation versus inhumation as a preferred form of burial.

---

[24] W-MZ (1971), (1972); and this report.

[25] "Elaborateness" in this discussion is a subjective appraisal of the status of an individual by the care with which his grave was constructed and the quantity of grave offerings.

Grave Elaborateness.

The variation in the elaborateness of graves in the West Cemetery is most striking. True, we would normally expect a wide range of funeral customs in a city of the Roman Empire. Among the people (and their graves) there would be economic and social stratification as well as religious differences. Stobi, being a provincial city and on the periphery of the Empire, would be exposed to a variety of stimuli. Interaction among the autochthonous cultures, Roman influences, and other more transient peoples would contribute to variability in many aspects of daily and religious life. What proved surprising was so much variability in funeral customs in the small (relative to the entire extent of the cemetery) area that was excavated.

In Period I, to cite examples,[26] Graves 89, 90, and 96 were those of infants inhumed in shallow pits.[27] The pit for Grave 20, the inhumation of an adult, cut for nearly a meter through compact Quaternary gravels. None of these inhumations, as well as some of the cremations, had any burial offerings.

Grave 79 was a shallow pit adult cremation with a bronze fibula and an iron blade found among the bones.[28] Adjacent to this grave was the

---

[26] The discussion that follows in the text above is rather subjective for several reasons:

a. A sample of 93 graves spread among five periods is small for an objective, statistical test of correlation, especially in light of the uncompleted study of materials from the excavations.

b. There are variables which are difficult to treat as discrete. There would be little problem to designate a grave with ten unguentaria as more elaborate than a grave with only five, but it would be more difficult to measure the difference between a carelessly constructed rock cairn and a more carefully built one.

c. Finally, there is the problem of equating different classes of grave offerings. How many unguentaria are required to reflect the same socioeconomic status as a single terracotta figurine? For that matter, could the oil represented by a single unguentarium equal several figurines? At this time it would be premature to present a rigorous assessment of socioeconomic implications of the West Cemetery. Such a study is intended for the future.

[27] The apparently casual interment of infants may indicate that, in some instances, a shallow pit was adequate for stillborn neonates or for infants under a certain age. The simplicity of these graves, then, would not necessarily reflect socioeconomic status.

[28] Both of these artifacts may be personal effects attached to the deceased's clothing when he was cremated, rather than grave offerings *per se*.

inhumation of an adult *Equus* which had been decapitated and carefully laid out in the pit.[29]

Grave 81, a double pit cremation,[30] had the remains of a funeral banquet, two strigils, and an iron arm band included among the bones. Graves 82 and 85 had no burial gifts. Grave 95 had a peribolos wall, and 18 unguentaria, an amphoriskos, and a glass needle as grave offerings.

Figure 78. Grave 60, an arched tile cremation surrounded by a peribolos. View from northwest.

Period II had four shallow infant graves, in one of which the corpse had been placed face down. As in Period I, none of these had any offerings. A few meters away the cremated adolescent of Grave 76 had been interred with a host of terracotta figurines. In this same period Graves

---

[29] This is the only certain evidence of an animal being slain as part of a funeral ceremony in these excavations. Another possible instance is the *Equus* femur from Grave 68 in Period II.

[30] Although present in Periods I—IV, double pits were never common. Graves with double pits were 20 and 81 of Period I, 12 and 60 of Period II, 38 and 39 of Period III, and 28 and 31 of Period IV. All except Grave 20 were cremations.

21 (which sported a peribolos wall) and 77 yielded a number of terracotta figurines. To mention some of the shallow pit cremations, Grave 18 had 18 unguentaria while Graves 19, 64, 73, and 75 had nothing.

In Period III, the complexity of graves ranged from the shallow pit cremation of Grave 43 to the carefully built rock cairn and libation spout of Grave 38. Also, one might recall the layer of gravel deposited over several of the graves bearing libation spouts.

The graves of Period IV were only ordinary tile graves, and grave offerings were rarer than in the preceding periods. Period V is difficult to assess since so many of the graves were disturbed after the area went out of use as a cemetery. The available evidence indicates that the graves of Period V were the most consistently simple of any period in the sequence.

By either of the criteria we use to assess the elaborateness of a grave (the quantity and kind of burial offerings, as in the case of Grave 76; or grave construction, as in the case of graves with cairns or peribolos walls), Periods I through III show more variation than Periods IV or V.[31] If we take elaborateness of a grave as an indicator of socioeconomic status, the data show no apparent use of one part of the cemetery by one class of people during the first three periods. During the last two periods it seems more likely that this sector of the cemetery was being used by the poorer classes.

Another possibility, although we have only negative evidence to support it, is that this part of the cemetery had always been reserved for the poorer classes. If so, what we now interpret as variation among socioeconomic classes is only variation within one of the less affluent classes. Perhaps we have yet to excavate the portion of the cemetery where there are elaborate columbaria or mausolea. If there were such elaborate tombs in the vicinity of Stobi it seems unlikely that they would have been so thoroughly destroyed as to leave no trace.

The Funeral Banquet.

Three cremations, Graves 21, 81, 59, all of Augustan date had carbonized but well-preserved walnuts, grape seeds, peach pits, and olive pits scattered amongst the bones. As mentioned earlier, there is no way to tell whether the grapes, peaches, or olives were consumed by the

---

[31] Periods IV and V combined have only some 25% of the total number of completely excavated graves. Sampling error may be a factor in their homogeneity.

funeral cortege and the inedible portions placed in the grave, or whether the whole fruit was thrown in for the enjoyment of the deceased. In all three graves, however, there were at least a dozen whole, unbroken walnuts as well as empty shells. We may assume that some of the other fruit was placed in the grave uneaten. That the food remains are carbonized indicates that the grave fire and the funeral banquet were simultaneous.[32]

That vegetal remains were recovered only from cremations is not surprising. Charred organic materials almost always have a better chance of being preserved than uncharred materials, and only cremations feature a grave fire. That only three cremations had such remains is more difficult to account for. Perhaps these graves had unusually thick concentrations of vegetal remains, insuring the survival of some specimens. Conversely, perhaps the funeral banquet was only rarely observed.

The Grave Fire.

The grave fire, as explained in the Grave Forms section of this paper, was a fire built within the grave pit as part of the funeral rites. In no case was there evidence that the fire was of sufficient magnitude to have cremated a corpse. However, the fire had been hot enough to scorch the sides and bottom of the pit and large enough in some instances to leave perhaps half a kilogram of ashes and carbonized wood (Graves 21, 38, 39, and 81).

Grave fires were limited to cremations, and in only seven cases out of 55 cremations was there no certain evidence that a grave fire had been built.[33] As Table I shows, there are cremations in each of the first four periods and in each period, between 80% and 100% of the cremations had had grave fires. Clearly, a grave fire was an important aspect of the funeral involving a cremation; but apparently a fire was considered unnecessary for an inhumation. Perhaps it was necessary for the deceased to be at least symbolically cremated in the grave. Srejović[34] points out that autochthonous elements have contributed to Roman burial customs in Yugoslavia. The grave fire as seen at Stobi may not be part of the Roman ethos but rather an indigenous modification of a Roman practice.

---

[32] Toynbee, *supra* n. 5, 50—51, mentions funerary meals eaten at the tomb.
[33] Graves 11, 13, 14, 52, 64 and 65 of Period II; and Grave 45 of Period III.
[34] "Necropoles Romaines du Haut Empire en Yougoslavie," *Starinar* XIII—XIV (Beograd 1965) 49—88.

Cremation versus Inhumation.

In the West Cemetery sequence, inhumations are absent only from Period III. Numerically, however, cremation is the preferred form of burial throughout Periods I, II, and III. In the last three periods, we are dealing with rather small samples (only ten or eleven graves opened in each period). Nonetheless, Periods IV and V show that during the later 2nd century A. C. to the 3rd century A. C. there was a shift from cremation to inhumation as a preferred means of burial. This date is consistent with that presented in Toynbee's[35] review, although the reasons for the shift remain uncertain.

"... the pagan thought of this period gives no hint of any dogma of bodily resurrection for mankind as a whole; and the fact that, for a time, in imperial Rome the two rites could co-exist in the same mausoleum suggests that the change in custom did not imply any significant change in actual doctrine. The abandonment of cremation was, moreover, too general to owe anything to Semitic, in particular to Jewish, habit and too early to be due to Christian influences. The explanation has, therefore, to be sought elsewhere ... inhumation could be felt to be a gentler and a more respectful way of laying to rest the mortal frame which has been the temple and mirror of the immortal soul and enduring personality. For this matter of sentiment neither funerary inscriptions nor the literature of the time provide explicit evidence. Nonetheless, the change of rite would seem to reflect a significant strengthening of emphasis on the individual's enjoyment of a blissful hereafter."[36]

PERIOD I

INHUMATIONS	20, 89, 90, 96	4
CREMATIONS	71+, 72+, 79+, 80+, 81+, 82+, 85+, 86+, 88+, 91+, 92+, 94+, 95+	13
NOT EXCAVATED	83*+, 84*+, 93?	3
		20

---

[35] *supra* n. 5, 40.
[36] *Ibid.* 40—41.

PERIOD II

INHUMATIONS	16, 17, 53, 63, 78	5
CREMATIONS	11, 12+, 13, 14, 15+, 18+, 19+, 21+, 49+, 50+, 51+, 52, 55+, 57+, 59+, 60+, 61+, 64, 65, 66+, 67+, 68+, 69+, 70+, 73+, 74+, 75+, 76+, 77+	29
NOT EXCAVATED	58?, 62?	2
		36

PERIOD III

INHUMATIONS	0	0
CREMATIONS	38+, 39+, 40+, 43+, 44+, 45, 46+, 47+, 48+, 56+	10
NOT EXCAVATED	42?	1
		11

PERIOD IV

INHUMATIONS	1, 6, 8, 10, 29, 30, 35, 36	8
CREMATIONS	28+, 31+, 37+	3
NOT EXCAVATED	32?, 33?, 34?, 41?	4
		15

PERIOD V

INHUMATIONS	2, 3, 4, 5, 22, 23, 24, 25, 26, 27, 54	11
CREMATIONS	0	0
NOT EXCAVATED	0	0
		11

+ Grave fire certain
? Grave not excavated, not known whether grave fire was present or not
* Almost certainly a cremation

ОБИЧАЈИ САХРАЊИВАЊА У ЗАПАДНОМ ГРОБЉУ

АЛ ВЕЗАЛОВСКИ

Ископавање Западног гробља у Стобима извођено је током 1970. и 1971. године.[24] Отворена је сонда 9.00 X 10.75 метара. Овај простор приближно је ограничен координатним линијама Ј81—87 и З135—140. На плану локалитета, који се налази на крају књиге, ова сонда означена је бројем 22. Анализа скелетних остатака и гробних прилога није још завршена. Тек кад се ове студије заврше имаћемо одговарајуће податке помоћу којих можемо да испитамо међусобно дејство погребних обичаја, морталитета и активности људи унутар самог града. Ово последње, укључило би не само шири римски свет, чији су Стоби били део, већ и трагове аутохтоних обичаја модификованих римском културом.

Ипак, постоје извесне карактеристике сахрањивања у Западном гробљу, које већ сада заслужују коментар.

1. Елаборација гробова и њен распон, нарочито унутар једног истог периода.[25]

2. Погребни банкет.

3. Гробна ватра.

4. Кремација наспрам инхумације као популарнији вид сахрањивања.

ЕЛАБОРАЦИЈА ГРОБОВА

Зачуђују нас варијације у квалитету израде гробова. Истина, нормално је очекивати широк распон погребних обичаја у граду римског царства. Између људи (а и њихових гробова) постоје економске и социјалне стратификације као и религиозне разлике. Стоби су, као провинцијски град на периферији царства, изложени различитим утицајима. Међусобно деловање аутохтоних култура, утицаја римског и других народа, који су се краће задржавали на овом простору, доприносе шароликости многих видова свакидашњег и религиозног живота. Врло је необична оволика разноликост обичаја сахрањивања на малом (у односу на читаву некрополу) простору који је откопаван.

У периоду I, цитирамо примере,[26] у гробовима 89, 90 и 96 била су сахрањена деца у плитким јамама.[27] Јама гроба 20, у коме је сахрањен одрастао човек, усечена је скоро читав метар у компактни слој шљунка из времена квартара. Ни у једном од ових гробова са инхумацијом, као ни код неколико гробова са кремацијом, није било гробних прилога.

Гроб 79 је плитка јама са спаљеним покојником, у коме су међу костима пронађене једна бронзана фибула и сечиво од гвожђа.[28] У близини овог гроба пронађен је скелет одраслог коња, коме је била отсечена глава. Тело је пажљиво било смештено у јаму.[29]

Гроб 81 је јама са два спаљена покојника,[30] у којој су пронађени остаци погребног банкета, две чешагије и гвоздена трака за руку. Гробови 82 и 85 нису имали прилога. Гроб 95 имао је кружан зид. У њему је пронађено 18 унгуентарија, амфориск и стаклена игла.

Период II заступљен је са четири плитка дечија гроба. У једном од њих тело је било смештено лицем на доле. Као и у периоду I, ниједан од ових гробова није имао прилоге. Пар метара даље, спаљени младић из гроба 76 покопан је са мноштвом фигурина од теракоте. Два гроба из истог периода, 21 (који је имао кружни зид) и 77 дала су велики број фигурина од теракоте. Споменимо неке од кремација у плитким јамама; гроб 18 садржао је 18 унгуентарија док су гробови 19, 64, 73, и 75 били без прилога.

У периоду III, комплексност гробова ишла је од плитке јаме са спаљеним покојником у гробу 43 до пажљиво саграђене купе од камена са отвором за жртву ливеницу гроба 38. Такође, можемо споменути слој шљунка насутог изнад неколико гробова који су имали отворе за жртве livenice.

Током периода IV гробови су били обични, саграђени од опеке. Гробни прилози су се у њима ређе налазили у поређењу са гробовима из претходних периода. Период V тешко је одредити пошто су многи гробови овог периода били уништени кад је овај простор престао да се употребљава као гробље. Ипак, према подацима које имамо може се закључити да су гробови периода V једнообразни и најпростији од свих гробова овде споменутих.

Без обзира којим се критеријумом служимо да би одредили степен елаборације гробова (квантитетом и врстом гробних прилога, као у случају гроба 76; или гробном конструкцијом, у случају гробова са купама или кружним зидовима), периоди од I до III показују више варијација од периода IV или V.[31] Ако узмемо да је степен елаборације гроба индикатор социјално-економског статуса, подаци не показују уочљиву употребу једног дела гробља од стране једне класе људи током прва три периода. За време последња два периода изгледа вероватно да је овај део гробља употребљавала класа сиромашнијих грађана.

Једна друга могућност постоји, иако поседујемо само негативне доказе који говоре њој у прилог, и то да је овај део гробља одувек употребљавала сиромашнија класа. Уколико је ово тачно, онда оно што сада објашњавамо као варијације међу социјално-економским класама јесу у ствари варијације унутар једне мање богате класе. Можда ћемо у будућности откопавати део гробља са савршено израђеним колумбаријумима и маузолејима. Уколико је у близини града било таквих гробница, изгледа невероватно да су оне биле тако разрушене да од њих ни трага није остало.

ПОГРЕБНИ БАНКЕТ

Три гроба са спаљеним покојницима, 21, 81 и 59, из времена Августа, садржала су угљенисане али добро сачуване орахе, семенке грожђа, коштице бресака и маслина разбацане међу костима. Као што смо и раније рекли, не постоји начин којим би се одредило да ли су грожђе, брескве или маслине појели људи из погребне пратње док је нејестиви део само смештен у гроб, или је све воће смештено у гроб ради забаве покојника. Ипак, у сва три гроба, пронађено је најмање туце целих, несломљених ораха као и празних љуски. Можемо да закључимо да је извесна количина неког друго воћа (нетакнутог) смештена у гроб. Пошто су остаци хране угљенисани, значи да су гробна ватра и погребни банкет били истовремени.³²

Не изненађује нас чињеница да су остаци воћа пронађени само у гробовима са спаљеним покојницима. Угљенисани органски остаци скоро увек имају већу шансу да се одрже од неугљенисане органске материје. До угљенисања може да дође само код погреба са спаљивањем кад се пали гробна ватра. Теже је објаснити зашто су само три гроба са кремацијом имала такве остатке. Могуће је да је у ове гробове стављена велика количина воћа, тако да су се могли сачувати остаци неколико плодова. У обрнутом случају произилази да је погребни банкет можда био само ретко примећен.

ГРОБНА ВАТРА

Гробна ватра пали се унутар гробне јаме и део је ритуала сахрањивања. Ни у једном случају није било доказа да је ватра била довољне јачине да би се могао спалити леш. Ипак, ватра је била јака тако да су опрљене стране и дно јаме. У појединим случајевима остало је и по пола килограма пепела и угљенисаног дрвета (гробови 21, 38, 39 и 81).

Гробне ватре ограничене су на гробове са спаљивањем, и само у седам случајева од 55 кремација није било сигурних доказа о гробној ватри.³³ Као што показује табла I, спаљивање се вршило у сваком од прва четири периода, а између 80% и 100% гробова са кремацијом имало је гробну ватру. Јасно је да је ватра била важна одлика погреба са спаљивањем; очигледно је да ватра није сматрана потребном приликом инхумације. Можда је било потребно да се покојник макар симболично спали у гробу. Срејовић³⁴ истиче да су аутохтони елементи утицали на римске обичаје сахрањивања на територији Југославије. Гробна ватра, виђена у Стобима, можда није била део римског обичаја већ локална модификација римског обичаја.

КРЕМАЦИЈА НАСПРАМ ИНХУМАЦИЈЕ

У откопаном делу Западног гробља, сахрањивања нема само у периоду III. Ипак, спаљивање је бројачно заступљеније у периодима I, II и III од сахрањивања инхумацијом. У последња три периода, располажемо са прилично малобројним узорцима (само је 10 или 11 гробова из сваког од ових периода отворено). Ипак, периоди IV и V показују да је крајем другог и почетком трећег века н. е. дошло до промене обичаја. Спаљивање (до тада популарније) уступа своје место инхумацији. Овај датум подудара се са резултатима Тојнбијеве[35], иако је разлог промене још увек неизвестан.

„... *паганска мисао овог периода не наговештава никакву догму о ускрснућу читавог човечанства. Чињеница да су извесно време у царском Риму оба обичаја могла да се примене у истом маузолеју наговештава да промена обичаја није била последица никакве значајне промене тадашње доктрине. Штавише, напуштање спаљивања било је сувише масовно да би било у ма каквој вези са семитским, а посебно јеврејским обичајем, а прерано да би било последица утицаја хришћанства. Стога, разјашњење треба тражити другде ... Могло се сматрати да је инхумација нежнији начин, пун поштовања, полагања смртног оквира који је представљао храм и огледало бесмртне душе и трајне личности. О овом питању осећаја не говоре изричито ни надгробни натписи, ни литература тог времена. Ипак изгледа да промена обичаја одражава значајно јачање веровања у блажени живот индивидуе после смрти.*"[36]

GODS, WAR AND PLAGUE IN THE TIME OF THE ANTONINES

by

JAMES WISEMAN

I. THE CENTURION

The most renowned native of Stobi is the scholar Ioannes who lived during the 5th century after Christ and whose collections of citations from ancient authors are extant. We know also that his son was called Septimius or Epimius. Nothing more, however, is known of the life of either and we are aware of the origin of Ioannes only because his name was customarily given as Ioannes Stobaeus.[1]

We also know of five bishops of Stobi whose names are preserved in the lists of bishops attending some of the most important of the early ecclesiastical congresses. The bishops are Budius, who attended the Council of Nicaea in 325; Nicolaus, Council of Chalcedon, 451; Phocas, Council of Constantinople, 553; Ioannes, the Sixth Ecumenical Council of Constantinople, 680; and Margaritus, who was present at the

---

[1] As author of the four books called 'Εκλογαί or 'Ανθολόγιον. He is mentioned by Photius *Bibl.* 167, where the son is named Septimius, and by Suidas, who records the name of his son as Epimius; s. v. 'Ιωάννης Στοβαῖος.

Second Trullanum Synod in 692.[2] Ioannes and Margaritus, however, belonged to a time when the city of Stobi had been in ruins for a century;[3] they, like many other bishops of the seventh and eighth centuries, never had the opportunity to celebrate the eucharist in their designated see.

Ancient literature records the name of no other citizen of Stobi. Even the city is mentioned rarely, except in reference to various military operations from the Hellenistic period to the late fifth century[4] and in connection with administrative reorganizations of Macedonia and Illyria. The historian, therefore, must rely chiefly on archaeological and epigraphical evidence for information about almost all aspects of public and private life in the ancient city.

Fortunately, the archaeological record is extensive, especially with regard to the city in early Christian times. The earlier periods are now becoming better known through the new series of excavations inaugurated in 1970, the results of which are also expanding even further our knowledge of the later city of Stobi.[5] The epigraphical evidence, too, is far from meager and touches on life in the city during the whole of its existence as a provincial city of the Roman Empire.

The present study offers some observations on the social and religious life of Stobi before the advent of Christianity. The chief evidence regarding the persons discussed here necessarily comes from inscriptions, a few of which have been previously published and others that are presented here for the first time.

---

[2] Budius (or Bunius): *Mansi* II, 696. Nicolaus: *Mansi* VII, 162. Phocas: *Mansi* IX 174, 191—192, where the ethnic Staliensis provinciae Praevaliensis is probably an error for Stobensis. Ioannes: M. le Quien, *Oriens Christianus* II (rep. Graz 1958) 176. Margaritus(or Margarites): *Mansi* XI, 993-994. A sixth bishop, Philippus, who lived in the late 4th or 5th century is known from an inscribed lintel of the Episcopal Basilica: Balduin Saria, "Neue Funde in der Bischofskirche von Stobi" *JÖAI* 28 (1933) 132—133.

[3] Stobi ceased to exist as an urban community in the last quarter of the 6th century: W-MZ (1971) 398; W-MZ (1972) 411, 421—422; Wiseman, *Guide*, "Historical Sketch."

[4] The site (called Στυπεῖον in the text) is mentioned also as the camp of a military garrison destroyed by Basil II in A. D. 1014; Cedrenus *CSHB* 2, 709A.

[5] The new excavations were begun in 1970 as a joint project of the University of Texas at Austin and the National Museum of Titov Veles under the auspices of the Smithsonian Institution.

1. Statue base. Figs. 79—80.

I-72-9. Green sandstone base. L. 0.572 m. W. 0.90 m. H. 0.266 m. H. of letters 0.054 m. The back and part of the two sides were cut into a rough semi-circle at some later date, perhaps when the base was removed from its original position. The inscription is on the front face.

    Λ I Δ
   Γ. Αἴλιον Πρεῖσκον

  Πρειμιπιλάριον

Figure 79. The inscribed statue base of C. Aelius Priscus (I-72-9).

Lines 2 and 3 are on a recessed face connected to fillets above and below by bevelled bands. Line 1 is inscribed partly on the bevel. The two cuttings in the upper surface of the base (D. 0.068 m. Depth 0.06 m.) were badly damaged when the original monument, almost certainly a bronze statue, was removed.

The base was found on July 13, 1972, in a wall of the 4th century located a few meters to the west of the Inner City Wall (Plan of Site, no.

25 and Fig. 81). The letters of the inscription are carefully cut and there are seriphs on several letters (Fig.80). The wall in which the inscription was re-used contains other material which had been removed from earlier buildings, including a coping block from the theater analemma (Fig. 80, upper left). The letter forms suggest a date in the 2nd century after Christ.[6]

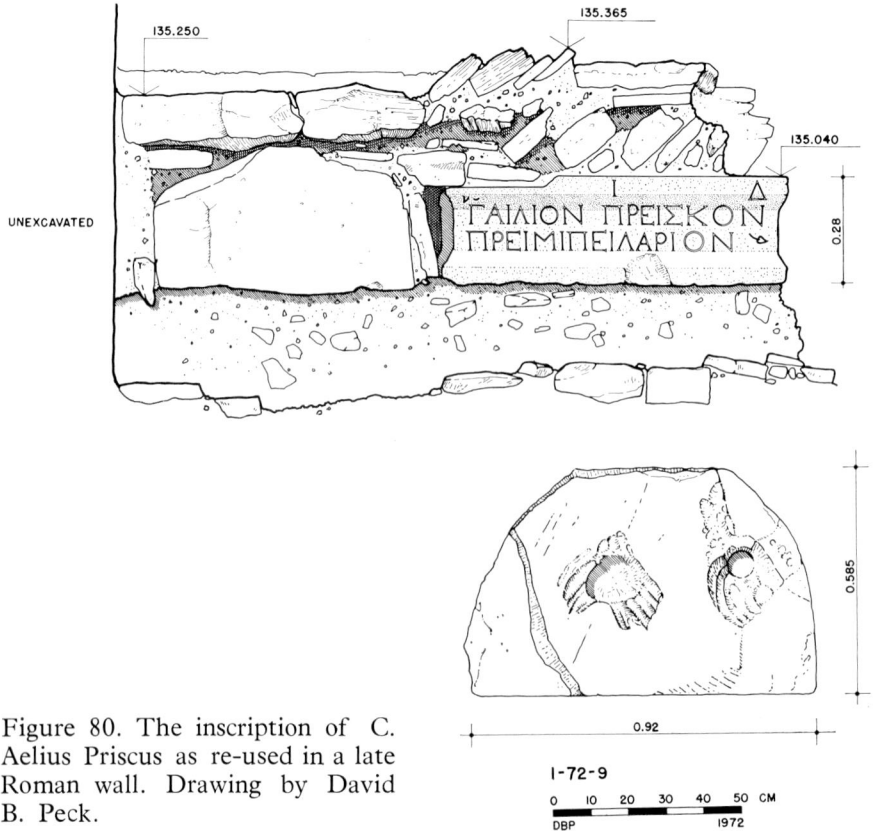

Figure 80. The inscription of C. Aelius Priscus as re-used in a late Roman wall. Drawing by David B. Peck.

---

[6] Letter forms are notoriously inexact chronological indicators, especially for the imperial era. It would be safer, perhaps, to date the inscription generally 1st-3rd centuries A. C. The tidy, boxlike letters with small, careful seriphs, however, suggest the middle of that long period. The 4-barred sigma would more *likely* be lunate or quadrate in the late 2nd or 3rd century and a 1st century inscription (if Greek at all) would be *likely* to have more elongated letters, more elaborate seriphs. The inscription seems only a bit earlier, for example, than Inscription (3) discussed below.

The name of the person in whose honor the monument was erected is in the accusative, as is often the case in imperial inscriptions.[7] The first line is problematic and even the reading of the first letter is uncertain; if it is a lambda it bears no resemblance to the other examples of the letter in lines 2 and 3. The second mark is a simple, vertical stroke in the exact center of the face of the block and is presumably an iota.[8] The third and final letter is unmistakably a delta. Perhaps the most likely explanation is that the letters represent the initials of the dedicator.

C. Aelius Priscus, a primipilarius, is a new name to Stobaean prosopography. An Aelius Priscus of the late 2nd century, who went mad and murdered his mother, is mentioned in the Digest (1. 18. 14),[9] but his home city is unknown and there is no reason to identify him with the soldier from Stobi. The cognomen Priscus, in any case, was a common one during the early and middle empire and was borne by several soldiers and provincial administrators.[10] C. Aelius Priscus himself may have served in some administrative post in Stobi after his retirement from the army or even during his tenure as first centurion of

---

[7] I list here a few Macedonian examples of the second and third centuries A. C. The Bragylii honor the Emperor Hadrian and Sabina Augusta, *SEG* XII (1955) 349; the Macedoniarch Silvanus Celer is honored, *SEG* XIII (1956) 400; C. Julius Crispus is honored by Lyca, *SEG* XXIV (1969) 488; Septimius Silvanus Nicomachus is honored in an inscription from Čepigovo, *SEG* XIII (1956) 404; T. Aelius Geminius is honored by the Thessalonicans in *SEG* II (1925) 410; M. Julius Severus, a primipilus, is honored by the Dostonei in *SEG* II (1925) 434. See also below, Inscription (3).

[8] The only other possibility is that it is a centering line.

[9] *PIR* I A (1933) 234.

[10] According to the lists of Iiro Kajanto, *The Latin Cognomina* (Helsinki 1965) 29—30, Priscus is represented by 1,269 examples, a number exceeded only by 13 other cognomina. A Priscus who was killed by Jews while serving as praefectus of the camp is mentioned by Josephus in *Bellum Judaicum* ii. 19. 7. Josephus also mentions a centurion of the same name, *ibid.* vi. 2. 10. An inscription of the late 2nd century records the name of a Priscus who served as subpraefectus vigilum and flamen Vulcanalis as well as in other offices: *CIL* VI, 1628: Rudolf Hanslik, s. v. "Priscus," *RE* 23 (1957) 5, no. 16. (- - - -)us Priscus was consul suffectus at some time between the years 128 and 133; *ibid.*, no. 17. Hanslik mentions two other Prisci of the 2nd century: one was an imperial procurator and the second was a native of Nicaea who built war machines; *ibid.*, cols. 4—5, nos. 9 and 12. P. Herrenius Macedo, son of P. and a member of the Roman tribe Aemilia at Stobi, served under the centurion Priscus in the XIII urban cohort during the early empire, but the home of the centurion is unknown: T. Mommsen, "Di una nuova silloge epigrafica del secolo XV," *RM* 5 (1890) 90; *MP* 466.

the legion.¹¹ The fact that a bronze statue of him was erected is indicative of some remarkable public service and/or membership in a family of such wealth and distinction that the magnitude of his service was irrelevant.

Figure 81. The late Roman wall in which the inscribed base, I-72-9, was found.

---

¹¹ Several examples of legionary officers, including primipili and other centurions, holding high administrative positions in provincial towns, especially under the Antonines and Severi, are discussed by Ramsay MacMullen, *Soldier and Civilian in the Later Roman Empire* (Cambridge, Mass. 1963) 64—67. See also, e. g., the inscription found in Peštani (a village southeast of Prilep) in which Τὸ κοινόν of the Dostonei honored M. Julius Severus, primipilus, as their benefactor and ἀρετῆς ἕνεκεν; G. I. Kazarow, "Inscriptions et antiquitiés de la Macédoine occidentale (regions de Mariovo et de Prilep)," *BCH* 47 (1923) 288, no. 4a, fig. 12; *SEG* II (1925) 434; cf. his tombstone, erected by his mother, Julia Severa: *SEG* II (1925) 433; *MP* 617.

An Aelia Priscila is also known at Stobi in the 2nd century. Considering the general contemporaneity of the names and the fact that we are dealing with families in a provincial city of only moderate size, the probability is high that Aelius Priscus and Aelia Priscila were related. If so, C. Aelius Priscus belonged to one of the most distinguished families of Stobi.

II. THE PRISCI

Aelia Priscila is named in an inscription noted first by J. G. von Hahn[12] and, independently, by Leon Heuzey.[13] The letters were already badly weathered at that time and von Hahn was unable to obtain a reading that yielded sense. Heuzey read as follows:

ΚΛΑΥΔΙΑΙ	Κλαυδία Πρείσκα
ΠΡΕΙΣΚΑΙ	καὶ Αἰλία Πρισκίλλα
ΚΑΙΑΙΛΙΑΠΡΙ	Μευστρία πισταῖς
ΣΚΙΛΛΑΙΜΕΥ	μετρασιν (peut-être
ΣΡΙΑΠΙΣ	μ[η]τέρασιν pour
ΤΑΙΣΜΕΡΑ	μητράσιν).
ΣΙΙΙ	

" À Claudia Prisca et à Aelia Priscilla; Mestria a élevé ce monument à celles qui ont été pour elle deux mères dévouées."

Neither von Hahn nor Heuzey described the stone; the location of the inscription was also left vague by the travellers.

The inscription was examined again and republished with a transcription by A. von Premerstein and N. Vulić.[14] They read as follows:

Κλαυδίαι
Πρείσκαι
καὶ Αἰλία Πρι-
σκίλαι. Με-
στριά Πρίσκα
ταῖς μητρά-
σιν.

---

[12] "Reise von Belgrad nach Salonik," *DenkschrWien (phil-hist Klasse)* 16, pt. 2 (1869) 166, no. 34.

[13] "Découverte des ruines de Stobi," *RA* 2 (1873) 38; *Mission archéologique de Macédoine* (Paris 1876) 335, no. 138. Followed by Dimitsas ἡ Μακεδονία (Athens 1896) 334, no. 295.

[14] "Antike Denkmäler in Serbien und Macedonien," *JÖAI* 6 (1903) Beiblatt, cols. 6—7, no. 8.

The new editors described the stone briefly, suggested a date of the 2nd century A. C. on the basis of letter forms, and commented that it was located "am Nordrande des Trümmerfeldes von Stobi an der Fundstelle."

The inscription was still visible during the First World War when German soldiers initiated excavations in some areas of the ancient site. The inscription was seen at that time by Dr. Hald, who was unaware of the previous publications and who was unable to read the inscription. He did, however, publish a photograph and sketch of the inscribed block and he located its position on a sketch map.[15] The monument was evidently rolled, not long after it was noted by Hald, so that the inscription was face down and therefore not visible. In any case, the inscription was not mentioned again in the published reports of the subsequent excavations.

When the new excavations at Stobi were begun in 1970 one of the first tasks inaugurated was the locating of all inscriptions, published or unpublished, that lay scattered about the site. Even during that initial season it seemed likely that: 1) the inscribed monument photographed and sketched by Hald was the same monument that had been published earlier by (among others) von Premerstein and Vulić, and 2) one of the two roseate marble monument bases at that time lying in the Via Sacra near the Porta Heraclea must bear the dedication of Meustria Prisca. Certainly they lay in the approximate location indicated on Hald's sketch. The pressure of other investigations, however, prevented our testing the hypothesis until the summer of 1972. At that time the monument base was rolled over, cleaned, measured and drawn, and finally set up vertically in a temporary location on the Via Sacra. The base is indeed the dedication by Meustria Prisca.

2. Monument base. Fig. 82.

I-72-2. Roseate marble monument base. H. 1.81 m. W. 0.84 m. Th. 0.785 m. The inscribed face is recessed slightly and framed by a small cyma recta. All faces except the back are bevelled at the bottom. The moldings are irregular and the letters unevenly carved. H. of letters 0.035—0.06 m.

---

[15] *Auf den Trümmern Stobis* (Stuttgart 1917) 23 and feature 5 on the sketch map, fig. 5, p. 19.

Gods, War and Plague in the Time of the Antonines

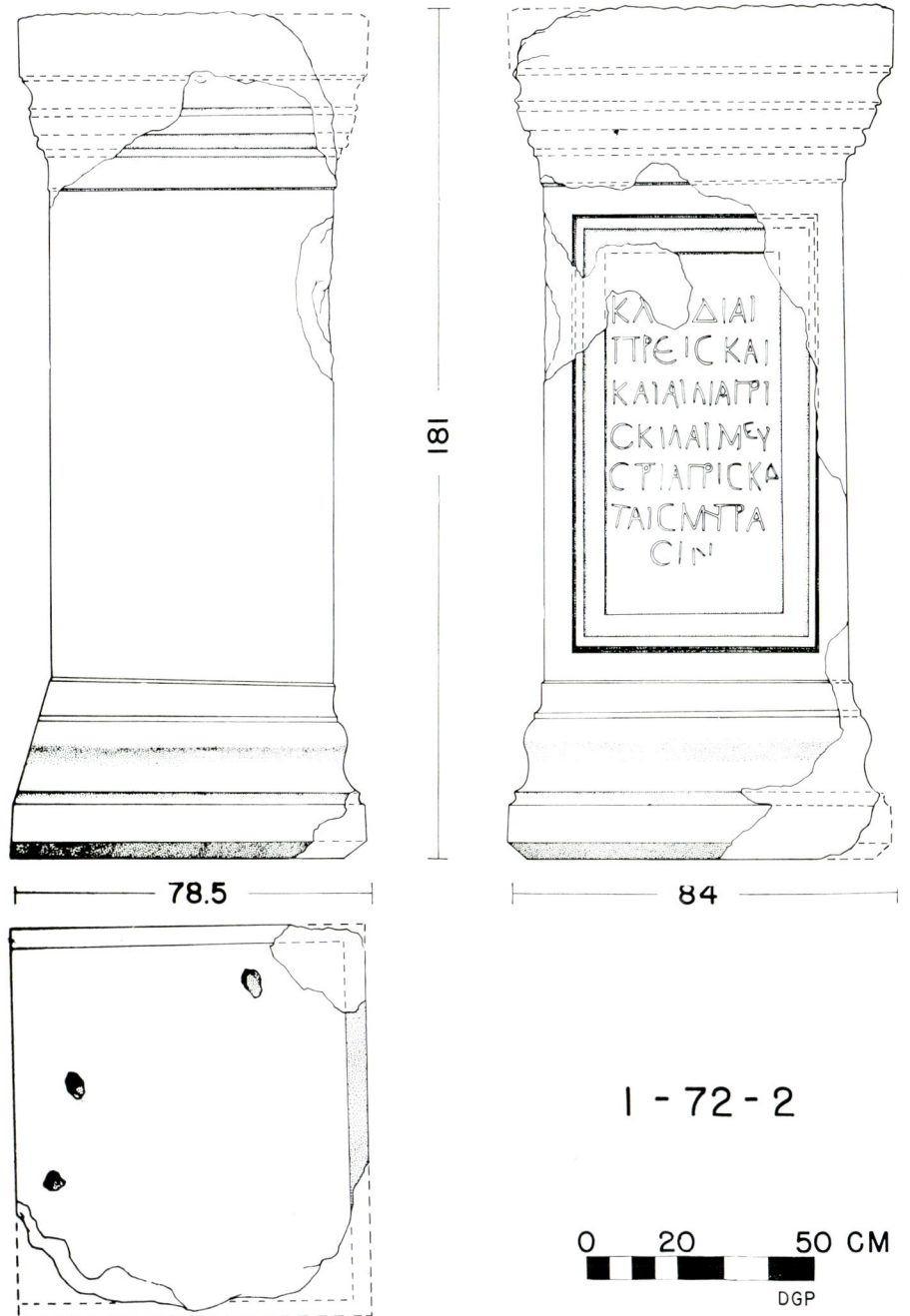

Figure 82. Base of monument dedicated by Mestria Prisca (I-72-2). Drawing by Diane G. Peck

K[λαυ]δίαι
Πρείσκαι
καὶ Αἰλία⟨ι⟩ Πρι-
σκίλαι. Μευ-
στρία Πρίσκα
ταῖς μητρά-
σιν.

"Meustria Prisca for her mothers, Claudia Prisca and Aelia Priscila."

There are four ligatures: line 3, pi-rho; line 5, tau-rho, pi-rho; line 6, mu-eta-tau-rho. Lunate sigma and epsilon suggest a date somewhat later in the 2nd century than the statue base of Aelius Priscus. Meustria for Mestria probably represents a local phonetic peculiarity, as Heuzey long ago pointed out,[16] and we shall hereafter refer to her as Mestria. The original location of the monument base is unknown, but during the late Roman period both the inscribed block and the nearly identical monument base found near-by almost certainly stood along the Via Sacra where they were re-used to support other, later dedications.[17]

One might suppose that ταῖς μητράσιν indicates that Claudia Prisca and Aelia Priscila were the grandmother and mother of the dedicant. But there is no need to speculate about which lady was which; the precise relationship of Mestria Prisca to Claudia Prisca is given in another inscription found at Stobi.

III. THE PRIESTESS

3. Statue base. Fig. 83.

I-70-20 (=*SEG* XVII [1960]319). White marble base, broken at upper left. L. 0.83 m. H. 0.57 m. Th. 0.628 m. H. of letters (lines 1—3) 0.025 m. (lines 4—5) 0.02 m. There are small mouldings above and below the inscribed face which continue around both end faces of the block.

---

[16] Heuzey, *Mission*, p. 335. Note also the single lambda in Priscila.

[17] Djordje Mano-Zissi, who found part of an imperial bust near the entrance to the Episcopal Basilica (see Plan of Site at back of volume), suggested that the two bases had been re-used to support busts of members of the royal family: "Iskopavanja u Stobima 1933 i 1934 godine," *Starinar* 10—11 (1935—36) 150; Kitzinger *Survey*, p. 115.

['Ἀρτέμι]δος· Λοχίας· ἱέρειαν καὶ Σεβαστῶν
[Κ]λαυδίαν· Πρεῖσκαν· ἱερασαμένην· ὁσιώτα-
τα· ἔτεσιν· ξ',· μαρτυρηθεῖσάν τε ἐπὶ ἁγνείᾳ
ὑπὸ τοῦ Κλαρίου· Ἀπόλλωνος,· Μεστρία Πρεῖσκα·
ἡ ἔγγονος· λαβοῦσα· τόπον· δόγματι βουλῆς.·

"The priestess of Artemis Lochia and the Divine Emperors, Claudia Prisca, who performed the sacred rites most devoutly for 60 years, and whose purity was attested by Clarian Apollo. Mestria Prisca, her granddaughter, (set up this votive) in this place which she received by a decree of the Senate (of Stobi)."
The base may have supported a statue of Claudia Prisca or a group of two statuettes, one of which might have been the figure of Artemis found near the base in 1931. The top of the base was severely damaged in antiquity (much of the left side is gone) and offers little help in determining the nature of the monument. The single, small cutting preserved on the right (L. 0.055 m. W. 0.04 m. Depth 0.04 m.) may have been for the attachment of a plinth between base and statue(s).

The monument base was built into a late Roman wall between the Episcopal Residence and the House of Parthenius (see Plan of Site at back of volume, nos. 16 and 13). The wall was discovered and largely removed during the excavations of 1931, but the base was left as it was found. The wall closed the east side of a rectangular room, the other walls of which were left standing by the excavators and are visible today. The inscribed base is also still to be seen in its find-spot.[18]

The inscription was published first by N. Vulić, but without commentary.[19] The text of the inscription was later treated briefly by Ch. Picard who thought, for some reason, that the stone had been removed to the near-by town of Gradsko. In any case, he records that

---

[18] The circumstances of discovery were made known to me by Djordje Mano-Zissi who was excavating in the near.-by Theodosian Palace and House of Parthenius in 1931. He recalled vividly the dismantling of the wall by V. R. Petković, the excavator, in order to free the inscription and the discovery in the immediate vicinity of a marble statuette of Artemis. The published report by Petković, "Istorisko-umetnički Muzej u 1931 godini," *Godišnjak Srpske akademije nauka* 40 (1931) 225, does not mention the inscription, but does mention the statuette of Artemis, „bez glave," ("without a head"). The statuette (still unpublished) is now in the National Museum at Belgrade.

[19] "Antički spomenici naše zemlje," *Spomenik* 71 (1931) no. 637.

Figure 83. Monument base honoring Claudia Prisca (I-70-20).

he sought it unsuccessfully both at Gradsko and at Stobi in 1956.[20] The chief contributions of the article are: 1) the observation that ἁγνεία in the inscription refers to "pureté du coeur" and 2) the suggestion that Apollo, Artemis and Dionysus were somehow closely associated at Stobi. The latter suggestion appears to have been prompted by the existence of a Greek inscription from Stobi identifying a certain Prepon as archimystes of the Βακχεῖον πρεσβύτερον.[21] Neither the inscription cited, however, nor any other inscription concerning Stobi implies a cult association of Dionysus with Apollo and Artemis.

Jeanne and Louis Robert have commented at some length on Picard's article.[22] They provide additional documentation for the meaning of ἁγνεία in this context but take issue with Picard on several other matters. The most important of the latter for our present considerations is that the Roberts show that the passive of μαρτυρέω in the inscription refers not merely to a certificate of spiritual purity obtained from Clarian Apollo, but to an oracle of the god. We shall discuss later the visit of a sacred embassy from Stobi to the Sanctuary of Apollo at Clarus, but we should first consider what else may be known about the family that includes such an illustrious lady as the long-lived priestess Claudia Prisca.

Since we are told explicitly in Inscription (3) that Claudia Prisca was the grandmother of Mestria Prisca, then we may be sure that the Aelia Priscila of Inscription (2) was her mother. Whether or not other members of the family can now be identified depends in part on our understanding of how women were named in the 2nd century after Christ. Although we may presume that the Roman practice at that time was general throughout the Empire, especially among the upper classes of the provincial cities, it will be more relevant to look most closely at the practice in Macedonia.[23]

---

[20] "D'Éphèse à la Gaule et de Stobi (Macédoine) à Claros," *REG* 70 (1957) 109—117.

[21] The original publication suggested βακχεῖον | πρεσβύτε|ρον πρέπον | Τίτῳ ἀρχι|μύστῃ: N. Vulić, "Antički spomenici naše zemlje" *Spomenik* 75 (1933) no. 55. The correct reading was offered by Louis Robert, "Antanoi" *REG* 47 (1934) 31, note 3: βακχεῖον|πρεσβύτε|ρον Πρέπον|τι τῷ ἀρχι|μύστῃ. Cf. MP 1222.

[22] "Bulletin epigraphique," *REG* 71 (1958) 266—269, no. 303.

[23] The names of slaves and those assumed by freedmen at the time of manumission are omitted from the discussion that follows. The prosopographical studies of D. Kanatsoulis have been of great value in the research involved in the preparation of this article; see also Fanula Papazoglu, "O onomastičkoj formuli kod Makedonaca u rimsko doba," *ŽA* 5 (1955) 350—372.

Both daughters and sons regularly took at least one of their names from the nomen of the father. Examples are numerous and we cite here an inscription from Tremnik (Antigonea?), located not far south of Stobi, because it is illustrative of both.

>Αἴλιος Ἑρμῆς ἐ-
>ξήρτισε τοῖς
>θρεψάντ[εσιν]
>Αἰλία[ι κα-]
>ὶ Αἰλίῳ [- - - -]
>μνήμης (χάριν).[24]

A secondary feminine name was customary and was usually derived from the father's cognomen, e. g., Geminia Olympia, daughter of Geminius Olympus of Thessalonica (2nd century);[25] Naevia Symphorusa, daughter of Naevius Symphorus, known from an inscription of early imperial date found near Philippi;[26] Pomponia Aquilina, daughter of C. Pomponius Aquila, a centurion of legion III Scythica (Dium).[27] The praenomen, however, was occasionally passed on from father to daughter who might then take a third name (a) from her father's cognomen, (b) from her mother, or (c) from her husband. A few instances of each will suffice as examples.

(a) Septimia Silvana Celerina was the daughter of Septimius Silvanus Celer, who were members of a distinguished family which even included a Macedoniarch.[28] Aelia Baebia Heliodora of Thessalonica was the daughter of Aelius Baebius Heliodorus in the 3rd century.[29]

(b) Marcia Junia Paula was the daughter of Marcus Athenagorus and Junia Votiana (Thessalonica, early 3rd century).[30] Caea Petronia

---

[24] Vulić, *Spomenik* 75 (1933) no. 164.

[25] *MP* 359.

[26] *MP* 959.

[27] *MP* 1175. Caelidia Secunda is probably the daughter of Sextus Caelidius Secundus of Scupi (*MP* 666) and Cornelia Asprilla was probably the daughter of P. C. Asper Atiarius Montanus (*MP* 783). Numerous other examples could be adduced.

[28] D. Kanatsoulis, Τὸ κοινὸν τῶν Μακεδόνων (Thessalonica 1956) 93.

[29] *MP* 52.

[30] *MP* 890. Paula may have been added from her husband's name after marriage.

Pacatiana was the daughter of Julius Pacatianus and Petronia Caea, known from a Greek inscription found near Prilep.[31]

(c) The high priestess Pontia Callistiana Cassia was the wife of Pontius Cassianus Proclus;[32] Flavia Aeliana Sempronia Artemidora was the wife of Flavius Sempronius Aelianus.[33]

What we might expect, then, at Stobi in the 2nd and 3rd centuries is that daughters of citizens would take two names from their father or, if the mother was from an especially distinguished family, they might take the nomen of the father and one name from the mother. Other names might or might not be added at the time of marriage. These possibilities should be kept in mind as we consider possible familial ties.

Inscriptions (1)-(3) provide us with three nomina (Claudius, Aelius, and Mestrius) and but a single cognomen (Priscus) spread over a minimum of three generations from about the late 1st century to the early 3rd century after Christ.

On the evidence of the feminine names we may construct a rudimentary genealogical tree as follows:

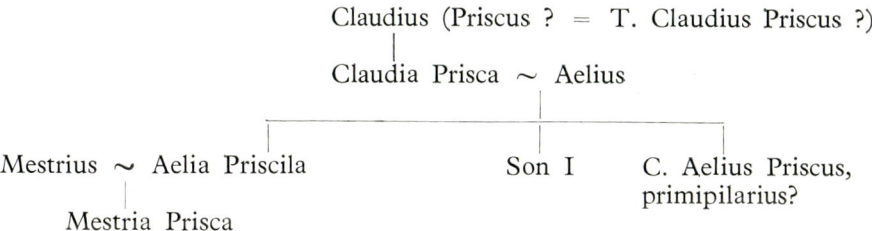

The women took one name, as customary, from the father's nomen. Their second name, at least after Claudia Prisca, they acquired from the mother, probably because of the importance of the maternal line.

We may now look for additional relatives and some clues to the identities of the males so far listed. We should turn first to the inscriptions at Stobi.

Only two other Claudians are known at Stobi. One is Tiberius Claudius Polycharmus, also known as Achyrius. There is little likeli-

---

[31] *MP* 1154 and 608. For additional comments and examples of feminine names derived from the paternal praenomen in Macedonia during the early and middle empire see Kanatsoulis, Τὸ κοινὸν τῶν Μακεδόνων, p. 92, esp. note 3.
[32] *MP* 1189.
[33] *MP* 1452.

hood, however, that Polycharmus, the "father of the synagogue" at Stobi, was in any way related to the priestess of Artemis and of the Emperors.³⁴ Other than Polycharmus and Claudia Prisca herself, we know only Κλω[δίου?], an abbreviated name inscribed on a seat in the theater at Stobi.³⁵ There may, however, be other Claudians indicated among the numerous monograms carved on the theater seats.

Aelius is only slightly better attested at Stobi. A fragmentary tombstone inscribed in Latin records the name of Ael(ius) [E]u[porus]. The cognomen, however, is manifestly uncertain and the names of the two women for whom the monument was erected, perhaps the wife and sister of Aelius, are nearly as conjectural.³⁶ Aelius S———and Aelius Tertius Ulpius are known from the theater.³⁷ None of the names

---

³⁴ On Polycharmus, see Martin Hengel, "Die Synagogeninschrift von Stobi," *ZNTW* 59 (1966) 145—182; W-MZ (1971) 406—411; W-MZ (1972) 408—411.

³⁵ Kerkis 2, row 12, seat 3. Most of the seats in the theater were inscribed by patrons who had evidently purchased the right to reserve their seats. Names are found not only on the horizontal surface of the seat but also frequently on the riser and on the lip. All names were written in Greek characters. Inscriptions from the first two kerkides and a small part of the third (moving clockwise from the west parodos) were published by Balduin Saria: "Die Inschriften des Theaters von Stobi," *WJ* 32 (1940) 1—34. Saria numbered the inscriptions consecutively: Κλω — is his no. 125 on p. 20. The third and fourth kerkides were uncovered during the 1960s. In 1971 the new Project Stobi undertook the recording of all theater inscriptions. Photographs were taken of each inscription and Apostol Keramidčiev made both paper squeezes and a provisional handwritten record. The locations of the inscriptions will be referred to hereafter by seat, lip, or riser and the number of kerkis (west to east), row (bottom to top), and seat block (west to east). See the theater plan by W. B. Dinsmoor, Jr., published in W-MZ (1972) 419, ill. 3.

³⁶ N. Vulić, "Antički spomenici naše zemlje," *Spomenik* 77 (1934) 40—41, no. 17:

> Noviae [Vere]cun-
> dae et Liv[i]ae Ni-
> cerot[is] Ael(ius) [E]u-
> [porus ux]ori [ca-
> [rae et sor]ori.

³⁷ Kerkis 1, row 2, seat 3: Αἰλί(ου) Σ[- -]λλ (—ου). Kerkis 1, row 16, seat 1: Αἰλί(ου) Τερτί(ου) Οὐλπί(ου). The inscription numbers in Saria are 2 (several names listed together) and 60, respectively. I note here also the conjectural reading of a fragmentary sandstone tombstone from the Episcopal Basilica published by Rudolf Egger ("Die städtische Kirche von Stobi," *JÖAI* 24 (1929) 86, no. 4): Φιλού[μενος Αἰ-] | λία Γε[μελλίνῃ] | τῇ ἰδί[ᾳ συμβίῳ] | [τ]ῇ πο[θεινοτά|τῃ] μν[ήμης χάριν].

suggests immediately a close relation with the persons named in Inscriptions (1)-(3).

Figure 84. The genitive of Mestrius as it appears on a theater seat.

Mestrius is also found among the inscriptions in the cavea of the theater (Fig. 84).[38] Mestria or Mestrianus occurs in a fragmentary Greek inscription that may have been a dedication to Asclepius.[39] And Mestrius appears on an inscription found in the Sanctuary of Nemesis in the scene building of the theater.[40] The inscription is on a sandstone slab that had served as part of the platform for an aedicula in the Nemeseum:

> Θεᾷ(ι) Νεμέσει κατ' ἐπιταγὴ[ν]
> Τ(ίτος) Μέστριος Λόγγος.

Titus Mestrius Longus, as Saria pointed out, presumably dedicated the entire aedicula of which several other pieces were recovered. The

---

[38] Kerkis 3, row 14, seat 5, on the riser: Μεστρίου. The epsilon and sigma are lunate and the genitive ending is a ligature. H. of letters 0.065/0.09 m.

[39] Rudolf Egger, *JÖAI* 24 (1929) 86, no. 4 (name in last line of fragment B). The inscription on white marble had been re-used in the construction of the ambo of the Episcopal Basilica. Egger dated the inscription (now Stobi No. I-70-17) to the early 4th century, but it could belong to the late 3rd century.

[40] Balduin Saria "Das Theater von Stobi," *AA* 53 (1938) 106 and fig. 18G; idem, *WJ* 32 (1940) 11—12, no. 2. It was published first, without commentary, by N. Vulić, *Spomenik* 77 (1934) 41, no. 18.

dedication occurred κατ' ἐπιταγήν, i. e., in accordance with a divine command conveyed to Mestrius in a dream or oracle. Saria assumed that the command came from Nemesis herself. The suggestion is reasonable and may be correct, but we should note that the phrases κατὰ μαντείαν, κατ' ὄναρ were also used when the dedication to a deity resulted from an oracle given by another god.[41]

Saria dated the inscription to ca. A. D. 200, evidently on the basis of letter forms.[42] Fanula Papazoglu, however, has recently argued that another inscription found in the sacellum and which would appear to refer to the dedication of the room to the goddess, dates to the late 3rd century.[43] The dates both of the construction of the theater and of its later conversion into an arena have long been disputed. The principal views have been presented by Saria, who argued for a Hadrianic construction and a Severan remodelling, and by Ejnar Dyggve, who placed construction in Severan times with remodelling in the late 3rd.[44] The new excavations at Stobi (1970 to present) have not as yet brought about the discovery of an intact archaeological deposit that can be definitely associated with either of the two chief building periods of the theater. We are prevented by the present lack of firm archaeological and historical evidence from settling the chronological issues involving the theater. In these circumstances, the cautious path is perhaps best, and we should leave the date of the dedication by Mestrius open: the letter forms might indeed belong to the late 2nd or the 3rd century A. C. The preference for lunate to quadrate letters (the latter do not appear at all) argues for, but does not prove, an earlier rather than later date.

The social and financial credentials of T. Mestrius Longus are certainly adequate for us to consider him a possible relation to the Prisci so far discussed. His dedication to Nemesis of a columnar aedicula is proof enough of his prosperity; that he should have been permit-

---

[41] The lexica discuss the general usage of ἐπιταγή: see, e. g., James Hope Moulton and George Milligan. *The Vocabulary of the Greek Testament* (London 1930). On ἐπιταγή as emanating from the deity honored see the discussion by Wilhelm Dittenberger in his commentary on *SIG*³ 786.

[42] Saria, *WJ* 32 (1940) 12.

[43] "Natpis iz Nemezejona i datovanje Stobskog pozorišta," *ŽA* 1 (1951) 279—293.

[44] Ejnar Dyggve, "Le theâtre mixte du bas-empire d'après le theâtre de Stobi et les diptyques consulaires," *RA* (1958) pt. 1, pp. 137—157; pt. 2 pp. 20—39. Saria, *loc. cit.* above in note 40.

ted to make such a dedication was not just concomitant with his wealth, but an indication of some social prominence. If Mestrius Longus was related to Mestria Prisca, the probable date of the inscription from the Nemeseum suggests that he was more likely a younger brother or nephew than her father. If Papazoglu is correct about the other inscription from the Nemeseum, he could be removed from Mestria by 3 or 4 generations.

We should not, however, restrict our search for other relatives to Stobi. There is ample evidence that the populations of the provincial cities were seldom, if ever, static during the Empire. The movements of the legions, the retiring of soldiers, the arrival of new provincial administrators were all occasions that naturally affected the local census. But such factors probably had less effect than more ordinary occurrences such as marriages between persons of neighboring communities, the arrival and departure of semi-transient trading families, or movements involving inheritances or a failure to inherit. The tomb monu-

Figure 85. The theater seat of F. Aufidenus Atticus

ment of Thessalonicus[45] that now stands just outside the Porta Heraclea at Stobi may serve to remind us that a Stobaean of the early Empire

---

[45] Inv. No. I-70-22. The inscription was published by N. Vulić, *Spomenik* 98 (1941—48) 43, no. 93.

need not have been born there. He may, in fact, have come from some distance, as some of the retiring soldiers doubtlessly did. The theater provides graphic evidence of distant homelands in the form of names; e. g., Φ. Αὐφιδήνου Ἀττικοῦ (Fig. 85).[46]

It is tempting to relate the Prisci of Stobi to Tiberius Claudius Priscus, the Macedoniarch at some time during the first two centuries of the Empire. He is known only from an altar at Beroea honoring a daughter, Tiberia Claudia Quintiana. The father is identified as Μακεδονιάρχης and the mother, Flavia Isidora, is called Μακεδονιάρχισσα.[47] Here certainly is a family distinguished enough to justify the perseverence of a maternal cognomen through at least three generations. Unfortunately, we know nothing more that is certain of the Macedoniarch or of his family. Even his date is unknown.

Another Tiberius Claudius Priscus, son of Tiberius, is known from the Paeonian city of Doberus. The town lay to the east of Stobi beyond the Vardar, perhaps near modern Strumica. The name occurs in a Latin inscription of early Imperial date which provides little information; he was a soldier and belonged to the voting tribe Aemilia. Other soldiers bearing the same name are known from Pannonia.[48]

The name Aelius occurs frequently in Macedonian inscriptions and Aelia is a common feminine name. There was, indeed, an Aelia Priscilla, wife of C. Julius Menelaus, who was the son of Menelaus, the πατὴρ συνεδρίου of the Macedonian League. It is of interest to note that the mother passed on a part of her name to her daughter, Julia

---

[46] Kerkis 3, row 3, seats 5 and 6. H. of letters 0.09/0.17 m. The second phi is diamond-shaped.

[47] Otto Walter, "Archäologische Funde in Griechenland von Frühjahr 1940 bis Herbst 1941," *AA* 52 (1942) 176, no. 7; Kanatsoulis, Τὸ κοινὸν τῶν Μακεδόνων, p. 86; *MP* 737.

[48] *CIL* VI, 3884, p. 2, 15; *MP* 1648. On Doberus and its possible location, see *MGRD* 248—252 and Map 3. A native of Pannonian Savaria, T[i. Cl]audius Priscus, was a praetorian before A. D. 209: Arpadus Dobo, *Inscriptiones extra fines Pannoniae Daciaeque repertae ad res earundem provinciarum pertinentes* (Budapest no date) p. 21, no. 46/b. Yet another Ti. Claudius Priscus is known from an inscription found in 1909 at Beočin near Sirmium. The inscription was on a boundary stone of the veteran's estate and identified him as the prefect of the *ala I Civium Romanorum*. The inscription has been dated to the late 1st century A. C. on the basis of letter forms and historical evidence regarding the movements of the *ala*; see Miroslava Mirković in *Sirmium* I, ed. Vladislav Popović (Beograd 1971) 81—82, inscription no. 79.

Priscilla.⁴⁹ The precise dates of the three inscriptions honoring members of the family are unknown, but are placed by Kanatsoulis in the last quarter of the 2nd century A. C. Aelia Priscilla II, then, was a contemporary of our Stobaeans and may well have been related to them.⁵⁰

Among the numerous other Aelians of Macedonia there are two that may be mentioned here as being of special interest: P. Aelius Mestrius, son of Publius, and M. Aelius Mestrianus, son of Marcus. Both were veterans and belonged to the tribe Maecia of Pelagonia, a town on the Erigon not far to the southwest of Stobi.⁵¹ The inscription recording the first name was dated by letter forms to the time of Domitian (emperor A. D. 81—96), but the second is specific: M. Aelius Mestrianus was discharged from the army in A. D. 177.⁵²

Mestrius Priscus, son of Gaius, a citizen of Dium in southern Macedonia, may also be related to Claudia Prisca through her daughter Aelia Priscila (I) and Mestrius. It is of interest that the probable sister of Mestrius Priscus, Mestria Aquilina, was a priestess.⁵³ A *possible* descent may be traced as follows:

---

⁴⁹ Walter, *AA* 52 (1942) 175, 184, inscriptions nos. 1, 28 a, b; see also Kanatsoulis, Τὸ κοινὸν τῶν Μακεδόνων, pp. 91—93. The inscriptions are all from Beroea, the capital of the League.

⁵⁰ Aelia Priscilla II is not likely to have been identical with Aelia Priscila I of Stobi, but she might have been the daughter of an Aelius Priscus, and so a descendant of Claudia Prisca and Aelius through a second son, perhaps even C. Aelius Priscus, our primipilarius. That is, a first son of Aelius would have taken his father's cognomen, which was presumably not Priscus, while a second son might well have the maternal cognomen. The use of a double-lambda in the spelling of Priscilla, wife of C. Julius Menelaus, and a single lambda in the name of the Stobaean is of significance only as another instance of the variability of spelling in Macedonian inscriptions.

⁵¹ Pelagonia was also a region of Macedonia. The ancient references are discussed, the epigraphical material cited and the possible location of the town is considered by F. Papazoglu in *MGRD* 203—210 and Map 3 at end of volume. The names occur in *CIL* III, 3530 and *CIL* VI, 2382 b⁸ respectively; cf. *MP* 1535—36.

⁵² *MGRD* 205, note 29 (where the reference should read *CIL* III, 3530 instead of 3350); *CIL* III, 3530: D. M. | P. AEL P. F. MA ECIA | MESTRIVS. PELA OPT. LEG. II. Ab | 7. ATTEI. DEXTRI | AN. XXXVIIII. STp | XVIIII. H.S.E. OPT | ONES.LEG.EIVSD; *CIL* VI, 2382 b⁸ reads: M. ∧ELIVS. M. F. MEC. MESTRI ∧ NVS. PEL.

⁵³ Dimitsas. ἡ Μακεδονία, nos. 190—191; *MP* 929, 931. We should also mention here a Julia Mestria and Julius [Me]s[t]rinus known from an inscription of the late 2nd-early 3rd centuries A. C. found in the courtyard of the monastery of Sveti Dimitri near Titov Veles: A. von Premerstein and N. Vulic, *JÖAI* 6 (1903) 3, no. 2.

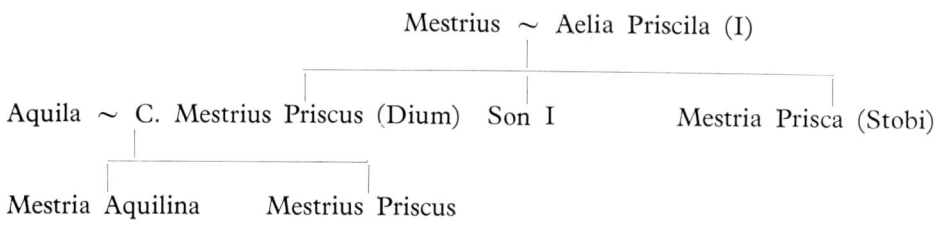

IV. CLARIAN APOLLO

The reverence held by the people of Stobi for Clarian Apollo is attested not only by our Inscription(3) but also by an inscription carved on the interior face of the west wall of the propylaea of the sanctuary at Clarus. The inscription concerns an embassy sent to the sanctuary by the citizens of Stobi.

4. Commemorative inscription. Fig. 86.

[Σ]τοβαίων
[ἐπὶ] πρυτάνεως Ἀπόλλω-
[νος]τὸ πζ', ἱερέως Γ(αίου) Ἰου(λίου) Ζω-
[τίχ]ου, θεσπι(ω)δοῦντος Γν(αίου)
[Ἰου(λίου)] Ῥηγείνου Ἀλεξάνδρου·
[προ]φητεύοντος Διογνήτου
[Ἄν]δρωνος β', γραμματεύ-
[οντ]ος Σέξ(του) Ἰου(λίου) Διογνήτου νε(ωτέρου)
[θεο]πρόπος Λ(ούκιος) Κορνήλιος
[Μου?]νδικιανὸς Κρόκος
[γέ]νους Φιλοπαππιδῶν·
[ἐπ]ετέλεσε καὶ μυστήρια.

The inscription was published by Th. Macridy in 1912 with no commentary and has since been referred to only briefly.[54] The Stobaean embassy took place during the 87th prytany of Apollo. Jeanne Robert,

---

[54] Th. Macridy, "Antiquités de Notion II," *JÖAI* 15 (1912) p. 52, no. 20. Ch. Picard, *Éphèse et Claros* (Paris 1922) 199, note 3; 205, note 9; 210, note 4; 303—304; 694. Picard refers to the inscription again in *REG* 70 (1957) 116; cf. Jeanne and Louis Robert, *REG* 71 (1958) 267—268. B. D. Meritt has informed me that the name Ζωτιχός (inscription lines 3-4) does not occur at least in Athenes, but Ζωτικός does; the name of the priest *could* be Ζω[τικ]οῦ (note accent).

Figure 86. Inscription recording an embassy of the citizens of Stobi inscribed on wall of propylaea of the Sanctuary of Apollo at Clarus.

who has made a special study of the chronology of the lists of delegations, places the date of the inscription between A. D. 162 and 168. It is of considerable interest that there is no other reference to Stobi among the vast number of inscriptions recording the visits of official delegations to Clarus.[55] Although we may not argue from this fact that there were no other official delegations to Clarus from Stobi, it does suggest that such visits were (at least) not numerous. For comparative purposes we note that more than 20 delegations from Laodicea in Caria are recorded.[56]

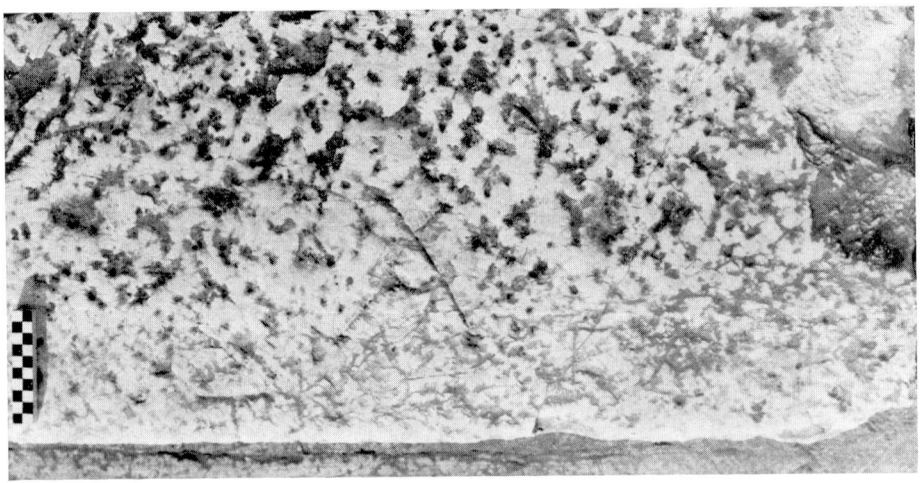

Figure 87. The name of A. Cornelius Gaius on a theater seat.

The *theopropus*, or sacred ambassador, from Stobi was Lucius Cornelius [Mu?]ndicianus Crocus, who speaks proudly of his descent

---

[55] The final publication of the great mass of inscriptions from Clarus is still in preparation. A group of 30 inscriptions was published by J. and L. Robert in *La Carie* II: *Le Plateau de Tabai et ses environs* (Paris 1954) 115—120, 203—216, 327—238, 380—383, and now 25 referring to embassies from Laodicea have been discussed by Louis Robert in *Laodicée du Lycos: Le Nymphée* (Quebec and Paris 1969) 298—305. The date of the Stobi delegation and the information regarding the uniqueness of the reference to Stobi at Clarus are based on a personal communication from Louis Robert to whom I am most grateful for his cordial and helpful response to my inquiry.

[56] See the preceding note.

Figure 88. The name of Cornelius Agathe ——— on a theater seat

from the Syrian family of Philopappus.⁵⁷ Surely he must have been a citizen of considerable prominence in his home city of Stobi. There is, however, no certain reference to him in the inscriptions so far found at Stobi.

Another distinguished Cornelian from Stobi is named in a Latin inscription of disputed date (2nd or 3rd century).⁵⁸ The inscription records the dedication of a statue of Ultrix Augusta (Nemesis) to the divine Caesar Augustus, *pater patriae*, and the Municipium Stobensium by the *Augustales*, Sextus Cornelius Audoleo, Gaius Fulcinius Epictetus and Lucius Mettius Epictetus.

Seats for several Cornelii were reserved by inscribing names in the cavea of the theater. They are Qu⟨i⟩ntilius Cornelius Agathocles,⁵⁹

---

⁵⁷ C. Julius Antiochus Epiphanes Philopappus, grandson of Antiochus IV (last king of Commagene) was consul of Rome in A. D. 109 and was also an Athenian Archon. *OGI* 409—413; *PIR* ii¹, 166, 199; ii², 262, 1086. On his funereal monument atop Museum Hill in Athens, see John Travlos, *Pictorial Dictionary of Ancient Athens* (New York and Washington 1971) s. v. "Philopappos."

⁵⁸ Supra, p. 160.

⁵⁹ Kerkis 1, row 2, seat 4; Saria no. 3. Κου⟨ι⟩ντιλί(ου) Κορν(ηλίου) Ἀγαθακλέους. H. of letters in praenomen, 0.05/0.085 m.; H. of letters in last two names, 0.04/0.055 m. The first two omicrons, the theta and the sigma are quadrate. The last name was superscribed by the name Παυλι[- -].

A. Cornelius Gaius (Fig. 87),[60] P. Cornelius,[61] T. Cornelius Maxi-(mus?),[62] Cornelius Agathe———(Fig. 88),[63] C. Ju(lius) Cornelianus (Fig. 89),[64] and, finally, Lucius Cornelius (Fig. 90).[65] There is no way of knowing whether or not the latter is the *theopropus* to Clarus.

The *theopropus* ἐπετέλεσε καὶ μυστήρια; no other member of the delegation, if there were others, is mentioned. The inscriptions from Clarus, however, indicate that the *theopropus* in the 2nd century was usually accompanied by choral groups made up of children (and the children are named); a priest (evidently also a child); and other officials.[66] The practice of honoring Clarian Apollo with a choral performance on the occasion of a visit by a *theopropus* seems to have been in accord with an explicit request of the priests of the sanctuary: κατὰ χρησμόν in several of the inscriptions.

The *theopropus* of Stobi seems to have come alone. We may at least assume that he brought no choral group to hymn the god. The inscription resembles closely two other inscriptions at Clarus dating to the same prytany and recording *theopropoi* from two cities in Moesia Inferior, Odessus and Dionysopolis. All three inscriptions were carved on the interior face of the west wall of the propylaea of the sanctuary. It is of some interest to note there is no other record of an embassy to

---

[60] Kerkis 1, row 4, seat 2. Ἀ. Κορ(νηλίου) Γαίου. The alpha has a broken bar and a hasta at top; the genitive ending of Gaius is a ligature. Saria no. 12 reads: Α ΓΑΙ ΚΟΙ.

[61] Kerkis 2, row 9, seat 3 lip. Π. | Κορνηλίου; Saria no. 112.

[62] Kerkis 2, row 12, seat 3. Τ. Κορν(ηλίου) Μαξι(μοῦ?). Saria no. 128.

[63] Kerkis 3, row 2, seats 1—2. Κο[ρ]νη(λίου) Ἀγαθη(μέρου?). H. of letters 0.05/0.10 m. Ligatures: kappa-rho, nu-eta; omicron is diamond-shaped. On seat 2 appears the same kappa-rho ligature followed by Ἀγα[θημέρου?]. The cognomen is restored here *exemplaris gratia*; cf *SEG* XVIII (1962) 277.

[64] Kerkis 3, row 7, seat 3. Κ. Ἰου(λίου) Κορνηλιανοῦ. H. of initial kappa 0.18 m., H. of other letters 0.04/0.07 m. Ligature in nomen.

[65] The name occurs on a seat block re-used as a part of the base for the mullioned screen in the north aisle of the Episcopal Basilica (westernmost block): Λο⟨υ⟩κίο(υ) Κορ(νηλίου). H. of letters in praenomen 0.07/0.13 m.; in nomen 0.05/0.07 m. The omicrons are diamond-shaped in the praenomen. The name Τίτου, written below in slightly smaller letters, indicates a person different from Lucius Cornelius.

[66] Groups from Heraclea of Salbakè, *La Carie*, nos. 135, 136, 137, 138, 139, 141, 143, 144, 145, 146, 194; from Tabai, *ibid.*, nos. 24, 25, 26, 27, 28, 30, 31, 192, 193; Sebastopolis, *ibid.*, no. 180; Laodicea on the Lycus, Robert, *Laodicée*, pp. 299—309, nos. 1, 2, 6, 7, 8, 10—19, 22—25.

Figure 89. The name of C. Julius Cornelianus on a theater seat.

Figure 90. The theater seat of Lucius Cornelius.

Clarus from Moesia Inferior and only one other from Macedonia.[67] The precise contemporaneity of the three inscriptions, their closely similar nature, the proximity of the three inscriptions, and the evidently exceptional circumstance of each embassy itself are all factors that, in their sum, suggest that Stobi and the two cities of Moesia Inferior may have been prompted by the same reason to send emissaries to Clarus. Indeed, they may even have traveled together part of the way and have made common cause to the god. What, we might well ask, might prompt cities in Macedonia and Moesia Inferior to seek the aid of the oracle in distant Clarus?

We may be reasonably sure that Stobi did not undergo the expense of sending an embassy, even a small one, to Clarus merely to have the spiritual purity of Claudia Prisca attested. Such a singular occurence must have been prompted by a matter of profounder significance, something touching on the welfare of the city at large. The matter of the purity of the priestess of Artemis at Stobi, of course, could have been raised by the nature of the inquiry and of the oracular response.[68] That is, the attestation of Apollo regarding Claudia Prisca may have been incidental (or even highly relevant!) to the content of the oracle. But it is the content of the oracle that we must first seek. The general summation by W. K. C. Guthrie of the functions of the god Apollo is worth recording as a reminder here:[69]

> "Above all he is the Averter of Evil (Apotropaios) (whether physical as of disease or exerting a less tangible influence), the god of purification (Katharsios) and the god of prophecy."

The mission of the emissary from Stobi, we might then suppose, was to seek relief for the city from some evil against which the oracles of Apollo were considered to be especially efficacious. The time of danger is rather closely limited by the inscriptions considered; i. e., sometime in the third quarter of the 2nd century. We might, in fact,

---

[67] Macridy, *JÖAI* 15 (1912) 50—51, inscriptions nos. 15—16. See Picard, *Éphèse et Claros* 905, note 9; 694.

[68] The account of the famous visit of Germanicus to Clarian Apollo in A. D. 18 seems to imply that the oracle did not, at least on that occasion, require an inquiry to be directed specifically to the priest before an oracle might be received, as if the god knew the question before it was asked (Tacitus *Annales* ii. 54). It is unlikely that such deception was practiced generally. It should be noted also that Apollo at Clarus received written inquiries from worshippers who did not visit the sanctuary: the evidence is discussed by Picard, *Éphèse et Claros*, 114—115.

[69] W. K. C. Guthrie, *The Greeks and their Gods* (Boston 1955) 87.

reasonably suppose that the oracle was sought when the danger was most imminent. Such an hypothesis requires a date in the sixth decade of the century. And the danger may well have threatened Macedonia and Moesia Inferior simultaneously. One thinks immediately of war or plague.

V. THE EASTERN CAMPAIGN OF LUCIUS VERUS

Parthia invaded Armenia in A. D. 162. Lucius Verus, who had been named Augustus in the preceding year, was immediately dispatched to the east by the Emperor Marcus Aurelius. The success of the Roman army under the nominal command of Verus was extraordinary. In 163 Armenia was regained and in the next year both Seleucia and Ctesiphon were destroyed by the victorious legions. The campaign ended with a raid into Media, the limit of eastern penetration by Rome. Lucius Verus was able to celebrate his generals' victories by a joint triumph with Marcus Aurelius in Rome on October 12, 166.[70]

But the victory was in a sense a Pyrrhic one. We recall the dramatic comment of M. Cary:

"But the spoil which the Romans stripped off the Parthians was a shirt of Nessus, for they brought back with them the germs of the most destructive plague in Roman history."[71]

The opinion of Cary regarding the severity of the plague is one that has been held by most modern historians who have dealt with the events of that period. Similar comments have been collected, along with the ancient sources on the plague and modern discussions of its scope, in a study by J. F. Gilliam.[72] Gilliam points out that some of the inscriptions and coins that have on occasion been cited as evidence

---

[70] *SHA*, Vita Veri 8. 3.

[71] M. Cary, *A History of Rome down to the Reign of Constantine* (2nd ed., London and New York 1957) 648.

[72] "The Plague under Marcus Aurelius," *AJP* 82 (1961) 225—251. The principal ancient sources are: Marcus Aurelius ix. 2; Lucian Quomodo hist. conscr. 15: Alexander 36; Aristides Orat. xxxiii. 6; xlviii. 38—39; 1.9; li. 25k; *SHA* Marcus Aurelius 13.3—6; 17.2; 21.6—7; 28.4; *SHA* Lucius Verus 8.1—4; Eutropius viii. 12; Orosius vii. 15. 5—6; 27.7; Xiphilinus on Dio Cassius lxxi. 2.4. The references to the plague(s) in Galen and Pseudo-Galen are collected by Gilliam in the article just cited, p. 227, notes 10—13, and by C. A. Behr (see next footnote) along with other possible mentions of plague under the Antonines. The important relevant passage in Ammianus Marcellinus is quoted in full below.

for the severity or persistence of the plague may, in fact, have been prompted by other conditions of the time. He concludes that comparisons of the plague with the Black Death, the 14th century epidemic that reduced the population of England by twenty percent in three years and ultimately by half over a period of 50 years, are unjustified. His arguments against such a heavy depopulation by plague are not altogether persuasive, but his warnings not to associate deaths by disease during the two following decades with a single plague are salutary.

It is by no means clear that the many literary references and several inscriptions cited all refer to a single plague. It is likely, in fact, that they do not, and several studies have attempted to identify in some of the ancient sources references to purely local plagues and famines that may have been prompted by, but were not identical with, the plague that spread from Seleucia.[73] C. A. Behr has argued recently that there were two plagues.[74] In his view Plague 1 was smallpox and began in the army at Nisibis or Seleucia in summer, 165; the epidemic had sporadic outbreaks until A. D. 189. Plague 2, with which Behr would associate all the inscriptional evidence that is considered below, was connected somehow with famines that followed closely on the first summer of Plague 1. Plague 2, according to Behr, lasted until A. D. 182. His division of the ancient references so precisely into associations with one or another plague is unconvincing chiefly because the references are often too vague to permit more than a general chronological identification. There is, however, sufficient evidence, especially in the inscriptions and in some of the ancient authors,[75] to be certain that not all of the deaths attributed to plague, ca. A. D. 165—189, were brought about by the germs from Seleucia.

But whether or not plague in the time of the Antonines was singular or multiple (and I believe it was the latter), there is no doubt that the result was wide-spread sickness and death.

And if the Antonine plague were less devastating than the Black Death of England, it was at any rate an epidemic more disastrous, more

---

[73] Among the earliest are J. Keil and A. von Premerstein, "Beiblatt über eine Reise in Lydien und der südlichen Aiolis," *DenkschrWien (phil.-hist. Klasse)* 53 (1908) 10—11, and J. Ilberg, "Aus Galens Praxis: Ein Kultbild aus der römischen Kaiserheit," *Njbb* 15 (1905) 276—312.

[74] *Aelius Aristides and the Sacred Tales* (Amsterdam 1968) 96—98, notes 8, 11—12; 166—167, notes 13—15.

[75] E. g., Aelius Aristides who contracted both diseases. The inscriptions are discussed below in Section VI.

far-reaching than the Empire had ever known before. The sources, collected so meticulously by Gilliam and Behr, speak unequivocally for a catastrophic pestilence, and not all the sources are impeachable. The inscriptional evidence has perhaps been overstressed on occasion, but it would be unreasonable to reject its existence. Even Gilliam, who would deny the plague a significant role in the process of depopulation and general decline of the Empire in the 3rd century, felt constrained to acknowledge that the Antonine Plague must have been an epidemic of major and devastating force.

"Nevertheless, after making due allowance for distortion and rhetorical convention, it is quite clear that there was a great and destructive epidemic under Marcus Aurelius. It seems probable, though by no means certain, that it caused more deaths than any other epidemic during the Empire before the middle of the third century."[76]

The plague, we are told, began in Seleucia and the victorious soldiers carried the disease with them on their homeward journey, infecting the communities through which they passed as well as, ultimately, inhabitants of their own homelands. The plague spread along the Danube, on the Rhine, in Gaul, even in Rome itself. Ammianus Marcellinus recalled the spread of the plague in describing events two centuries later.[77]

"When this city was stormed by the generals of Verus Caesar (as I have related before), the statue of Apollo Comaeus was torn from its place and taken to Rome, where the priests of the gods set it up in the temple of the Palatine Apollo. And it is said that, after this same statue had been carried off and the city burned, the soldiers in ransacking the temple found a narrow crevice; this they widened in the hope of finding something valuable; but from a kind of shrine, closed by the occult arts of the Chaldeans, the

---

[76] *AJP* 82 (1961) 249.

[77] XXIII. 6. 24. Qua per duces Veri Caesaris (ut ante rettulimus), expugnata, avulsum sedibus simulacrum Comaei Apollinis, perlatumque Romam, in aede Apollinis Palatini deorum antistites collocarunt. Fertur autem quod post direptum hoc idem figmentum, incensa civitate, milites fanum scrutantes invenere foramen angustum, quo reserato, ut pretiosum aliquid invenirent, ex adyto quodam concluso a Chaldaeorum arcanis, labes primordialis exsiliunt, quae insanabilium vi concepta morborum, eiusdem Veri Marcique Antonini temporibus, ab ipsis Persarum finibus ad usque Rhenum et Gallias, cuncta contagiis polluebat et mortibus.

The translation is from the Loeb text by J. C. Rolfe (rev. ed. 1950).

germ of that pestilence burst forth, which after generating the virulence of incurable diseases, in the time of the same Verus and of Marcus Antoninus polluted everything with contagion and death, from the frontiers of Persia all the way to the Rhine and to Gaul."

Among the contingents that took part in the Parthian War was a detachment from the VII Claudia stationed then at Viminacium on the Danube (Moesia Superior). Its losses during and after the campaign were so great that a conscription of twice normal size resulted in 169. The losses have been attributed, with good reason, more to the virulence of the plague than to Parthian arms.[78]

VI. PLAGUE AT STOBI

The recruits listed in the inscription from Viminacium that is cited in footnote 78 include, not surprisingly, a number of names from the south. There are, for example, at least 27 from Scupi (modern Skopje) and even one from Thessalonica. We may be sure, then, that soldiers from Macedonia as well as Moesia Superior were among those of the VII Claudia who served in Parthia, and very likely some even from Stobi. Only one soldier who served in that legion, however, is presently known from Stobi.

5. Funereal relief. Fig. 91.

I-70-3. Green sandstone with low relief of standing soldier above, inscription below. H. 1.225 m. W. 0.75. m. Th. 0.17 m. H. of letters 0.03—0.05 m.

C. Aeficio · Maximo
L. f · Aem · Stob[- -]s
[an] · XXV · m[ili]tavit · an · V
[- -] · Titia · Mater
[- -]sibi · viva.

---

[78] The inscription recording the names of the new recruits was found at Kostolac, the ancient Viminacium, not far east of Belgrade (ancient Singidunum), on the right bank of the Mlava River. The inscription is studied and the spread of the plague discussed in F. Ladek, A. von Premerstein, and N. Vulić, "Antike Denkmäler in Serbien," *JÖAI* 4 (1901) Beiblatt 81—98, no. 3. Gilliam (*AJP* 82 [1961] 237—238), however, suggests that the increase in enlistments was not extraordinary for the time since war was at hand.

Figure 91. The funereal relief of C. Aeficius Maximus.

Aeficius Maximus, son of Lucius, who belonged to the Roman tribe Aemilia at Stobi, was a soldier in the VII Claudia for 5 years before dying at the age of 25. His mother, Titia, erected the inscribed monument in his honor.[79] The date of the inscription is early imperial, no later than the 2nd century. We may not, of course, claim that Aeficius Maximus himself died of the plague (though he may have), but we do have in the inscription evidence of a direct tie between Stobi and a legion that sent detachments to the Parthian War.

Another inscription from Stobi includes what appears to be a poetic, but explicit allusion to plague on the Danube.

6. Epitaph in verse.

   Τᾶς Σεμ[νᾶς ὅδε] τύμβος·
   ἐδείμα[τό μιν ?Θεό]δωρος
   εὐν[ήτης δρο]σερῷ
   τεγ[γόμενος] δακρύῳ,
   Τᾶς νο[ύσου θ]οινᾶντο
   βοραῖς [περὶ εὐ]ρέα Ἴσ[τ]ρον

"This is the tomb of a worthy woman.
Theodorus, her husband, full of horror, moistens
 her (body) with his dewy tears.
Those in the north along the wide Ister
 are eaten by the disease..."

The reading given above is essentially that of A. von Premerstein and N. Vulić.[80] The two fragments of the sandstone inscription were taken to the Austro-Hungarian consulate in Skopje in 1890 after being discovered at Stobi ca. 1870 during the construction of the railway for the Orient Express. Von Premerstein and Vulić dated the inscription to the 2nd half of the 2nd century.

There can be little doubt that the νοῦσος on the "wide Ister" was, as von Premerstein and Vulić maintained, the plague that ravaged the

---

[79] The relief was found at Stobi before 1970. The exact find spot was not recorded.

[80] *JÖAI* 6 (1903) Beiblatt 7—9, no. 10. The inscription was first published by A. Struck, "Inschriften aus Makedonien," *AM* 27 (1902) 317, no. 41. Struck published a slightly different transcription of the two fragments and was unable to offer a reading. P. and V. wrote Σέμ[νας in line 1.

Empire in A. D. 165—168, and perhaps during the following two decades. It may be inferred that the wife of [Theo?] dorus died of the same plague in Stobi and that it was brought to the city by the victorious, but diseased soldiers who campaigned with Lucius Verus against the Parthians. The carriers may have been legionaires of the VII Claudia.

I would suggest that wide-spread pestilence, once it brought death to inhabitants of the city itself, would be a danger sufficiently threatening to prompt a delegation to a sanctuary of Apollo, a God who Averts Evil (Alexikakos), and who gives oracular responses through his priests to direct queries. It is true that Delphi was closer and since the time of Hadrian had seen a revival of influence. But the second century after Christ marked the high point of influence of Clarian Apollo. And did the plague not spread to Pannonia and Moesia and Macedonia from the East? It may even have been a matter of minor relevance to the city of Stobi that the emissary should have had a direct tie to the East, as L. Cornelius [Mu]ndicianus Crocus, a descendant of the family of a Syrian prince, surely did.

Knowledge of the nature and content of the oracular responses of Clarian Apollo would of course be helpful in our present considerations. Fortunately a few oracles and actions directed by oracles have been preserved for us on stone.

(a) The Pamphylians of Syedra erected a group of statues in accordance with an oracle. The statues represented Ares bound in chains that were held by Hermes, while Dike stood to the side rendering justice. The dedication of the statues may have been directed by the oracle in response to an inquiry concerning pirates operating from the territory of Syedra.[81]

The erection of the group may have coincided with the issuance of coinage in Syedra depicting Ares in the center, Hermes to the right and a female to the left. The type occurs on coins of Lucius Verus, Decius and his wife Herennia Etruscilla, Valerian the father, and Gallienus. The inscription had previously been dated to the 1st century B. C., but Robert suggests that the oracle was delivered during the time of Lucius Verus, and in any case no later than his reign.[82]

(b) The dedication of a similar group of statues at Iconium is recorded in a fragmentary inscription that Louis Robert has identified

---

[81] Louis Robert, *Documents de l'Asie mineure meridionale* (Genève and Paris 1966) 91—95. On the significance of the subject see below, note 83.
[82] *Ibid.*, pp. 97—100, where the numismatic evidence is discussed in detail.

as an oracle of Clarian Apollo.[83] The fragment refers first to deities who are both the protectors and destroyers of cities. The next three lines of the inscription refer to statues of Hermes Argeiphontes and Thesmus placed on either side of Ares. The date of the inscription must be close to that assigned to the oracle concerning Syedra.

(c) An inscription found at Pergamum in 1818 preserves a large part of the text of an oracle delivered to the city by Clarian Apollo.[84] The oracle instructs the city to honor by sacrifices and hymns a number of gods in order for the city to be saved from a plague (lines 11—12: [ὡ]ς μὴ δηρὸν ὑπ' ἀργαλέῃ [τ]ρύοιτό γε νούσωι | Αἰακίδης λαός). Four choral groups of young males were to hymn Zeus, Eiraphiotes (Bacchus), Tritogeneian Athena, and Asclepius, and the nature of the sacrifices was specified. The inscription must belong to some time between the reign of Antoninus Pius and Caracalla because of the reference to the fact that Pergamum was twice νεωκόρος.[85] Most scholars, beginning with Boeckh, have identified the *nousos* of the inscription with the Antonine plague,[86] while others have followed Keil and Premerstein in supposing that the plague at Pergamum, as well as the one at Trocetta (cited in the next paragraph), was local only.[87]

---

[83] *Ibid.*, pp. 95—97. The bibliography both of this inscription and the preceding one are included in the discussion by Robert. The new dating of the inscription of Syedra to the time of the Antonines obviates the chief reason for the previous association of the group with problems involving pirates (of the first century). The similarity of the statue groups at Syedra and Iconium suggests that the two oracles *might* have concerned a similar, or identical danger to the cities. I consider plague at least as likely a danger as pirates; moreso, if we could be sure that the two inscriptions date to the time of Verus. Hermes is the conductor of souls to the underworld, and it is the God of War, Ares, who is in chains in the presence of divine judgment and retribution. The great plague, it will be remembered, was thought by some to have been brought upon the Empire by impious acts of soldiers in the midst of war; see especially the account of Ammianus quoted above in Section V.

[84] The inscription is *CIG* II, 3538 = Kaibel, 1035 = *IGRR*, IV, 360. The text has been discussed in a number of studies, the most important of which are Buresch, *Klaros*, pp. 70 ff., and J. Keil and A. von Premerstein, *DenkschrWien (phil.-hist. Klasse)* 53 (1908) pp. 10—11.

[85] Pergamum was νεωκόρος a third time under Caracalla; see the commentary on this inscription by Boeckh in the *CIG*.

[86] E. g., Ch. Picard, "Un oracle d'Apollon Clarios à Pergame," *BCH* 46 (1922) 193—194.

[87] *DenkschrWien (phil.-hist. Klasse)* 53 (1908) 10—11; Gilliam, *AJP* 82 (1961) 235—236.

(d) Another oracle of Clarian Apollo concerning a plague was delivered to the city of Trocetta at about the same time as the oracle for Pergamum.[88] The prescription for salvation was similar to that sent to the Pergamenians but added the specific request that the Trocettans erect a statue of Saviour Apollo (=Alexikakos). Again, most commentators have related the oracle with the plague of the soldiers of Verus.[89]

(e) A fragmentary inscription from Callipolis on the Thracian Chersonese records an oracle that may also have come from Clarus.[90] The city was directed to dedicate a statue of Apollo holding a bow, in his aspect as the god who drives away pestilence; το[ξο]φόρον Φοῖβον, λοιμοῦ [ὑ]ποσ[ευ]αντῆρα. Apollo Toxophorus appears on the coins of Callipolis as early as the reign of Marcus Aurelius; the type may have been prompted by the statue dedicated by the city in accordance with the oracle,[91] and the date of the oracle suggests that the λοιμός was the Antonine plague.

It is evident from our examination of the five oracles above that Clarian Apollo was not only a suitable deity to petition for advice on a plague, but appears even to have been consulted specifically and repeatedly about pestilence in the time of the Antonines.

It is striking that of the five Clarian oracles preserved on stone that have so far been published, all date to the late 2nd century. It is even possible that the oracles were all delivered during the reign of Marcus Aurelius and Lucius Verus. It is even more remarkable that three of them (perhaps all) have to do with plague. And that plague, as we have already seen, spread not only to the Danube, but south of the Danube to Stobi.

VII. STOBI AND CLARUS

There is as yet no evidence for a close tie between Stobi and the sanctuary at Clarus. We are certain, in fact, only of a single official embassy, and that one seems to have consisted of a single member, L. Cornelius [Mu]ndicianus Crocus. The embassy seems then to have

---

[88] *IGRR* IV, 1498.
[89] See especially Buresch, *Klaros* 1—29, 67—68.
[90] Kaibel 1034. Buresch, *Klaros*, pp. 81—86.
[91] The evidence of the coins is discussed by Otto Weinreich, "Heros Propylaios und Apollon Propylaios," *AM* 38 (1913) 62—72.

been extraordinary, one prompted by extraordinary circumstances. The hypothesis suggested here is that those circumstances were the deaths from the plague brought to Macedonia, and Stobi itself, by soldiers who campaigned in Armenia and Mesopotamia with the generals of Lucius Verus.

The response of the god at Clarus is likely to have included commands for dedications to specific gods at Stobi, just as the oracles cited in Section VI did. The oracles seem to choose, in fact, the chief deities of the city concerned. Such consideration for the local gods is especially notable in the Pergamenian oracle and other commentators have called attention to the general practice.[92] Apollo was not the only oracular deity who called for honors to other gods; ancient literature abounds with examples from the oracular shrines. The inquiries were often even phrased to require a response of that sort as we find at the Sanctuary of Zeus at Dodona:

> "God. The Corcyreans inquire of Zeus Naios and Dione, to what god or hero by making sacrifice and prayer they may dwell in the fairest and best way both now and in time to come."[93]

Specifying that honors be paid to the local deities of the city that inquired something of the oracle was, of course, a matter of considerable practicality. It involved the welfare both of the local priesthood and of the oracular shrine. A panhellenic sanctuary such as Clarus had to depend for its reputation in some large measure on the cooperation and good will of local cults. The local sanctuaries, in turn, could expect to receive (and often did) support from the greater sanctuaries.[94] In the case of plague in Macedonia we might expect Clarian Apollo to advise special requests and offerings to Asclepius, Hygieia, and Telesphorus,[95]

---

[92] See, e. g., the remarks by Kaibel on his no. 1035.

[93] H. W. Parke, *The Oracles of Zeus* (Oxford 1967) 260. The inquiry took place in the second half of the 5th century B. C. For other examples see *ibid.*, pp. 260—261, and among the inquiries by private persons, e. g., no. 9. on p. 266.

[94] As the examples cited from Clarus and Dodona show. Picard stresses the general advantages to paganism, which was under frequent attack in the second century, when the god at Clarus used the prestige of his sanctuary to enhance the reputations of other shrines; *BCH* 46 (1922) 195.

[95] On the existence of their sanctuary at Stobi from at least the 1st to mid-3rd century, see W-MZ (1971) 401—402, 406. The close ties of Asclepius with the god at Clarus are emphasized not only by the inscription from Pergamum, but also by a number of recorded deeds involving mutual benefits to worshippers of Asclepius and Clarian Apollo. Patients might even be accepted for incubation at Clarus; see Picard, *Éphèse et Claros*, p. 390.

to his own sister Artemis,⁹⁶ and almost certainly to himself, among other deities.⁹⁷

The purity of Claudia Prisca might reasonably have been touched upon in the oracle concerning the manner or the appropriateness of offerings to Artemis, who might even have sent the plague. It is impossible to know precisely how the matter arose. Was the purity of the priestess of Artemis questioned by the city because of the presence of the plague?⁹⁸ If so, Clarian Apollo protected her and thereby the cults of Artemis Lochia and the Emperors at Stobi.

There is yet another inscription that may offer a tie between Clarus and Stobi in the late 2nd century.

7. Marble inscription fragment. Only the left side of the block is preserved; the inscribed face is framed by a simple cyma recta. The inscription was found by Petković in the Theodosian Palace and was published first by N. Vulić, *Spomenik* 71 (1931) 46, no. 104. Two supplemental readings were subsequently published, the first by Balduin Saria.⁹⁹

Ἀρτεμίδ[ωρος...
Τὸν βωμ[ὸν ἔθηκε κατὰ
Θεοῦ χρη[ματισμὸν μετ-
ὰ τῶν τέ[κνων πάντων ἐ-

---

⁹⁶ Both Apollo and Artemis, after all, were often considered the deities who sent plague among men as divine vengeance taken upon mortals for their sins. Picard discussed briefly this manifestation of divine wrath and cites examples of the involvement of Artemis in imperial times: *Éphèse et Claros*, pp. 379—383. Artemis and Leto were also worshipped at Clarus: the temple of Artemis has been uncovered by the French excavators of the 1950 s immediately to the north of the great temple of Apollo.

⁹⁷ Titus Mestrius Longus, as we have seen above in Section III, honored Nemesis with an expensive dedication κατ' ἐπιταγήν. It is at least *possible* that the ἐπιταγή came not from Nemesis, but Clarian Apollo. If so, we have epigraphical evidence for the early dating of the theater. But the date of Mestrius and the sense here of ἐπιταγή must remain conjectural for the time-being.

⁹⁸ A Hellenistic inquiry at Dodona might serve as a model for that type of inquiry: "The Dodonaeans ask Zeus and Dione whether it is on account of the impurity of some human being that god sends the storm," Parke, *The Oracles of Zeus*, pp. 261—262, no. 7. On plague and Artemis, see note 94 above.

⁹⁹ *JÖAI* 28 (1933) 139, no. 12, and fig. 70. The figure bears the caption "Weihinschrift an Artemis," though Saria's reading does not suggest that he thought so. The brackets in lines 3 and 4 of the published text were reversed.

πιμελη[τῶν τοῦ ἱεροῦ
Ζωΐλου κ[αὶ Διοσκου?-
ρίδου κα[ὶ

Vulić later suggested the following (in majuscules and without brackets):[100]

Ἀρτέμιδι Ἐφεσία(ι)
Τὸν βωμὸν ἔθηκεν
Θεούχρηστος μετ-
ὰ τῶν τοῦ θιάσου ἐ-
πιμελητῶν Σύρου
Ζωΐλου καὶ Διοσκου-
ρίδου καθ' ὅραμα.

Obviously a variety of supplements are epigraphically possible, but τὸν βωμ[ὸν] in line 2 and [...ἐ] πιμελη[τῶν...] in lines 4—5, at least, seem certain. Ephesian Artemis was indeed worshipped in Macedonia during the early Empire[101] and the reading is basically preferable to that of Saria because it places the deity honored first (the normal practice); in Saria's restoration, indeed, the reason for setting up the altar is not given. I suggest, however, that Ἀρτέμιδ[ι Λοχίαι] is not only possible, but more likely since her worship is specifically attested at Stobi while that of Artemis Ephesia may only be conjectured.

The restoration of line 4 by Vulić is to be preferred as yielding better sense. "Theouchrestus with the epimeletes of the priesthood, Syrus, Zoilus, and Dioscurides, set up the altar to Artemis (Lochia?)." It should be noted that τοῦ ἱεροῦ, a restoration by Saria in line 5, would fit in line 4 in place of τοῦ θιάσου and produce equally good sense. Syrus in line 5 and Dioscu — in line 6 of the text by Vulić should be taken only as examples of possible names.

We should also note that both Saria (Κατὰ θεοῦ χρηματισμόν) and Vulić (κα[θ' ὅραμα]) attribute the decision to set up the altar to a divine oracle or dream. κα[τὰ χρησμόν] is also possible in the last line; if we could be sure that the dedication resulted from the oracle of Clarian Apollo, which I think is likely, it would be the preferable reading.

[100] *Spomenik* 77 (1934) 41, no. 20.
[101] On the evidence for the worship of Artemis Ephesia in Macedonia see J. and L. Robert, *REG* 71 (1958) 268.

Finally, if the suggestion is correct that Stobi dispatched an emissary to Clarus for divine aid against the plague, it is possible to see the continuing gratitude of the citizens towards Apollo as Saviour in an inscription of the 3rd century.[102]

[Δία Ὀλύμ]πιον βασιλέα κὲ Ἥραν βασίλιαν
[κὲ τὸν Σωτ]ῆρα Ἀπόλλωνα Ἰουβεντία Σαβινι-
[άνη ψηφίσ]ματι καθιε ⟨ie⟩ ρομένη ὑπὸ τῆς
[βουλῆς ἐ]πύησεν τὰ ἀγάλματα.

---

[102] The inscription was found by Saria in 1927 in the village of Čičevo near Stobi and is now in the Archaeological Museum at Skopje. N. Vulić, *Spomenik* 71 (1931) 47, no. 109; Saria, *JÖAI* 28 (1933) 137, no. 8.

БОГОВИ, РАТ И КУГА У ВРЕМЕ АНТОНИНА

ЏЕЈМС ВАЈЗМАН

Грчки натпис на основи статуе, који спомиње Гаја Елија Приска (C. Aelius Priscus), пронађен је током ископавања 1972. године у Стобима, у близини унутрашњег градског бедема (види план локалитета, бр. 25). Гај Елије Приск био је вероватно у сродству са свештеницом Клаудијом Приском (Claudia Prisca), која потиче из угледне стобске породице другог века н. е. Чланак такође садржи сугестије о другим могућим рођацима.

Један од натписа из Стоба који спомиње Клаудију Приску каже да је њена ,,чистота" проверена од стране Кларијског Аполона. У чланку су изложене везе између Стоба и Кларуса, као и важност натписа у Кларусу, у коме се говори о посети стобског посланика у другом веку н. е.

Разлог посете посланика из Стоба Кларусу вероватно је била велика куга која је харала за владе Антонина. Та могућност детаљно је приказана, као и дискусија о ширењу заразе.

Други докази о присуству куге у Стобима изложени су а предложено је да је Кларијски Аполон потврдио чистоту Клаудије Приске за време епидемије.

STRATIGRAPHIC PROBLEMS AND THE URBAN DEVELOPMENT OF STOBI

by

DJORDJE MANO-ZISSI

1. INTRODUCTION.

The importance of the site called "Pusto Gradsko" was realized thanks to its early recognition by J. G. von Hahn[1] and Leon Heuzey,[2] its overall appearance at the confluence of the Crna and the Vardar Rivers, and finally the testing by Krischen[3] in 1916—1918. This realization led to systematic excavations of the site by the National Museum of Belgrade from 1924 to 1940.[4] During those years parts of the urban complex of Stobi, as well as the Cemetery Basilica and the Palikura Basilica located *extra muros*, were exposed (see Plan

---

[1] J. G. von Hahn, "Reise von Belgrad nach Salonik," *DenkschrWien* (*Phil.-hist. Kl.*) 11, pt. 2 (1861) 175, 231—236; *idem*, "Reise durch die Gebiete des Drin und Wardar," *ibid*. 15, pt. 2 (1867) 158—188.

[2] Leon Heuzey, "Découverte des ruines de Stobi," *RA* 2 (1873) 25—42.

[3] Dr. Hald, *Auf den Trümmern Stobis* (Stuttgart 1917). H. Dragendorff, "Archäologische und kunstwissenschaftliche Arbeit während des Weltkrieges in Mazedonien," *Zeitschrift für bildende Kunst* 54 (1919) 269—270.

[4] See the Bibliography by Ž. Radošević published in this volume.

Figure 92. Stobi: Aerial photograph taken in 1940.

of Site at the back of this volume). An aerial photograph taken in 1940 shows the urban features of a late antique city (Fig. 92).[5]

The site is on a long, narrow terrace, the northern end of which is a narrow spur on the right bank of the Vardar. The southern and eastern sides of the terrace slope gradually toward the Crna. The area within which excavations were conducted by the National Museum extended from the Porta Heraclea on the south along the slope to the North Basilica (Plan of Site, nos. 21 and 1 respectively).

Material from earlier times was found to be included in the buildings of the late antique city (4th-6th centuries A. C.). It seemed likely, therefore, that the late settlement had been built above the earlier Roman, Hellenistic, and possibly even earlier Macedonian and Paeonian urban complexes, sanctuaries, and cemeteries. The architects of the latest city re-used architectural pieces, sculptures, and inscribed votive and burial monuments as building material and decoration in the new houses, baths, streets, and courts. The discovery of such re-used material indicated that Stobi had been a prosperous city for a very long time and there was an obvious need to study the deeper stratigraphic layers.

Test excavations performed before the Second World War in the apse of the Civil Basilica (Plan of Site, no. 2) brought to light a few bronzes of the Greek Archaic period.[6] Similar tests carried out by the Archaeological Museum of Skopje in 1955—1957 indicated a complex stratigraphic situation below the Civil Basilica. In the course of conservation in 1963—1966 by the Conservation Institute of Macedonia, small-scale excavations revealed deep cultural deposits below the Large Bath and the Synagogue Basilica. In 1960 the Archaeological Museum of Skopje investigated deposits beneath the House of Peristerias and discovered a Hellenistic cemetery.[7] Most recently, the excavations of the Stobi Project, sponsored by the Smithsonian Institution and jointly organized by the University of Texas at Austin and the National Museum of Titov Veles, have revealed the stratigraphy in deep test trenches

---

[5] The early excavations were concentrated in the latest levels of the city. See also Dj. Mano-Zissi, "Urbanistički lik Stobija," *Umetnički pregled* (Beograd 1939) 262.

[6] Dj. Mano-Zissi, "K pitanju stratigrafije u Stobima," *Zbornik* (1958—1959) 355—357.

[7] V. Sokolovska, "Stobi, II: Peristerijeva palata," *Arheološki pregled* 7 (1965) 128—129. I. Mikulčić, "Stobi-(Peristerija)-kasnohelenistički grobovi," *Arheološki pregled* 8 (1966) 113—114.

in several areas: inside the Synagogue Basilica, on the Acropolis, by the Inner City Wall, in the Fuller's House, and in the Casa Romana (Plan of Site, no. 26) by the bank of the Crna River. Excavation of Hellenistic, Early Roman, Late Roman, and Christian cemeteries has also been undertaken.

2. PRESENT KNOWLEDGE OF THE STRATIGRAPHY AND THE URBAN DEVELOPMENT.

Stratified habitation horizons at Stobi have been ascertained by a careful comparative control of elevations and cultural deposits. The cultural layers deposited during the successive periods of occupation were covered in the end with windblown, sandy layers in the upper part of the city, while in the lower part they lie under the deep inundation silt of the Erigon (Crna) River.[8]

B. Saria mentioned the discovery of a stone axe and fragments of prehistoric pottery in early excavations. There have also been occasional discoveries of a few small pieces of worked flint and handmade pottery that might be prehistoric. Unfortunately, none of these artifacts was found in equally early context. Still, their presence may indicate Neolithic habitation of the plain that extends from the ridge to the Erigon. Some fragments of ceramic vessels found below the Civil Basilica, but in uncertain context, were dated by their discoverers in the 1950s to the Halstatt (Iron Age) period. Autochthonous ceramics similar to Paeonian finds elsewhere appear also in other deep layers that had been disturbed by the later foundations.[9]

The discovery, mentioned above, of bronze vessel fragments of an Archaic Greek character below the apse of the Civil Basilica, at a depth of 3 m. in the greenish-gray sand close to virgin soil, constitutes the first material document for the existence of a Paeonian horizon from the 5th century B. C. at Stobi. The historian Livy referred to Stobi as a Paeonian city.[10] Historical sources also speak of good relations between Athens and the Paeonian kings, and even of the re-

---

[8] See Robert L. Folk, "The Geologic Framework of Stobi," in this volume.

[9] W-MZ (1972) 411—412. Garašanin, Sanev, Simoska, and Kitanoski, *Les civilisations préhistoriques de la Macédoine* (Štip 1971) 31. I. Mikulčić, *Pelagonija*, (Beograd 1966) 15—19.

[10] Livy. xxxix. 53. 14—16.

settling in Paeonia of Attic colonists from the region of Olynthus where they had been menaced by pressure from Macedonia.[11] However, no signs of Greek classical elements, such as those found at Demir-Kapija,[12] have been discovered so far at Stobi.

The penetration of the Macedonians through the valley of the Crna River could have isolated Stobi from the rest of Paeonia rather early. If an oppidum existed at Stobi at that time, it might have occupied the space of the narrowing cliff which extends to the northeast and ends near the bank of the Vardar. Such a Paeonian-Illyro-Thracian "refugium" of the "Gradina" type, situated on that height, would have rendered more easy the task of the defenders. Unfortunately, the railroad and the highway cut through and thereby destroyed much of the northeastern part of that area. A large test trench to the southwest of the highway, however, uncovered no evidence of occupation earlier than the late 3rd and 2nd centuries B. C.[13]

Excavation, as we have seen, has so far provided very little evidence for habitation at Stobi before the 3rd century B. C. and there may simply have been no town at the site earlier. The accounts of the victory of Philip II in 356 B. C. over the Paeonian-Illyro-Thracian alliance and his conquest of Paeonia, which remained under Macedonian control for a short time, include no mention of Stobi. In 284 B. C. Lysimachus brought the region under control again, only to have it devastated five years later by the Celtic invaders. Sometime later Antigonus Gonatas reconquered Paeonia, but in 229 B. C. the region was lost to the Dardanians after they had inflicted a defeat on Demetrius II. Philip V conquered Paeonia, including Bylazora (Titov Veles), in 217 B. C. Stobi may have served as one of his bases at that time, but the earliest specific reference to the town occurs in connection with Philip's victory near Stobi in 197 B. C.[14] The resulting period of peace was brief and ended with the defeat of Philip near Pydna in 168 B. C. It is, therefore, not surprising that the finds of the Hellenistic period are so modest. The town, after all, apparently came into existence as a military outpost

---

[11] Menelaus, basileus of Pelagonia, was Hipparch of the Athenians; F. Papazoglu, *MGRD*, 200, 308. Thucydides ii. 99.6. About the emigration from Chalcidice to the interior of the Balkans, see Dj. Mano-Zissi and Lj. Popović, *Novi Pazar* (Beograd 1969) 116—117; Mikulčić, *Pelagonija*, 52, 72—73. *RE* XIV 705—720.

[12] D. Vučković-Todorović, "Antička Demir Kapija," *Starinar* 12 (1961) 240—267.

[13] W-MZ (1972) 411—412.

[14] Livy xxxiii. 19. 3.

in the midst of war, and in an area dominated by a succession of different powers.

In 167 B. C. Stobi fell under the Roman protectorate of Macedonia and became a part of the third *meris* whose capital was at Pella. In 148 B. C., after an unsuccessful uprising, Macedonia became a Roman province.[15] It seems to me improbable that a mere half century of Macedonian control was sufficient to Hellenize Stobi to such an extent that its residents would continue to use the Greek language and way of life even under Roman administration. We might have expected such Hellenization to have required even three centuries, between the 5th and the mid-2nd centuries B. C. This enigmatic period of possible Hellenism, however, is not now visible in the stratigraphy of Stobi.

Some works of Hellenistic art have been found which may have some significance regarding cults in Stobi. Examples include the marble heads of Artemis (Fig. 93; until now considered to be Cora) and of Apollo (Fig. 94; until now considered a nymph). Other well-known Hellenistic sculp-

Fig. 93. Marble head of Artemis, National Museum, Beograd (Inv. No. 812/I).

Fig. 94. Marble head of Apollo, National Museum, Beograd (Inv. No. 821/I).

---

[15] *MGRD*, 55, 235. H. Bengtson, *Griechische Geschichte*, 474. J. Larsen, *Roman Greece*, 303, 441, 452.

tures from Stobi are the two bronze satyrs and a marble relief of Pan with dancing nymphs, all in the National Museum of Belgrade. Their origins were New Attic, Ionian, or Alexandrian workshops, and they must have been imported by contemporary worshipers, or by admirers who dwelled in later living horizons.

The cult of Artemis was popular in Macedonia and Paeonia because it was combined with an analogous autochthonous cult of Bendis. Following the investigations of Ch. Picard and of J. Wiseman on mutual relations between Stobi and Ionia, I propose an identification of Artemis Lochia and Clarian Apollo in Stobi with the above-mentioned marble heads which were found on the central plateau of Stobi: specifically, in the Theater and in the Theodosian Palace.[16]

3. THE HELLENISTIC PERIOD AT STOBI AND THE EXCAVATION OF THE CIVIL BASILICA.

Much of our knowledge of the Civil Basilica was obtained during two short excavation seasons (1955—1956) conducted under the auspices of the Archaeological Museum of Skopje and directed by D. Koco and Dj. Mano-Zissi. The field method employed involved step terracing, beginning at the level of the Via Principalis Inferior and ending, at the lowest point, in the apse (Fig. 95).[17] The foundations of a three-aisled basilica with west compartments and numerous interior walls had been uncovered in 1937. Some of the walls in the nave and north aisle were attributed at that time to an earlier building (Fig. 96).[18] The walls

---

[16] M. Grbić, *Choix de plastiques grecques et romaines* (Beograd 1958) 37, 43—44. M. Bieber, *The Sculpture of the Hellenistic Age* (New York 1955) 160, 139. G. Rodenwaldt, *Die Kunst der Antike*, 687. Ch. Picard, "Un bronze alexandrin importé à Stobi," *RA* 6 (1956) 217. V. Petković, "Antičke skulpture iz Stobija," *Starinar* (1937) 12, 19. Mano-Zissi, *Antique in the National Museum* (Belgrade 1954) 4; idem, "Antiquité Gréco-Romaine," *L'Art en Yougoslavie* (Paris 1971) 43—48. V. Dautovska, "Srebrni medaljon od Bučin," *Zbornik Skopje* (1966) 19. P. Lisičar, "Artemida Efeska i Dioskuri," *ŽA* (1958). Ch. Picard, "D'Éphèse à la Gaule, de Stobi macédoine à Claros," *REG* 70 (1957) 109—117. J. Wiseman, "Gods, War and Plague in the Time of the Antonines," in this volume.

[17] Members of the staff: Dragi Trajkovski (architect), B. Aleksova, K. Petrov, V. Sokolovska and A. Keramidčiev. Contextual material was destroyed in the earthquake of 1963 at the Museum in Skopje. No detailed report of these excavations has yet been published.

[18] Dj. Mano-Zissi, "Bericht über die Ausgrabungen in Stobi," *Der 6. Kongress* (1940) 593.

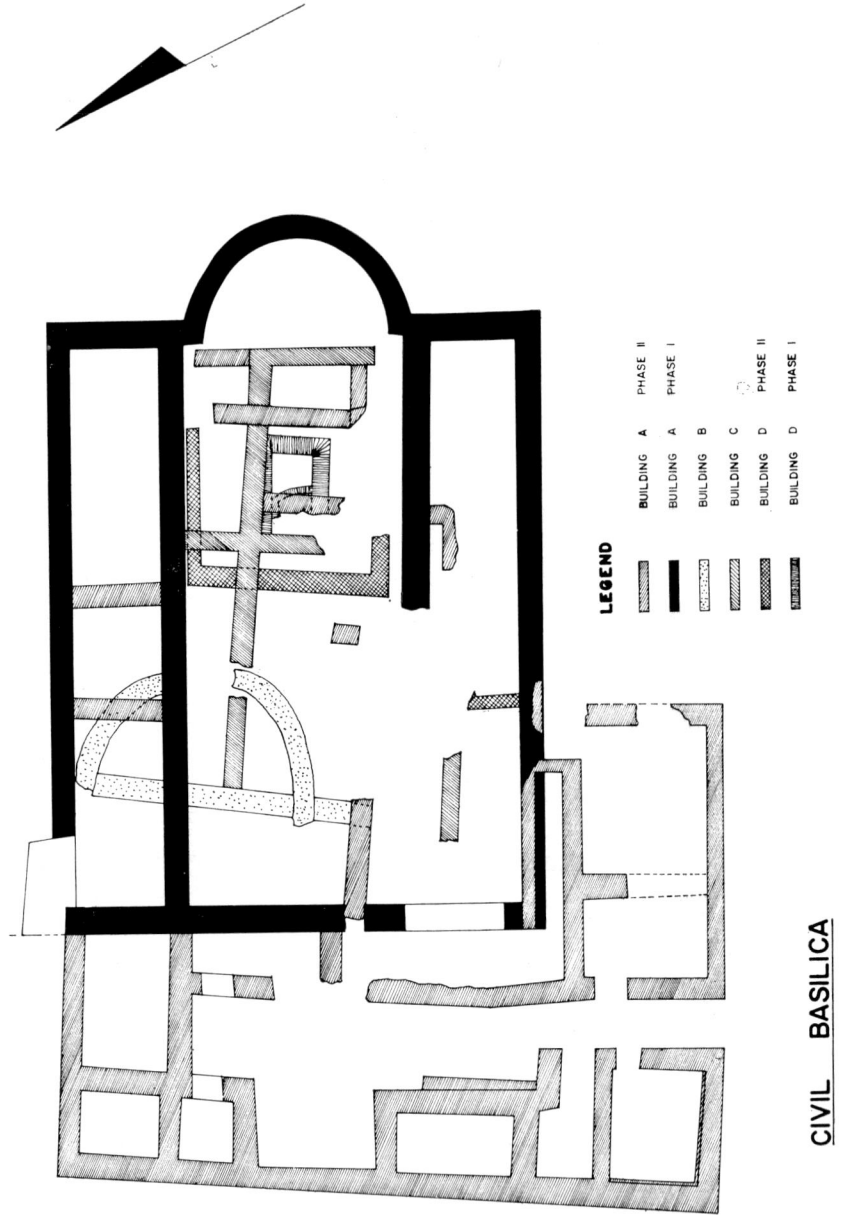

Figure 95. Civil Basilica.

were not preserved to a great height above the foundations and much of the re-usable architectural material appeared to have been removed shortly after the final destruction of the building and before its burial beneath an overburden of wind- and water-laid deposits.

During the 1955—1956 excavations a series of four building periods and one non-architectural deposit were investigated before bedrock was reached. After we had removed a deposit 0.50 m. deep, a difference in construction between the east and west parts of the basilica (Building A) became evident. In the western portion, which included a transverse corridor and a number of small rooms, the walls were built with stones in earth mortar; in the east the stones were set in lime mortar with occasional courses of brick. The central part of the building was paved with mortar and tiles. There were no traces of a stylobate for a partition except in the western half, where fragments of Ionic bases, columns, and capitals, and perhaps also of an architrave and of window mullions were found. Traces of a burned wooden ceiling and beams were noted in the dark destruction deposit. The pottery was coarse and decorated with parallel grooves. On the basis of a bronze key with teeth bent out, stucco fragments, and 5th century coins, the earthquake of A. D. 518 has been suggested as the cause of the destruction.

Later in the 6th century the basilica may have been repaired and the corridor and rooms at the west added (later phase of Building A). The floor level in the south aisle was 0.20 m. lower than in the nave and north aisle, and in the south aisle a stone bench extended along the wall next to the apse.

During this final phase of Building A the Civil Basilica was used for living quarters; it might even have served as a xenodokeion or valetudinorium. Since it is flanked by churches--the Synagogue Basilica and the North Basilica--and because the complex resembles a refectorium and cells, one may speculate that the residents were priests or monks; however, no trace of religious symbolism has been found.

Later use of the area is shown by the discovery of Slavic graves, built of stone slabs, beside the stone bench in the south aisle of the basilica. Slavic graves were also found north of the building in the space extending as far as the North Basilica.[19]

---

[19] On the Slavic graves at Stobi see D. Koco *et al.*, "Izveštaj sa iskopavanjata vo Stobi vo tekot na 1955 godina," *Zbornik Skopje* (1961) 69—72. B. Aleksova, "Slovenska nekropola u Stobima," *Glasnik Instituta za Nacionalna istorija* (Skopje 1958).

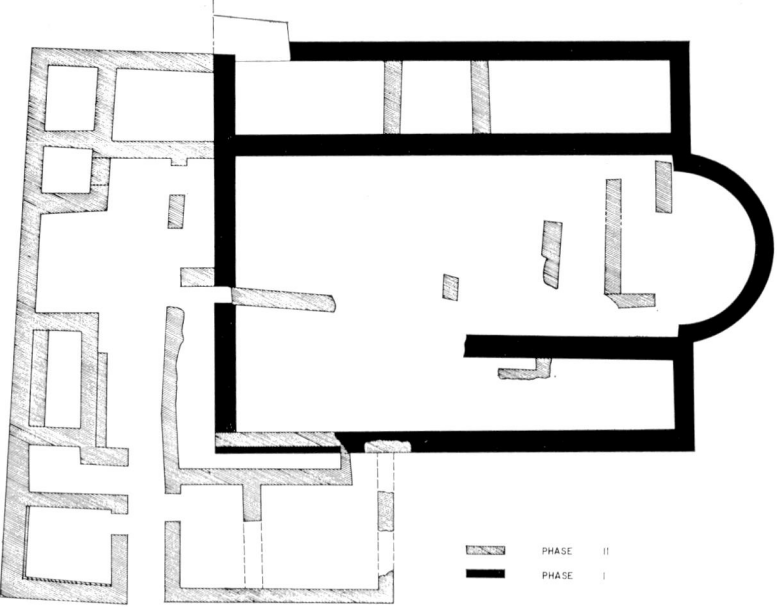

Figure 96. Civil Basilica. Building A.

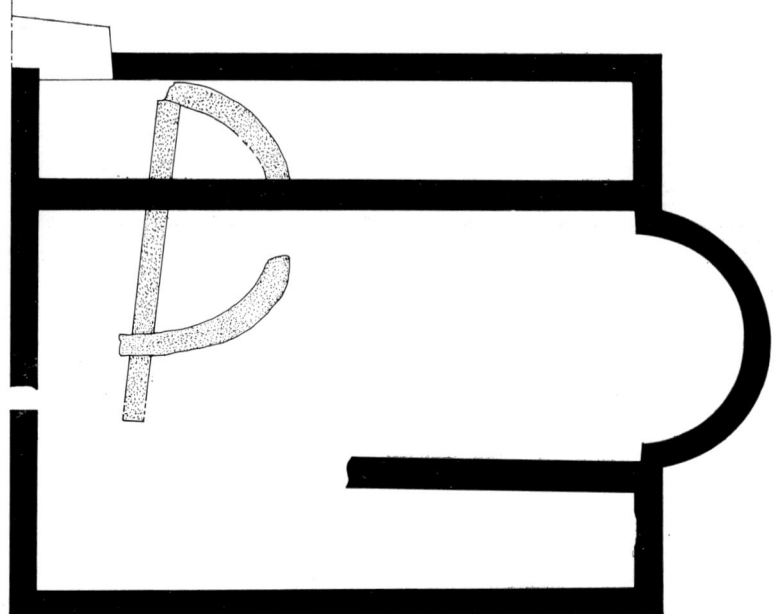

Figure 97. Civil Basilica. Building B.

At a depth of 0.90—1.00 m. below the surface, excavation below the mortar and tile floor of the nave and north aisle of Building A revealed the levelled walls and apse of Building B. The walls were built of dressed stone in mortar and the floor was paved with stone slabs. The apse of Building B had a southeast orientation, different from that of Building A. In the firmly packed dark earth with bits of charcoal, there were stucco fragments, fragments of fresco imitating variegated marble, pieces of fluted Ionic columns (similar to those in the narthex of the Episcopal Basilica), fine-grooved pottery, and coins of Theodosius I. Building B was probably constructed in the 4th century A. C.; it and earlier structures were badly disturbed when the foundations of Building A were laid.

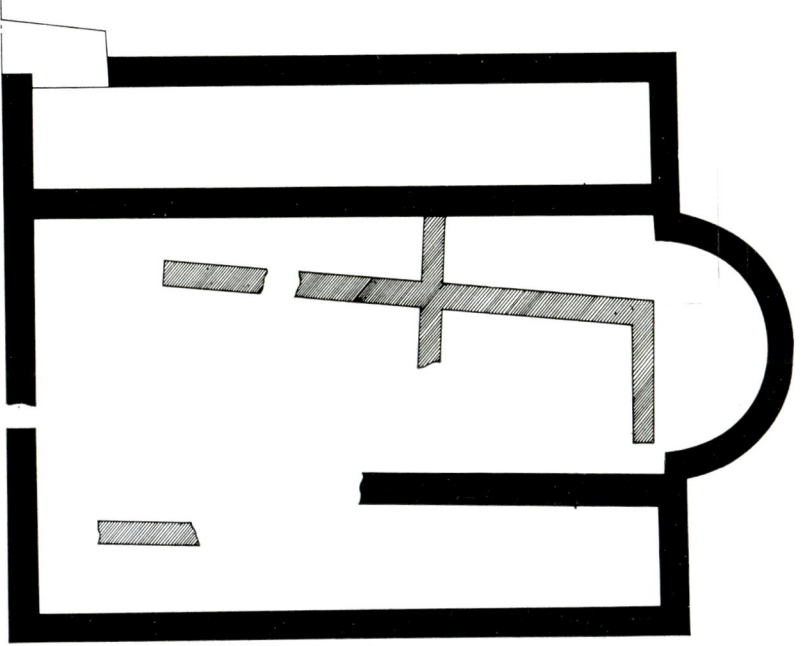

Figure 98. Civil Basilica. Building C.

At a depth of 1.56 m. below the surface in the eastern part of, and below, the apse of Building A appeared walls (Building C) with an orientation similar to Building A. A solid mortar floor was uncovered 1.86 m. below the surface. A canal running north-south along the west side of the basilica, outside the complex, seems to have been associated with this mortar floor. The walls of Building C were of dressed stone alternating with vertically set bricks and cemented with clayish mud. Finds above the mortar floor included fresco fragments with floral and geometric designs, bricks, imbrices, fragments of pithoi, terra sigillata,

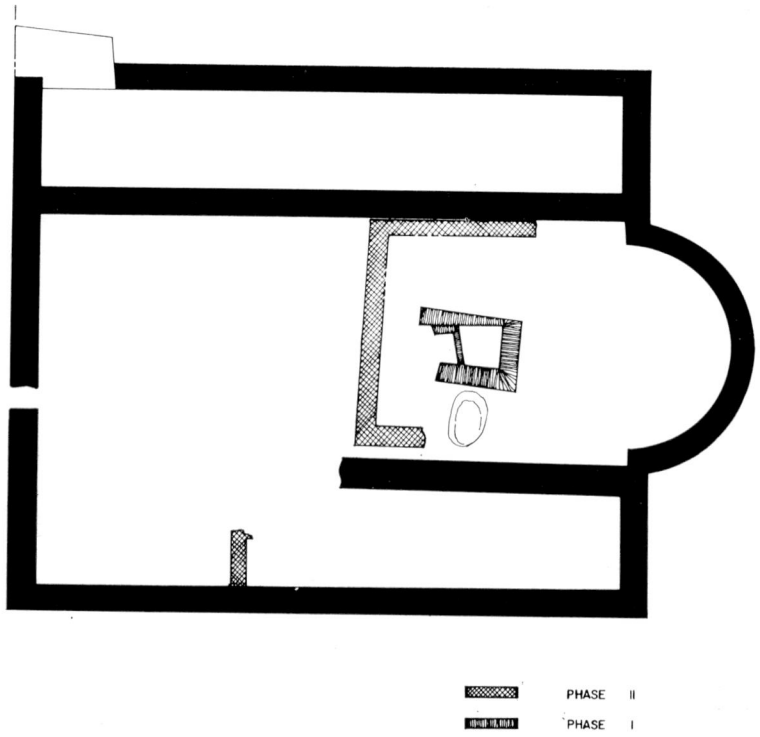

Figure 99. Civil Basilica. Building D.

terra nigra ceramics with grooved concentric patterns or three relief zones showing wave molding, astragal, and palmette; a lamp, a squat vessel with a Lesbian molding, and pottery with a golden sand glaze. The deposit was dated to the 2nd-3rd centuries A. C.

Beneath the mortar floor of Building C appeared the walls of Building D which extended down to approximately 2.60 m. below the surface. The foundations and socles were constructed of dressed stone, while the upper part of the walls was of brick with clay mortar. Frescoes were preserved on the wall. Fragments of fresco and of molded stucco were also found in the associated destruction deposit which contained much charcoal. The evidence suggests that the room was decorated with fluted pilasters and geometric frames of light-ocher stucco enclosing medallions of painted fresco. The painting of a duck probably came from such a medallion (Fig. 100). The bird was painted on a blue background although most of the other fresco fragments show a background of Pompeiian red. The head of the bird was painted a dark color with yellow and green highlights around the eyes. The plaster on which the paintings were done included bits of reed.

Figure 100. Fresco painting of a bird from Building D beneath the Civil Basilica.

Among the bits of burned roof beams in the center of the room we found amphora fragments, terra nigra ceramic sherds with incised or stamped decoration, and small pieces of Boeotian Homeric vases and Megarian bowls showing a warrior with shield, an astragal, and leaves of swamp vegetation. A dark brown oinochoe and two moldmade lamps were almost completely preserved (one in the form of a crescent, the other of a Negro's head). A terracotta disc with an owl (Athenian molded ware?) was also found. The deposit dated to the early Roman period, 2nd century B. C. to 1st century A. C.

The floor of Building D was a red mortar pavement, the color of which was evidently produced by an admixture of ground red brick. Beneath this floor was a layer of greenish sand which covered a floor of stone slabs. Below the earlier floor, in the central part of the area west of the apse, a large pit of irregular oval shape appeared, framed with large stones. It was filled with ashes, charcoal, and animal bones, but at the east side were found a handmill, carbonized grain, a bronze handle adorned with a small greyhound's head, and a hairpin.

A few decimeters to the south, a second pit was found. This pit also contained ashes, animal bones and teeth as well as pieces of a black-figured kylix, two ceramic lamps with strap and lug handles (probably belonging to the 3rd-2nd centuries B. C.), and a bone stylus. We were inclined at first to consider the pit merely a fireplace; I now suspect that it may have been a burial. But cremation without an urn, contrary to the Greek custom of the period, and the lack of proof that the pit might represent the continuation of a Paeonian funeral tradition leave this interpretation uncertain.

Further tests were carried out in 1971 in the nave of the Civil Basilica. Ceramic material of the 2nd to early 1st century B. C. was found in a clay-lined pit directly above sterile soil, which lay at an elevation of 135.95 m. above sea level.[20] In the 1955—1956 excavations bedrock had been reached beneath the similar near-by pits (mentioned above) approximately 2.80 m. below the surface. It is significant that the earliest cultural deposits below the Civil Basilica date to the Hellenistic period.

South of the Civil Basilica a few other pits containing Hellenistic pottery have recently (1972) been found cut into virgin soil. Late Hellenistic gray pottery was also found in the eastern end of the north aisle of the adjacent Synagogue Basilica.[21] Below the atrium of the same building at an elevation of ca. 136 m. a hearth with ashes, amphora fragments and bricks was discovered in 1972; the hearth may also be Hellenistic. Part of a 2nd or 1st century B. C. building was found below the narthex; the Megarian bowls and molds noted there indicate the existence of a kiln in the vicinity.[22] In the space between the Synagogue

---

[20] W-MZ (1972) 412.
[21] W-MZ (1971) 408.
[22] W-MZ (1972) 409—410.

Basilica and the Civil Basilica a spacious semicircular fireplace with lime coating and filled with amphora handles and other pottery was excavated in 1972. If we take the above finds as evidence of ancient ceramic workshops, we may speculate that here on the probable outskirts of the Hellenistic settlement was located the potters' quarter, the Ceramicus of Stobi.

If the Hellenistic city of Stobi was organized according to Macedonian patterns[23] by Philip V in the 2nd century B. C., we may assume the existence of an Acropolis, a Polis, and a Necropolis.[24] On aerial photographs of Stobi, the Hippodamian system of parallel and intersecting streets with terraces is clearly visible and it remained a factor in later urban phases. However, it has not yet been possible to define the boundaries of the late Hellenistic city. Now, with the evidence from the Synagogue Basilica, the Civil Basilica and from the House of Peristerias (to be discussed below), we may suggest that a line running from the Civil Basilica through the Synagogue Basilica and ending at the House of Peristerias might mark the periphery of the Polis. The city would have been located in a semicircle on the eastern slope of the ridge running north toward the Vardar. Testing on the Acropolis revealed a coin of Philip V near the bottom of the trench, thus proving late Hellenistic use of the area.[25]

There is a second possible location for the Acropolis. It is the trapezoidal plateau with widened south side--the longitudinal axis of the Episcopal Basilica (Plan of Site, no. 19). Dyggve provided some support for this hypothesis when he suggested that a site below the terrace of the ancient Acropolis had been chosen for the Theater.[26] The Theater of Dionysus in Athens and the theaters of Pompeii and Salona provide parallels for such a location.

If we assume that the potters' quarter lay at the edge of the city, we might expect to find the Necropolis nearby, just outside the boundary or the city wall, if one existed at that time. A Hellenistic

---

[23] Livy xxx. 19; xlv. 29; Diodorus xvi. 4; Strabo vii. 32. Papazoglu, *MGRD*, 12—34.

[24] Dj. Mano-Zissi, "Pogled na pitanja urbanizacije i urbanizma u Ilirikumu," *Zbornik* 4 (1964) 96—97. A. Gerkan, *Griechische Städteanlagen* (1924). Collart, *Philippes, ville de Macédoine* (Paris 1937). Papazoglu, *MGRD* 37, note 1; 49.

[25] W-MZ (1972) 412.

[26] E. Dyggve, *Den senantike faellesscene belyst ved Teatret i Stobi og ved Diptychonfremstillinger* (Copenhagen 1938) note 44.

cemetery was discovered during excavation by the Archaeological Museum of Skopje in 1957—1958. At that time Hellenistic graves were found below the west apsidal room and in the courtyard of the House of Peristerias.[27] Further investigation during the 1972 season in the court of the House of Peristerias brought to light four graves from the 2nd century B. C, two of which were covered either with stone slabs or Laconian tiles. All the burials were inhumations. Significant finds from those four graves include coins of the time of Philip V, a fusiform unguentarium, and an anklet of glass beads.[28]

Further investigation in near-by areas may prove or disprove these hypotheses concerning the location and extent of the Hellenistic city, the location of a potters' quarter, and the situation of the cemeteries of that period.

We have a few documents of the transition from the Hellenistic to the Early Roman period at Stobi. The most outstanding is the very fine coin hoard discovered beneath the earlier Synagogue. A trench in the west end of the nave of the Synagogue Basilica revealed a jug and a glazed lekythos which contained over 500 silver denarii and one Attic tetradrachm. The coins are mostly from the 2nd century B. C. and were probably buried in the last quarter of that century, possibly in 119 B. C. as a result of the forays of the Scordisci.[29]

4. THE EARLY ROMAN PERIOD.

Stobi became a municipium, an "Oppidum civium Romanorum," belonging to the tribe of Aemilius Paulus,[30] perhaps as early as the reign of Augustus. It received the "ius italicum" during the Augustan period. From the Flavian emperors to the reign of Elagabalus (69—221 A. D.) Stobi minted its own coinage: MUN STOB, bearing a representation of Tyche with twin nymphs.

---

[27] *Supra,* note 7.

[28] W-MZ (1973) 401—402.

[29] W-MZ (1972) 410—411. See now also Michael H. Crawford, "The Stobi Hoard of Roman Republican Denarii," in this volume.

[30] The Roman tribe Tromentina was also represented at Stobi: see Wiseman, "Historical Sketch," in *Guide,* where there is also a list of the known tribes of Stobi. Pliny iv. 10. 34.

During the Early Roman period the urban complex of Stobi expanded, although the greatest expansion probably did not occur until the 2nd or 3rd century. All levels of the east slope of the terrace were occupied from the Fuller's House and the Acropolis on the ridge to the Casa Romana by the Erigon. The city probably extended to the area of the Porta Heraclea and the line of the City Wall on the south, and at least to (perhaps across!) the Axius on the north. Other areas where Early Roman material has been found include the court of the House of Peristerias, the Synagogue Basilica, and the Civil Basilica. During Early Roman and later times the Hippodamian layout of the city continued, but with modifications. Over the centuries the lines of streets were altered, the streets themselves were widened or narrowed, and porticoes were added or removed.

The location of the administrative center of the city during the Early Roman period is unknown. We may suggest, however, that it and other important buildings were situated on the low plain by the Crna River (see discussion of the Casa Romana below). The construction date of the Outer City Wall, lying near the Crna River, is as yet unknown; if the Agora/Forum of the Early Roman city did exist on the plain, we cannot say at this time whether or not it was fortified.

Where were the initial Oppidum civium Romanorum, the Forum, and temples? According to the aerial photograph, the plateau northwest of the Via Principalis Superior resembles a Roman castrum with a Cardo-Decumanus system. The extension of the Cardo, which is oriented north-south, runs along the west perimetral wall of the Fuller's House up to the Porta Heraclea (Fig. 92).

An inscribed monument base of C. Priscus, primipilarius, a respected resident of Stobi, was found re-used in a structure west of the foundations of the Inner City Wall, which was built later, during the 4th century A. C. This discovery may indicate that the Forum was located near-by.

The area east of the Inner City Wall certainly suffered from floods. By the end of the 3rd century A. C. it ceased to be used for public or private buildings and was probably given over to agriculture.

Beneath four meters of sandy river silt, the Casa Romana, a complex of (at least) four large halls has been discovered. The walls were constructed chiefly of sandstone set in lime mortar. A great amount of stucco was still *in situ* on the walls, bearing witness to the tenacity of plaster reinforced with reeds. The stucco represents pilasters with framed relief orthostates of light-ocher color. Fragments of fresco fallen from the walls had a Pompeiian red background with floral and geometric designs in a wide range of colors. Portrait faces were also discovered, painted on the same red background with accentuated black contours.[31]

There are clear parallels between the decoration of the Casa Romana and Building D below the Civil Basilica. The style and the use of reeds in the plaster are similar. There is little doubt in my mind that the frescoes of Building D below the Civil Basilica and of the Casa Romana originated from the same workshop.

Other early wall paintings were discovered in 1972 in a room on the north side of the House of the Fuller (Plan of Site, no. 15). The walls had been coated first with clay, reinforced with reeds, as had the decorated walls of the Casa Romana. The plaster bearing the painted scenes was then applied to the clay, though not uniformly; some of the scenes were painted directly onto the clay near the bottom of the walls. Figures of four-legged animals as well as floral motifs have been recognized. Contextual material indicates that the structure was destroyed in the 1st century A. C.

Further evidence for this expansion of the urban community in Early Roman times is offered by the distribution of the burial grounds. A Hellenistic cemetery, as we have seen, lies under part of the House of Peristerias while Early Roman structures appear above them as well as further south (House of the Fuller). Early Roman burials, on the other hand, have not been found even within the limits of the (later) City Wall, but are numerous to the south and southwest of the Porta Heraclea.[32] The necropolis in that area, along both sides of the road to Heraclea which passed by the Christian Cemetery Basilica, continued in use until late antiquity. The earliest graves uncovered were Augustan in date. They contained terracotta figurines of a still Hellenistic character (workshop of Amphipolis?), which testify to certain popular domestic cults: of Telesphorus, Dioscuri, and the Thracian Rider. These and other autochthonous elements in the burials will have persisted into later times; for example, tiny bronze statuettes of Mercury, perhaps domestic works from the foundries of Stobi, appear in later burials.

---

[31] The structure was partially excavated in 1972; W-MZ (1973) 394—397.

[32] W-MZ (1971) 404—406; W-MZ (1972) 413—417; see also the articles in this volume by Al B. Wesolowsky and I. Mikulčić.

5. THE MIDDLE IMPERIAL PERIOD.

Stobi's period of greatest prosperity during pagan times seems to have occured in the 2nd and 3rd centuries A. C. Judging from the large number of architectural pieces and other objects preserved by re-use in the Early Christian period, we may conclude that urban life and organization had reached a high level and that the urban complex had achieved its greatest expansion. Stobi at that time seems to have become one of the largest cities in Macedonia. A number of inscriptions and sculptural works allows us to draw some conclusions regarding institutions of both cult and civic nature. But the influence of those institutions on the architectural appearance of the city can as yet only be hypothesized.

The presence of the sanctuary of Asclepius, Hygieia, and Telesphorus near the Episcopal Basilica is suggested by the re-use of a votive inscription as a mullion in a window of the Episcopal Basilica.[33] In the same manner the discovery of a marble statuette of Artemis and an inscription of Claudia Prisca, the priestess of Artemis Lochia, suggests that the Temple of Artemis could have been situated on a raised platform designated as the Prison Area (Fig. 101).

Deities represented by sculpture or named in inscriptions of the Middle Imperial period include Asclepius, Hygieia, and Telesphorus; Artemis Lochia; Clarian Apollo; Dionysus; Jupiter; Juno; Bacchus; Hercules; Mercury; Fortuna, and Nemesis. The only sanctuary yet located, however, is the Nemeseum in the scene building of the Theater. The statue of a Roman Emperor found in the Theater may have been set up at the same time as the famous inscription in the Nemeseum (see note 38).

The House of the Fuller exhibited the most prosperous appearance of its long architectural history during this period. The great apsidal hall and a large room heated by a hypocaust were constructed in the 3rd century. A small hoard of silver coins dating to the reign of Gordianus III (A. D. 238—244) provides a further indication of the prosperity of the residents of the house at that time.[34]

The first phase of the Large Bath (Plan of Site, no. 8) was also constructed in the 3rd century A. C. The early floor lies 2.50 m. below the 4th century reconstruction. In the earlier building the apodyterium

---
[33] W-MZ (1971) 401—402.
[34] W-MZ (1971) 402—403; W-MZ (1972) 420.

Figure 101. Marble statuette of Artemis, National Museum, Beograd.

was separated from the tepidarium by a row of columns, and the frigidarium included the southern part of the later enlarged apodyterium. Sculpture from the earlier bath includes a marble torso of Amphitrite and a *togatus*.

The Theater is the principal and most representative monument of the Middle Imperial period so far discovered. The Theater is an archaized Greek type similar to structures known in Asia Minor (e. g., Sagalassos in Pamphylia). There is no stage platform, but the scene building does include a stairway that descends directly into the orchestra. The cavea is separated from the scene building by the parodoi and seated over 7,600 persons in two tiers.[35]

Figure 102. Pilaster-capital with a tragic mask.
National Museum, Beograd (Inv. No. 889/IV).

The construction date of the Theater is still disputed. B. Saria suggested a 2nd century date for the original construction with conversion to an arena in the early 3rd century.[36] E. Dyggve argued that both construction periods belong to the 3rd century.[37] The later date is

---

[35] W-MZ (1972) 417—419 and ill. 3, the plan by William B. Dinsmoor, Jr.
[36] B. Saria, "Das Theater von Stobi," *AA* 53 (1938) 106 and "Die Inschriften des Theaters von Stobi," *WJh* 32 (1940) 11—12.
[37] E. Dyggve, "Le théâtre mixte du bas-empire d'après le théâtre de Stobi et les diptyques consulaires," *RA* (1958) pt. 1, pp. 137—157; pt. 2, pp. 20—39.

supported by F. Papazoglu who dates an important Latin inscription found in the Nemeseum of the scene building to the late 3rd century A. C. because the phrase *Deo Augusto* was used instead of *Divo Augusto*.[38]

Little new evidence for the construction date has yet resulted from the recent excavations of the Stobi Project. These excavations, however, have provided ample evidence that the structure was abandoned and partially destroyed before the middle of the 4th century.[39] The abandoning of the Theater may have been the result of the campaign of the church against gladiatorial combats.[40]

After the Theater went out of use, the large marble seat blocks and pieces from other structures were re-used in the construction of 4th and 5th century churches, palaces, and fortifications. A large number of re-used architectural pieces were found in the Episcopal Basilica, including pilaster capitals from the *scenae frons* (Figs. 102, 103).

Figure 103. Pilaster-capital with a venator, National Museum, Beograd (Inv. No. 1592/IV).

The water supply system and the sewer lines of the latest city seem to have their origin in the transition from Middle to Late Imperial/ Early Christian times (late 3rd and early 4th centuries A. C.). The remains of an aqueduct in the vicinity of the near-by village of Rosoman may indicate the direction of the main pipe-line. But how the water was distributed in all five elevation zones of Stobi is not yet clear. A line of the aqueduct has been uncovered in the third elevation zone; it follows

---

[38] "Natpis iz Nemezejona i datovanje stobskog pozorišta," *ŽA* 1 (1951) 279—293.

[39] W-MZ (1971) 402; W-MZ (1972) 417; Wiseman, *Guide*, Section 23. A single test in the east parodos, dug in 1972, does support a 3rd century construction, but the evidence is not conclusive; W-MZ (1973) 400—401. Neppi Modona, *Gli edifici teatrali greci e romani* (Firenze 1961) 230—233.

[40] Dyggve, *op. cit.* (in note 25), p. 16.

the line of the buildings between the Casino and the House of Peristerias down to the Large Bath and the Central Fountain (Plan of Site, nos. 8 and 7 respectively). The main distribution pipes are oriented north-south and built into walls of the buildings. There are indications for a parallel line which runs from the Porta Heraclea up to the Fuller's House and further along the Via Principalis Superior. It had collateral connections from the Fuller's House to the Casino, from the House of Peristerias to the Synagogue-complex and the North Basilica. This line would probably be the earlier, because it is in connection with building structures of the 3rd century.[41] An aqueduct forked from the Via Sacra to the south towards the Theater. It could have been constructed on pillars connected by arches in a manner similar to the aqueduct by the Large Bath, and might have extended alongside the stairway which descends from the narthex of the Episcopal Basilica and in the line of the column that was found in situ. Near the column by the corner of the stairway was found a trough of a fountain with shaft and canalization. I presume there were "Healer fountains" (there was one at the place of the Baptistery) both before and in the earliest Christian times. Because of the several periods of building and reconstructions of the Basilica and Baptistery and because of the catastrophic earthquake of 518, this complex of the water conduit was the most badly damaged structure in the area.

The City Walls may even have been utilized in the water system. A large tower-like construction in the wall east of the Porta Heraclea, for example, could have been a water reservoir with mains, as in the case of the Porta Caesarea in Salona or a similar one in Doclea. A large, circular tower at the southwest angle of the Theodosian Palace may have served the same function.

The mains along the buildings normally consist of ceramic pipes, while leaden ducts supply the houses, nymphaea, and other fountains. The joints of the terracotta pipes were cemented with red hydraulic mortar. There was a special arrangement of the aqueduct, supported by props, to supply the big angular reservoir of the Large Bath. Water was then distributed into pools and tubs of the caldarium, while the pools of the tepidarium and the frigidarium were also supplied by the city's network.

---

[41] Dj. Mano-Zissi, "Bemerkungen über die altbyzantinische Stadt Stobi," *Atti di Studi Bizantini* (Roma 1940) 230. K. Petrov, "Le systeme de conduite d'eau à Stobi," *Annuaire-Faculté Philosoph. de Skopje* 19 (1967) 303—306.

Water was quite rationally brought from higher to lower levels in the city and maximum use was made of the differing elevations of the terraces. Latrines and sewage, with street cloacae, became routine facilities by the early 4th century. In case of a siege, cisterns were available in the form of large pithoi.

The nymphaean fountains are of exceptional significance. It is probable that their system also originates from that epoch when it was already known in the whole Mediterranean (Leptis Magna, Antioch). Such fountains were a form of public wealth and are characteristic of palaces and churches in the 4th and 5th centuries A. C. From an upper set of basins lined with hydraulic mortar and marble, and with niches in the background, water gushes out of adorned openings or leaden tubes and falls into other stone-lined basins. The lower, sideways built intermediate basins, the arched and shell-like acoustic niches, and the ceramic receptacles all served to amplify the murmur of water and create the impression of waterfalls. In the triclinia (House of Psalms, House of Peristerias, and the Casino) fountains with water-jets seem to have been obligatory.

6. THE LATE IMPERIAL PERIOD (LATE 3RD TO LATE 4TH CENTURY A. C.).

There is evidence of a caesura between the buildings of the late 3rd and of the 4th century A. C. The Gothic invasion of A. D. 279 may have been responsible for the destruction levels found over 3rd century structures in the House of the Fuller, the Synagogue of Polycharmus, and elsewhere at Stobi. The large storage vessels found sunk in the burnt earth floors of the 3rd century storerooms of the House of the Fuller may be taken as contemporary indicators of the uncertainties of life, perhaps even of anticipations of siege.

A recognizable construction phase existed up to the end of the 3rd century A. C. whose techniques were adopted to some extent after the end of the above-mentioned caesura. Characteristic examples are from the Synagogue and the House of Psalms.

The inscription on the column of the Jewish Synagogue originates from the end of the 3rd century.[42] Above the pavement of the Early Roman period below the nave, coins of Marcus Aurelius have

---

[42] M. Hengel, ZNTW (1966) 145—183.

been found. In that same space, on the wall of the 3rd century building, fresco paintings existed with the votive formula of Polycharmus in drawing frames of "Tabula ansata." Also here was found a bronze votive plaquette of a certain Posidonia.[43] The portico in front of the House of Psalms has an Ionic capital with masks, also from the 3rd century (Fig. 104). In the sewage canal a bronze sealing plaquette with a menorah bearing the name of Eustathius was found. The House of Psalms communicated at the same time with the rooms of the Synagogue through a corridor oriented northwards.[44]

The Synagogue was rebuilt in the early 4th century and now included in the main hall a large base, probably for the Torah, against the wall that faced towards Jerusalem. The walls of that room were covered with frescoes of geometric and floral patterns while some features were set off by decorative stucco moldings. The floor was a mosaic pavement with geometric motifs that included six-pointed stars made of intersecting circles (Fig. 105). The contiguous House of Psalms communicated directly with the Synagogue during this phase and the earliest mosaics in that building may date to the same time.

Figure 104. Capital with masks from a porticus in the House of Psalms.

Building B below the Civil Basilica was constructed at the end of the 3rd or beginning of the 4th century. The Large Bath, too, had been reconstructed and enlarged at that time.

The Little Bath was built in the 4th century A. C. east of the Synagogue. It was probably a bath for women, judging by the jewels found

---

[43] W-MZ (1971) 408—410. F. Fülep, "Intercisa," *Acta Archaeologica* 18 (Budapest 1966) 93; D. Pinterović, "Mursa," *Osječki Zbornik* 9—10 (1965) 72.

[44] Lj. Popović — Dj. Mano-Zissi et al., *Antička bronza u Jugoslaviji* (Beograd 1969) fig. 343; B. Saria, *Starinar* (1933—34) 8—13.

in the test trenches dug before conservation in the 1960s. On that occasion, earlier remains of apsidal structures, not connected with the Bath, were noted at the level immediately above bedrock. However, it seems that the Little Bath itself had two phases of construction. The apodyterium and the frigidarium belong to the first phase, while the second is represented by the apsidal rooms along the south facade, dated to the 5th century A. C.

Baths are known in two other later structures: one is a part of the Casino and the other is in the House of Peristerias. They both are of a simplifed construction and consist of a room with basins and a praefurnium. The Casino has not as yet been thoroughly excavated. The rooms of its bath open from a nearly square room which is adjacent to a larger, apsidal room. In the center of the latter room is a fountain with water jets, surrounded by three marble mensae. The floors were ornamented with mosaics (Fig. 106) whose motifs correspond to those of the Synagogue. The name "Casino" was applied to this building because of the discovery in the large room of a bronze pan in the form of an elongated mask for throwing dice, together with numerous dice (Tabula lusoria, Fig. 107). The House of Peristerias is discussed in the next section.

The big apsidal hall and the peristyle with a small apse in the Fuller's House also belong to this period. Traces of benches and of supports destined for the triclinium have been recognized in the small apse. Dressed stones and mortar were used as building material. The floors of the apses were of hydraulic mortar and must, therefore, have been built for piscinae or for fountains. The apses have niches. In the elevated west area,

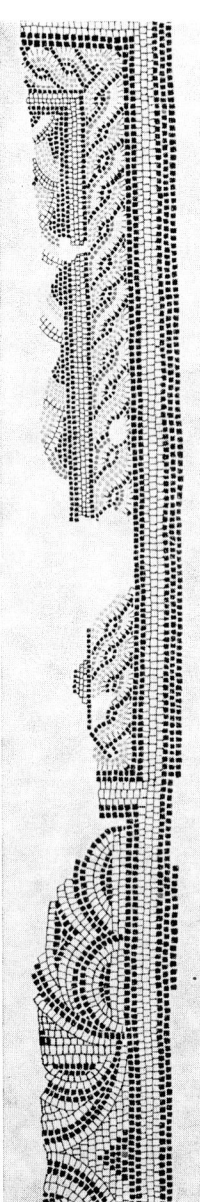

Figure 105. Mosaic from the Synagogue Basilica. Drawing by M. Petrovski and B. Damjanovski.

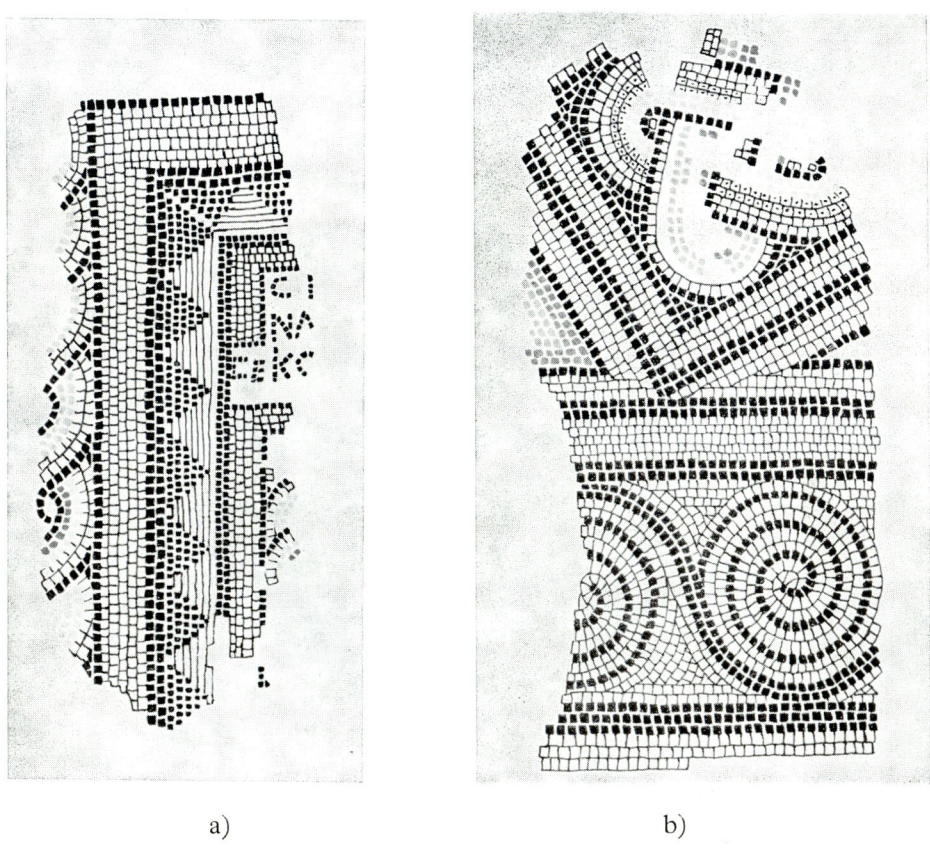

Figure 106. Mosaic from the Casino: a) in the corridor; b) in the apsidal room. Drawings by M. Petrovski and B. Damjanovski.

which was reached by two steps, the apodyterium and the hypocaust with the praefurnium represented the earlier phase. The floor levels were raised in the later phase and the room ceased to serve as a caldarium. The presence of Arcadius coins (A. D. 392) indicates the time of the 2nd destruction of that building. In the 5th century after the Gothic invasion in A. D. 479, the big hall with the large apse became a roofless courtyard. The rooms were partitioned and transformed into storage rooms and workshops. Among the latter, the textile factory with remains of looms and other spinning tools is worth mentioning. A multitude of sea shells, used for producing purple dye, found in stone troughs and canals in the corridor of the peristyle, indicate that part of the structure was a textile workshop for dyeing and fulling fabrics.[45]

Figure 107. Tabula lusoria from the Casino.

7. THE EARLY CHRISTIAN PERIOD (4TH TO LATE 6TH CENTURY A. C.).

Two residential complexes are among the outstanding representatives of the great architectural renaissance at Stobi between A. D. 386 (when it became the capital of Macedonia Secunda Salutaris) and A. D. 479, the year of the catastrophe it suffered from the Gothic invasions. They were formerly called the Palaces of Peristerias and Parthenius; the first after a mosaic inscription, and the second according to the text of a seal. The former has been renamed the House of Peristerias and the latter, actually two residences, comprises the Theodosian

---

[45] Mano-Zissi, *Starinar* (1935—36) 162. W-MZ (1971) 402; W-MZ (1972) 420.

Palace and the House of Parthenius (Plan of Site, nos. 10, 12, and 13 respectively).

Two major construction phases have been distinguished in the House of Peristerias. The eastern part of the complex (peristyle, two apsidal rooms, and the bath) belong, according to plans and building material used (dressed stones in mortar), to the earlier period, while later partitionings destroyed to a large extent the character of the entirety of that complex. After the Gothic plunderings, the great residence was transformed into workshops, storerooms, modest living quarters, etc., all constructed of spoils, fragments of blocks, rubble stones, and mud.[46]

Much more interesting is the differentiation of phases in the major part of the neighbouring Theodosian Palace. The architectural sculpture of the peristyle (columns, bases and capitals) included even spoils originating from the end of the 3rd century A. C. On the whole, however, organized as it is around the big peristyle with the nymphaeum, it is quite sumptuous enough to deserve its new name, the Theodosian Palace. The splendid nymphaeum in particular, with its decorative moldings; the peristyle with spirally-fluted columns and capitals that alternate with variegated marble columns and Ionic capitals; the triclinium and the elegant cubicula (museum, library, separés for meetings) with classical sculptures, on top of a raised platform--they all reflect the Hellenizing, oriental atmosphere of Constantinople during the reign of Theodosius and Arcadius. Opus sectile, frescoes and mosaics from the palace date to the end of the 4th century.[47]

Such a palace could have been inhabited by Theodosius in A. D. 388 when he issued his edicts at Stobi. The smaller southeast part of the complex, however, has no communication with the palace nor is there any element of unity between them, except for the fact that they form a block of buildings limited by streets. Although the architectonic plan and the concept of the structures surrounding the peristyle and the nymphaeum are similar, the method of construction and the ornamentation are entirely different. While the big palace was built of dressed stones in mortar, the small palace has single courses of stone alternating with four courses of brick cemented with mortar liberally applied. The green granite of the nymphaeum and of the columns in the peristyle is harmo-

---

[46] Wiseman, *Guide*, Section 10.
[47] Kitzinger, *Survey*, 124—128. E. Krischen, *Milet* (1938) 94: Museum Exedra. Keil, *WJh* 15 (1912) Beibl. 196.

niously combined with a red marble of capitals with carved crosses. Polychromy prevails. This house was the home of a rich patrician and merchant named Parthenius, whose seal was found in a storeroom full of large pithoi.[48]

The House of Parthenius may not have been built until the end of the 4th or the beginning of the 5th century A. C. The mosaic in the triclinium, resembling that of the Casino, also belongs to that period. It is interesting to note that a marble mensa which was uncovered in it is similar to those that surround the fountain of the Casino. However, in view of the fact that capitals with carved crosses are present in the House of Parthenius and that the mensa is situated on a higher podium of the room oriented towards the east, one might imagine that religious ceremonies took place here.

In the course of a continuous process of alternating destructions and constructions in the late 5th and 6th centuries A. C., a new late antique urbanism developed at Stobi.

Christian cult buildings played an increasingly important role at Stobi during this period of late antiquity. The urban and historical disposition of those buildings in the contemporary city of Stobi present special problems.

E. Dyggve has described the transformation of suburban pagan heroa into martyria and the urban martyria into churches during the 4th century A. C.[49] In the course of the 5th century the funeral liturgy was being transformed into the eucharistic rites. In this connection, it is of interest to note that a martyr's crypt (or bishop's tomb) has been uncovered underneath the south aisle of the Episcopal Basilica.[50] The building situated north of the Episcopal Church, which later became a residence, perhaps of the bishop himself, may have served originally as an oratorium.

The relationship of the early church and funeral liturgy may also be seen at Stobi in the form and location of the Episcopal Basilica. The location of that great Basilica above the Theater, where bloody scenes of Christian martyrdom may have been enacted, is significant. Although

---

[48] Dj. Mano-Zissi, "Stobi," *Enciklopedija Jugoslavije* 8 (1971) 153—155. K. Petrov, "Parament arasé," *Zbornik Skopje* (1955) 71—78 and *idem, op. cit.* (in note 41) p. 301, note 53. Lj. Popović, Mano-Zissi, et al., *op. cit.* (in note 44) fig. 342.

[49] E. Dyggve in *Atti VIII Byzant. Congress*, vol. II (Palermo 1953) 137.

[50] W-MZ (1972) 422; W-MZ (1973) 398. A. Grabar, *Martyrium* (Paris 1946) I, 457.

a temple of pagan healers was probably standing at that very place, the city cathedral was built on its ruins above the Theater/arena, as a sign of triumph of the new religion, perhaps as early as the middle of the 4th century A. C. What is more, the presbyterium includes a confessio with fenestella, and was visited by believers through a subterranean ambulatorium. The arrangement is very similar to that of the 4th century Basilica of St. Demetrius in Thessalonica. There, the place of martyrdom was the bath house while at Stobi it was the Theater.[51]

We should also mention that by the Palikura Basilica, which was probably in the vicinity of an ancient heroum,[52] an octagonal martyrium had also been constructed on the site of a Roman bath. The Basilica was erected next to it by the end of the 5th or at the beginning of the 6th century A. C. (Plan of Site, no. 29).

The Cemetery Basilica, dated to the late 4th or early 5th century A. C., also has the double apse that is characteristic of martyria. There is also a large funeral chamber with arcosolia at the basilica.[53]

If we may judge by construction technique (the use of dressed stone cemented with mortar), the North Basilica may be one of the oldest churches at Stobi.[54] It should be noted that the Episcopal Basilica shows the same method of construction in the apsidal part of the altar area and in the north shoulder, up to the line of the north aisle. This seems to indicate that it was initially a single aisled martyrium. It is also possible that the construction of the Episcopal Basilica was in progress over a long period of time, because the site had to be levelled and reinforced by masonry, so that the church in the northern part of the city could have served as the Episcopal Church for a while.

The North Basilica, on the other hand, may initially have been an oratorium. It had an apsidal nave with no side aisles; the shoulders of the apse were not connected with the east walls of the lateral aisles. Later, as a three-aisled basilica, it had a tribelon with an open narthex on columns and is, therefore, reminiscent of the Basilica Extra Muros at

---

[51] G. Sotiriou, *Hag. Demetrios Thessalonikes* (Athens 1952) figs. 7,59.

[52] A dedication to Heracles was found in the vicinity early in this century; Dr. Hald, *op. cit.* (in note 3), p. 41.

[53] Grabar, *loc. cit.* (in note 50). G. Sotiriou, "Basilikai tes Hellados," *Archeol. Ephemeris* (1929) 124, 177. A. K. Orlandos, Ἡ ξυλόστεγος παλαιοχριστιανικὴ βασιλικὴ τῆς Μεσογειακῆς Λεκάνης (Athens 1952—1954) 555 ff. R. Hoddinott, *Early Byzantine Churches in Macedonia and Southern Serbia* (London 1963) 167. R. Krautheimer, *Early Christian and Byzantine Architecture* (1965) 95, 328.

[54] Koco et al., *op. cit.* (in note 19) 69.

Philippi, or of two basilicas at Salona (Urbana and Manastirine).[55] Mosaics found in the basilica resemble those mentioned already in the House of Psalms. Both the mosaics and the small baptistery may be as early as the 4th century.[56]

The North Basilica appears to have been destroyed in the Gothic invasion of A. D. 479, and was not reconstructed before the end of the 5th century.

The church above the Synagogue may, by its very location, also mark the triumph of Christianity. The tripartite nave with colonnades ends in a tripartite sanctuary that suggests Syrian influence. The Corinthian capitals and the window imposts probably date to the middle of the 5th century A. C. After the earthquake in A. D. 518, smaller columns with arcades were used, and the initially axially-centered atrium-tristoon, with a nymphaeum, was narrowed and decentered.

The Episcopal Basilica, with its three aisles, presbyterium and atrium, was built before the time of Bishop Nicolas, who took part in the Chalcedonian Council in A. D. 451, by Bishop Philip, whose inscription on the lintel over the west door has been recovered. Judging by the style of the sculpture on the

Figure 108. Doorway lintel with a frieze of birds from the Episcopal Basilica.

---

[55] S. Pelekanidis, *Archaiolog. Ephemeris* (1955) 196; E. Dyggve, *Salonitan Christianity* (Oslo 1951) 27.

[56] I. Nikolajević-Stojković, "Ranohrišćanske krstionice u Jugoslaviji," *Zbornik Vizantološkog Instituta* 9 (Beograd 1966) 223.

Figure 109. Pyramid of the baldachino from the Episcopal Basilica.

lintel (grapevine and birds), it could be dated to the late 4th or early 5th century A. C. (Figs. 108, 109).[57] Investigations in the presbyterium in 1970—1972 revealed two building phases of the floor and the chancel screen. The older, rather lower level corresponds to the floor in the central nave. There were visible remains of the mensa, while the floor was decorated with opus sectile, which also corresponds to the opus sectile floor in the central nave. Moreover, the floor suggests a date at the end of the 4th century A. C. contemporary with the aedicula-

---

[57] The molding of the lintel resembles that of the pyramid of the ciborium baldachino found at the Exedra. Analogies in Thessalonica: the chancel screen of Hag. Demetrios and the baldachino of Hag. Georgios.

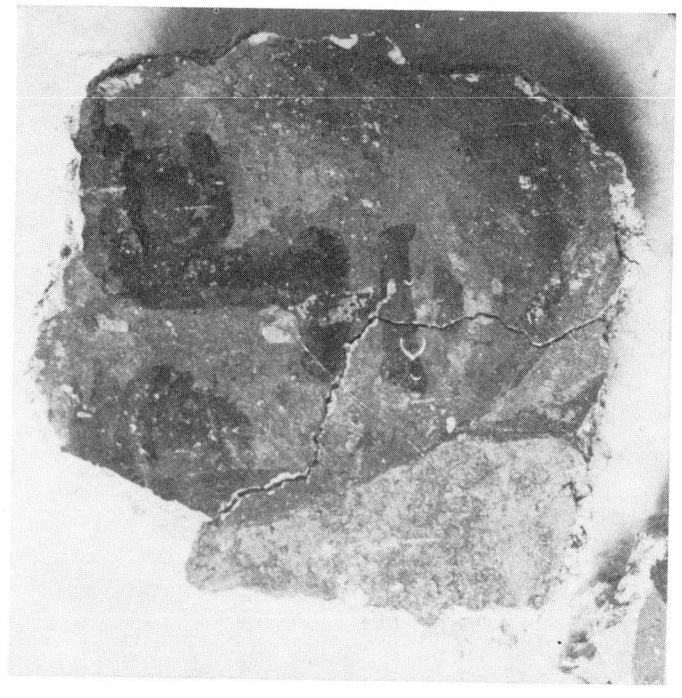
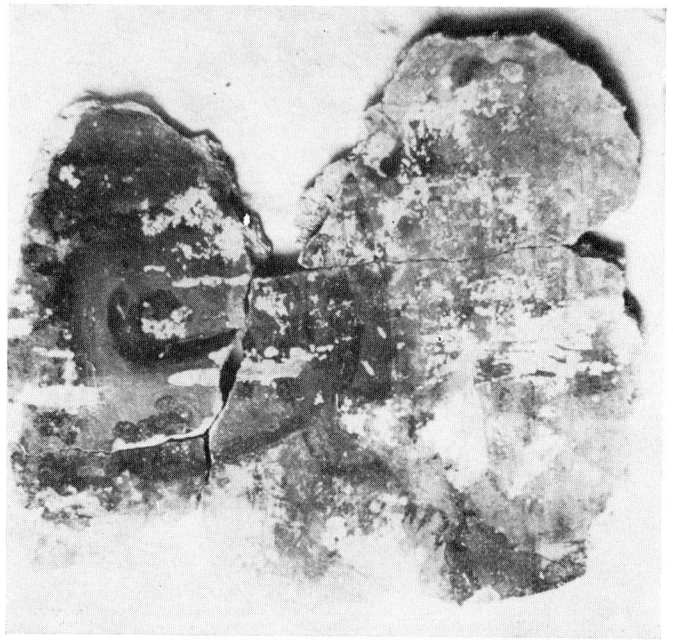

Figure 110. Two fresco portraits from the Baptistery.

Figure 111. Mosaic from the House of Psalms.

exedra rooms of the Theodosian Palace. The situation of the crypt and the confessio also points to the early period. Pilaster-capitals, stucco and frescoes document an earlier phase of the nave and the Baptistery (Fig. 110). In the south aisle that phase is evidenced by the mosaics which lie underneath the later, exterior stylobate. The inscribed name of the patron links the mosaic with Peristeria (or Peristerias), while its motifs and style are that of the House of Psalms (Fig. 111).

The discovery of a second mosaic dedicatory legend, specifying the gift of a deaconess, in the same mosaic and in the same general area, makes it likely that "Peristeria" refers to a woman and that the south aisle was used by female catechumens.[58]

The church was reconstructed in the 5th century following the example of the Acheiropoietos Church in Thessalonica and that of the John Studion in Constantinople. It obtained rich colonnades with Corinthian, Theodosian and composite capitals (the stylobates were reused seats of the earlier theater). The second base courses, parallel to the first ones, supported the parapet for the separation of insufficiently initiated believers in the lateral aisles. Ionic imposts were in the galleries. The chancel screen had been reconstructed, set more into the nave which was dominated by a luxurious ambo with twin stairways. Mosaics of this late period are preserved in the south aisle and in the narthex. The frescoes from the narthex probably also belong to the same period (Fig. 112).[59]

The Baptistery (Fig. 113), which presumably belongs to the earlier period, had also been reconstructed and may now have been used for ablutio, out of the big marble kantharos, instead of immersio, as in the earlier practice. The kantharos was placed beneath the narrowed baldachino on columns set at the angles of the parapet of the piscina.[60] The reconstruction probably occurred towards the end of the 5th century, after the Gothic invasion. The north outer wall of the basilica, which is preserved to a considerable height is characteristic for that

---

[58] On the new inscription see Wiseman, *Guide*, Section 19 and W-MZ (1973) 398. The dedications had been in connection with the ideology of the eternal life: see G. Babić, *Zbornik Vizantol. Instituta* (1971) 263 and Bitrakova-Grozdanova, *ŽA* (1970) 163.

[59] Dj. Mano-Zissi, *La mosaïque gréco-romaine* (Paris 1963) 287—295. Finds in the presbytery indicate the existence of a workshop of glass mosaics as in Salona. For frescoes see J. Maksimović, *Cahiers archéologiques* 10 (1959) 207—216.

[60] W-MZ (1972) 422—423; Wiseman, *Guide*, Section 20.

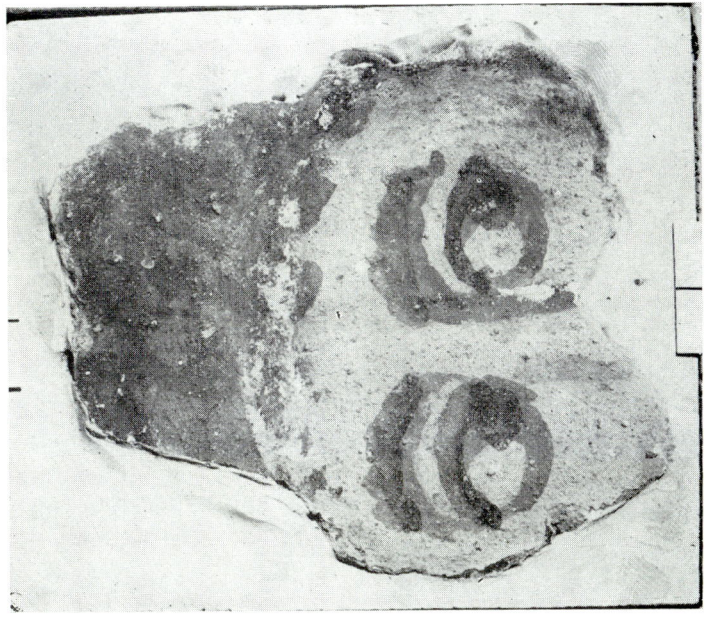

Figure 112. Two fresco portraits from the narthex of the Episcopal Basilica.

period with its alternating courses of dressed stones and (four) bricks set in mortar.

The building complex situated below and to the north of the Episcopal Basilica, which has been identified as the Episcopal Residence, also has two building phases. That building possesses a monumental stepped access down from the Via Principalis Superior along a corridor with colonnade and an exedra in front of the main hall. It has not yet been entirely excavated. In the second phase (late 5th century A. C.), the colonnade was framed and closed by walls, while the apsidal hall was decorated with luxurious stucco work imitating the motifs and the style of marble sculptures of the Episcopal Basilica.

It is clear, I believe, from the discussion above that by the early 5th century the urban plan of Stobi was no longer dominated by the Theater and the Thermae, but by ecclesiastical buildings. These structures were axially disposed along the streets and aqueducts. Irregularities in the terrain that disrupted the axial, rectangular *insulae* and system of traffic were "corrected" artificially by means of accesses or stairways. Levelling of the terrain was practiced on a large scale.

The axial system compelled architects to observe the obligatory lines of facades. Such obligations are witnessed by the irregular design of atria or exo-narthexes. This feature is especially perceptible in the case of the North Basilica.

It is only in the vicinity of the Episcopal Basilica that the street (the Via Sacra) was obliged to modify its normal direction. Coming from the Porta Heraclea to the Semicircular Court the Via Sacra deviates eastward in order to meet the street formed by the west side of the middle palaces and the east side of the Fuller's House (the Via Principalis Superior).

The eastward orientation of the Episcopal Basilica, which deviates slightly to the northeast, contrary to the direction of the other churches, is a problem in itself. Is it the result of the available space or the terrain configuration? Or was the angle of the sunrays on the occasion of the construction, at that time of the year, the decisive factor?[61] Or did the heavy, indestructible mass of the Theater force certain changes? One might expect *a priori* that a Christian acropolis of such importance would impose itself on, and be a dominant factor of, urban organization. Bošković reverses the question and thinks that the urban disposi-

---

[61] G. Gerola, *L'orientazione delle chiese di Ravenna antica* (Roma 1936).

tion had cut the Basilica's atrium, thus giving it an irregular shape.[62] But the initial direction of the Via Sacra from the Porta Heraclea was rather more westward. We may assume that the initial street was tangential to the Semicircular Court; in that case the atrium of the Episcopal Basilica could have extended to the edge of the street. Perhaps the situation was precisely that in the first phase of the Basilica. If so, it is likely that the street with porticoes and the Semicircular Court had been built *after* the catastrophic Gothic plunderings, when a probably undamaged atrium-tristoon, or one with a nymphaeum, was not so indispensable from the liturgical point of view as before. We must wait for an archaeological explanation of that problem. I admit,

Figure 113. Mosaic from the Baptistery.

however, the possibility of a change of the direction of the street in order to bind the Via Sacra with the Via Principalis Superior and to accentuate the Basilica with a monumental access through a piazetta.

[62] Dj. Bošković in *Charisterion eis Anastasion Orlandon* IV (Athens 1967—68) 184—189.

The city underwent further great changes after the Gothic destruction of A. D. 479. The Porta Heraclea may have been enlarged at that time with a double gate between towers like the Porta Aurea in Constantinople and Thessalonica, which had been built during the reign of Theodosius II.[63] Although the system of Hippodamus was maintained, there was a condensation of rooms and a transformation of large residences in insulae into small living quarters. At that time of uncertainty and influx of inhabitants into the city, additional stories had even been built upon some living units.

In order to embellish the streets, the construction of porticoes had been especially encouraged, after the patterns of Constantinople and Ephesus. Colonnades of the 4th century were replaced in the 5th century by arcades on pillars, as along the Via Sacra and in the Semicircular Court in front of the Episcopal Basilica. Consoles of balconies and window mullions were often ornamented with carved crosses, creating a truly Byzantine atmosphere in the city.

At a time when life was uncertain, everything, including the architecture and the urban plan, served the source of eternal life. After the time of hidden martyria, crypts, and oratoria, Stobi entered a period when more splendid, and open, Christian rites were celebrated. The idea of Eucharist triumphed[64] not only on the mosaics of two Stobi Baptisteries but throughout the Christian city.[65]

---

[63] E. Krischen, *Die Landmauern Konstantinopels* (Berlin 1938). Tafrali, *Topographie de Thessalonique* (1913) 105.

[64] A. Grabar and Hubert, "Fin de l'Antiquité et le Moyen Age," *Cahiers archéol.* 19 (1969). I. Nikolajević-Stojković, *Starinar* 21 (1970) 184.

[65] I am grateful to James Wiseman and Carolyn Snively for their help during the preparation of this article; however, I retain all responsibility for the interpretations presented.

ПРОБЛЕМИ СТРАТИГРАФИЈЕ
И УРБАНИ РАЗВОЈ СТОБИЈА

ЂОРЂЕ МАНО-ЗИСИ

Новија послератна истраживања, а посебно она у сарадњи Народног музеја у Титовом Велесу са Универзитетом Тексаса у Остину (1970—1972) поставила су извесне проблеме стратиграфије упоредо са урбаним развојем Стобија.

За познавање *стратиграфије* овог локалитета, после ранијих случајних налаза приличан допринос су дала испитивања 1955—57. од стране Археолошког музеја у Скопљу, на којима сам учествовао. Пробна ископавања у *Цивилној базилици* по систему терасастог силажења у дубље слојеве, идући од улице према апсиди, издиференцирала су 4 карактеристична хоризонта.

I. Још у 1937. години откривена, једноапсидална тробродна базилика са разгранатим анексима, са доста каснијих дозиђивања, дубоко је фундирана на чврстим каменим темељима. У највишем слоју карактеристична је градња наизменичним редовима камена и опеке са дебљим малтером. Контекстни материјал новаца из 5. века говори за живот до земљотреса од 518. године, после кога се у фази пропадања дограђивало дрветом и блатом. Ова А фаза представља грађевину Oikos у цивилној употреби. Може се схватити и као Xenodochion или Valetudinarium. Постављена између две цркве, без остатака је икаквих хришћанских знакова. Иначе би се, по систему рефекторија са редовима ћелија, могло мислити на њену монашку, општежитељску функцију.

2. Силазећи дубље до 0,90—1 m у другој трећини зграде, наишло се на остатке раније грађевине. У северном делу средњег брода појавила се апсида осовином помереном према југоистоку. И остали зидови, грађени тесаним каменом и малтером, немају везе са темељима Цивилне базилике. Камени под, остаци штукатуре и фресака, одломци канелираних јонских стубова (сличних онима у нартексу епископске базилике), фина канелована керамика и новци Теодосија I говоре за датовање *хоризонта* B на крај 4. века н. е.

3. У *слоју* C, на 1,56 m дубине, у трећој трећини зграде, указали су се остаци зидова (сличног смера хоризонту B) одаја које су се пружале до пречника апсиде цивилне базилике. Зидови грађени у техници бондрука (насатке постављени редови опека између редова камена, повезани глинастим малтером) имали су фреске флоралних и геометријских мотива. И овде су примећена дограђивања и прерађивања, али се овај слој може везати за период од 2. до краја 3. века. На то упућују и фрагменти тере сигилате и нигре, пергамонске керамике и керамике златне пешчане површине.

4. На 2,60 m дубини, у *слоју* D, у четвртој трећини зграде *Цивилне базилике*, појавили су се најзад остаци западног дела једне одаје. На бочном зиду правца СЈ сачуван је у ствари само његов високи сокл, са структуром камене основе, изнад ње са опекама малтерисаним мешавином глине. На зиду су местимично били још сачувани стуко-панели у виду ортостатних плоча, профилираних оквира између редова канелираних пиластара, од стукатуре. Одломци фресака су наговештавали емблеме усред помпејанско црвено обојене зидне површине. Сачувана је делимично *представа иловке* на плавој води. Њено мрко перје живо је контрастирало са жутим, зеленим-белим светлосним ефектима. Нарочито је обрађена партија око очију. Под је био од камених плоча изнад слоја црвеног кречног малтера. Присуство одломака беотских хомерских ваза и мегарских пехара, као и калупљених жижака (месечасти, негерска глава, диск са атинском совом), датују овај најзначајнији хоризонт у раздобље између 2. века пре и 1. века н. е.

5. Испод пода ове до сада најстарије грађње, у центру, испред пречника апсиде, у зеленом пешчаном слоју (на 3 m дубине), наишло се на овалну јаму, правоугаоно озидану каменом са источне стране. У њој је нађено само пепела, гара и животињских костију. Ван ње, источније, камени точак млина, бронзана дршка са главом хрта и двојна игла наговештавали су још старији хоризонт који је могао имати везе са ранијим касноархајским налазима. Међутим

до ње јужније, друга јама са градњом опет сличном керамичкој пећи, показала је изразити материјал касног *хеленизма* 3—2. века пре н. е: црнофирнисни kylix, два керамичка жишка дужих дршки и коштани стилус.

У јужном броду Цивилне базилике, и јужније између ње и Синагоге, и у самом оквиру *Синагоге* вршени су тестови 1970—72. На просечној дубини око 3 m од површине, а на 135 m надморске висине, на целом овом простору су нађени остаци јама, огњишта и трагови пећи и керамичких фрагмената 2. века пре н. е. (амфоре, мегарски пехари и калупи теракоте). То нас наводи на питање нисмо ли наишли на стобски Kerameikos, односно на *периферију насеља хеленистичког* Polisa? Истраживања јужније од Синагоге и у оквиру Перистеријине палате потврдила су крај насеља и појаву *хеленистичког хекрополиса*. Ископавања у дворишту јужно од апсида Перистеријине палате 1972. пружила су убедљиву документацију каснохеленистичких гробова, са контекстним материјалом унгвентарија и стаклених амфориска, сличним онима из околине Охрида и Битоља, и новцима Филипа V.

Хеленистички Polis *Стобија* је лежао према томе у благом конвексном полукругу североисточно према Еригону и Аксиосу, спуштајући се са првих благих тераса, са видним традиционалним заостацима Хиподамовог урбаног плана у конфигурацији терена. Истраживање Акрополе на северозападној узвишици према Вардару донело нам је потврду постојања хеленистичке градње на дну са новцем Филипа V. *Пеонски* претходни Refugium можемо претпоставити да је постојао на врху крај Вардара. На жалост градње жељезнице и аутопута уништише већ највећи део тог пункта.

Хеленистички период указује се дакле до тада само у својој последњој фази од 2. века пре н. е. до Аугустовог времена. То показују и налази ван бедема града, у некрополи већ римског доба, са теракотама амфипољске традиције и са култовима који су већ од почетака повезани са домаћим (Бендис, Диоскури, Трачки коњаник и Телесфор). Није ли то кратак период за онакву снажну хеленизацију која се одражава кроз цео римски период све до Византије? Култови Артемиде Ефеске и Лохијске и Кларијског Аполона указују на вероватно и старију повезаност Македоније са Јонијом, што је већ из ранијих културних сродности још од архајског доба непобитно. Уз постојеће натписе касније провениенције изгледа да постоје главе њихових мраморних статуа у Стобима. Поред њих знамо за 2 сатира и рељеф Пана са нимфама. Та хеленистичка скулптура пореклом је из Јоније, Александрије и из новоатичких радионица. Питање је само да ли су ова дела прибављали обожаваоци — сувременици, или тек љубитељи каснијих хоризоната.

Прелазни момент у римско доба документује један занимљив налаз сребра откривен 1971 испод нивоа најстарије Синагоге у једном крчажићу и лекиту: 506 денара римских и 1 атичка тетрадрахма, из 119 г. пре н. е. кад су Римљани поражени од Скордиска у Стобима.

Старији *римски материјал* везан је за појам ,,Oppidum Civium Romanorum'' и њиховог Municipiuma ca Ius Italicum, као и са ковницом MUN.STOB (са Tychom и двема нимфама). Из тог доба је и значајан почасни натпис Хадријана (у скопском лапидариуму). Распрострањеност града већ од тада обухвата оквире од Вардара и Еригона до линије бедема са Порта Хераклејом. Одатле почиње гробље и пружа се дуж друма према каснијој гробљанској цркви. Питање локације Castruma, Foruma, храмова за сада остаје без одговора. На југозападној узвишици уз (иначе традиционално одржани Хиподамов систем) у конфигурацији терена запажају се нешто одсечније повучене линије Cardo — Decumanus-a. Иначе овај комплекс могао би се тумачити и као Акропола над Театром, слично Атини и Салони.

Карактеристични налази почетне римске епохе, после Цивилне базилике, откривени су и *испод прве Синагоге*. Међутим, аналогно њој указује се у погледу унутрашње архитектонске декорације Casa Romana на Erigonu. Она се отвара последње две године у низу просторија. Првобитно припада Аугустовом добу, али евидентна су повремена каснија прерађивања зидова, до 3. века н. е. После једног хиатуса са траговима тешке поплаве, у 4. веку грађевина доживљује обнову у римску вилу, са карактеристичном ренесансом класицистичке традиције. У оквиру овог објекта занимљива су и стратиграфска померања, промена и враћање система ортостата са пиластрима, премазивања са новим слојевима фресака, сем тога и налази фигуралних људских ликова. — Развој и продужетак зидне декорације у флавијској и антонинијанској фази има свој карактеристичан случај у западној просторији Domus Fullonica. На зидовима грађеним бондруком, на глиненој подлози појављују се остаци фресака са живахним флоралним емблемама.

Средње римско царство је доба највеће експанзије и развоја града. Тада су се већ најзначајније зграде подизале на средњој тераси Стобија. На простору између Театра и комплекса палата нађени су, како натписи тако и статуете божанстава, чији би се храмови могли овде локализовати: Асклепија, Хигиеје и Телесфора, као и Артемиде. Споменик Баховог свештеника и многих статуа и рељефа наговештавају и његово светилиште. Да ли се Форум налазио у нижој равници пред Еригоном? Тамо је приликом испитивања унутрашњег бедема констатовано да је он грађен касније у 4. веку, изнад ранијег римског слоја 3. столећа. Због поплаве напуштен је међупростор до обале реке. Ту се указао портикус са степеништем, а испред њега мермерна база статуе са натписом Г. Приска, примипиларија.

Главни и најрепрезентативнији објекат тог времена је *Театар*. Кад се прихвата Саријина поставка о градњи и обнови полуамфитеатра и арене, према разлозима Дигвеа и Папазоглу, -те прекретнице могу се сагледати у почетку и крају 3. века. Један натпис exempli gratia нађен је као *сполиа* Баптистериума у част Марка Аурелија и Луција Вера. Натпис у Немезејону Театра Deo Augusto са краја је 3. века. Још увек није сигурно кога претставља торсо царске статуе, нађене у арени Театра. У то доба су постојале већ *велике терме* са статуом Togatusa и Amfitrite. Крајем 3. века је грађена *Полихармова Синагога*, према натпису на стубу и фреско-дедикацији у оквирима tabule ansate. Већ из тог доба је и портикус са капителом са маскама у *Кући Псалама*. Печатна плакета са Менором Еустатија биће да је припадала већ 4. веку, када су и синагога и ова кућа до ње обновљене и повезане међу собом и добиле раскошне фреске, стукатуру и мозаике. После театра, дошло је и до рушења синагоге, а са подизањем хришћанске цркве над њом и до адаптације куће у црквену резиденцију.

Domus Fullonica пружа највише могућности за праћење стратиграфских промена. Између остава Антонијана и Гордијана зграда је имала свој монументални грађевински изглед, са двема у осовини супростављеним апсидалним двоеранама и перистилом у средини, а на западној страни са простором грејаним хипокаустом. На крајњим западним и источним деловима зграде, крај улица, налазиле су се радионице и економске просторије. Упадљива је ливница са јамама и каналима, на вишем нивоу западне стране. Рушење зграде почиње већ крајем 4. века, и она је у току 5. века до 518. коришћена као Gynaeceum и Fullonica (према већим количинама нађених шкољки за бојадисање пурпуром, вретена и других одломака текстилних справа).

Подизање *великих палата* није без везе са просперитетом насталим у вези боравка Теодосија I у Стобима, крајем 4. века. О томе сведоче нарочито две највеће резиденције. Обе имају и две грађевинске фазе. *Перистеријина палата* задржала је свој раскошни карактер у источном делу (својим перистилом и нимфејем, делом обновљеним, мозаиком украшеним, триклинијем из 4. в. и купатилом), док су западни делови секундарно преграђивани у радионице и инсуле за масовно становање. *Други*, већи *комплекс палата* задржао је такође свој класицистички перистил, triclinium и exedre за библиотеку и музеј, мраморне оплате и opus sectile, у духу и стилу доба када је у њему, као најрепрезентативнијем, могао боравити сам Теодосије, приликом издавања својих едиката. Одвојени југоисточни део, са мањим перистилом, екседром и триклинијем и великим магацинима са питосима одговара кући богатог трговца Партенија, чији је печат и ту нађен. Капители овде имају крстове и мензу хришћанског карактера са поч. 5. в. И у градњи постоје разлике. У већој палати само камен и малтер, а овде има и цигле и дебљег малтера. Употреба менза, затим сличност употребе фонтана, нимфеја и обраде мозаика исте радионице везују за исто прелазно раздобље и новију Синагогу, Кућу Псалама, Перистеријину палату, а нарочито Партенијеву палату и Касину. У *Касини* сличне мензе коришћене су за коцкање, где је уз њих нађена tabula lusoria са коцкама за хазардну игру, уз атмосферу фонтане и купатила.

Водоводни систем са канализацијом изгледа да је постепено постављан већ од средњег царског времена, почев са Хадрианом. Он се потпуно развио до 4. века, улазећи и у домаћи комфор. За сада су познате две паралелне линије акведукта, са почетним извориштем од пиргокастела крај капије, који рачва воду доведену из правца Сиркова. Једна иде уз Via Principalis Superior, друга уз Inferior. Горња, старија, кроз структуре 3. века, рачва се према Перистеријином купатилу, великом купатилу, Синагоги, све до северне Базилике. Доња је евидентна идући од театра преко Касине до Терми. Један крај ишао је од Domus Fullonica ка Касини, а други се спуштао од Via Sacra акведуктом (сличним оном код Терми са ступцима и луцима) уз јужни зид Епископске базилике (крај степеништа које води из нартекса) ка Баптистерију и Театру. Корита чесми са шахтом и канализацијом у углу степеништа базилике и у излазној просторији из Баптистерија (у последњој са новцима из 4. века) говоре за то да су се на тим местима налазиле „*чудотвор-*

не чесме исцељења''. Велика *јавна чесма* се налазила на углу Перистеријине палате насупрот великом купатилу. *Нимфеји* својим системом степенасто постављених басена нису биле само у цивилној употреби, већ и у храмовима. Две *крстионице* у Стобима изгледа да су се смењивале у употреби у вези са насталим катастрофама. Два *јавна купатила* имала су такође две грађевинске фазе. Мање купатило је било женско судећи по накиту нађеном у њему.

Хришћенска епоха дубоко засеца у урбани развој Стобија. Од тада црквене грађевине дају специфичан карактер урбанизму, у двема маркантним фазама. 1. од краја 4. века до готске навале 479., 2. до земљотреса 518. У првом новом успону мартирија и ораторија са култом мучеништва и опсесијом вечитог живота дала су основне локације још скромним једнобродним грађевинама, које су затим победоносно развијане у репрезентативне тробродне базилике, са еухаристичком атмосфером, по узорима из Цариграда, Солуна и Ефеза. На месту некадашњег храма паганских исцелитеља најпре је подигнут martirium, а затим *Епископска базилика*. Крај Театра, у коме пролазећи Via venatorum умираху мученици (слично онима у термама крај Св. Димитрија у Солуну), чуване су њихове мошти и гробови првих епископа: у конфесији апсиде и у ходнику крипти под јужним бродом цркве. Из једнобродног oratoriuma претварана је и *северна базилика* у тробродну са трибелоном и отвореним нартексом, у истом 4. веку. Тада постављеном *нимфеју* касније се придружује и *крстионица*. Као *мартиријуми* су постављани и *гробљанска базилика* у 5. веку и *Манастириште* (Паликура) у 6. веку. Почетком 5. века и *над синагогом* се победнички диже хришћанска *базилика*. Већ крајем столећа доживљује преграђивања: пресбитериум постаје трипартитни, колонаде наоса се претварају у аркаде на ступцима, а атриум са нимфејем постаје дисцентриран. Око половине 5. века *Филипова базилика* означава врховни триумф хришћанства у Стобима. Надвратник са његовим натписом има фриз са птицама који се стилски уклапа са таквим датовањем. Наша последња истраживања су утврдила 2 фазе Presbiteriuma са померањима екстензије канцела. Триумфална фаза базилике имала је opus sectile и стубове сличне оним у Теодосијанској палати и класицистички укус при примени пиластеркапитела и других сполија из Театра. Утврђена су и два слоја мозаика у јужном броду. Онај дубљи има дедикацију познате личности (по палати) Перистерије. Слична дедикација Диаконисе по налогу Матроне у источном делу истог брода, названом ,,exedra'', наговештава да је овај простор био намењен женским верницима, те је и Перистерија жена. Базилика је поново обновљена у предјустинијановском периоду са раскошном декоративном пластиком. Отада су мозаици са емблемима у вишем слоју јужног брода и у нартексу, и фреске. Baptisterium епископске цркве грађен је крајем 4. века и служио је за immersio, после 479. вероватно је преображен за ablutio, са мермерним кантаросом на балустради писцине. Мозаици су остали из прве фазе, а изнад првих фресака су пресликаване друге.

Урбанистички лик Стобија добио је завршни изглед и атмосферу хришћанског и *византијског града* у току 5. века, са портицима, (у којима колонаде замењују аркаде на ступцима), са пиацетом екседре, са збијенијим инсулама (због нахрлелог становништва које због несигурности бежи у град), створеним надградњом спратова и преграђивањем раскошних палата. Ипак су при свем том исправљани правци улица, а *терасе* града повезиване су *степеништима*. Како је изгледала приватна *резиденција* тог времена, то наговештава она северно од епископске цркве. Са горњом улицом повезана је степеништем, коридором-портикусом и екседром, а имала је дворану украшену раскошном стукатуром. По укусу предјустинијановске декоративне пластике која је триумфовала у базилици.

Екседра-пиацета, грађена пред епископском базиликом, плод је урбанистичког захвата на штету атриума, али ради добијања репрезентативнијег приступа идући Via sacrom. На тај начин је иста повезана и са Виа Супериор. Porta Heraclea је обновљена, са *фортификацијом*, после готске навале по узору на Порта Аyреа у Солуну и Цариграду са propilonom и proteichismom.

6. век за Стоби значи период наглог опадања и пропадања. Крпљења, дозиђивања и преграђивања вршена су слабијим матејалом и настала је рурализација и мучно одржавање тековина. Велики делови града су остали у рушевинама, још док се у њему живело.

THE STOBI BIBLIOGRAPHY*

compiled by

ŽIKA RADOŠEVIĆ

Table of Contents

Ancient and Byzantine Sources	235
Studies of Sources	236
Historical Accounts	236
Topographical Studies	238
Coins	238
Inscriptions	239
Polycharmus' Inscription	241
Travelers' Accounts	242
General	242
Architectural Sculpture	244
Figural Sculpture	245
Mosaics	246
Wall Paintings	247

* The Stobi reference files assembled by Professor James Wiseman were extremely helpful in preparing this bibliography. The form is based on the analytical compilation in Ernst Kitzinger's article, "A Survey of the Early Christian Town of Stobi," *DOPapers* 3 (1946) 154—161. I am deeply grateful to Ruth Kolarik for her help in the preparation of this manuscript and the thorough revision of the entries.

Stuccos 248
Technical Studies 248

MONUMENTS

Aqueducts 248
Basilica Trans Erigon 249
Casa Romana 249
Casino 249
Cemetery Basilica 250
Central Fountain 250
City Walls 251
Civil Basilica 251
Episcopal Basilica 252
Episcopal Basilica Baptistery 255
Episcopal Residence 255
Hellenistic Cemetery 255
Horreum 256
House of the Fuller 256
House of Parthenius 256
House of Peristerias 257
House of Psalms 257
Large Bath 258
Mediaeval Graves 259
North Basilica 259
Palikura Basilica 260
Palikura Tomb 261
Porta Heraclea 261
Prison 262
Semicircular Court 262
Small Bath 263
Synagogue Basilica 263
Theater 264
Theodosian Palace 265
Via Axia 266
Via Principalis Inferior 266
Via Principalis Superior 267
Via Sacra 267
Via Theodosia 267
West Cemetery 268

ANCIENT AND BYZANTINE SOURCES

Cedrenus Georgius	Historiarum Compendium, *CSHB* 2, pp. 457—461.
Codex Theodosianus	16. 5. 15.
	16. 4. 2.
Cohors I Hispanorum Veterana	Papyrus fragment published by G. Cantacuzène, *Revue historique du sud-est européen* 5 (1928) 38.
Digest	I. 15. 8.
Diodorus Siculus	XVI. 4.
Hierocles	Synecdemus 10.
Ioannes Stobaeus	Eclogae.
Iordanes	Romana et Getica LVI. 285.
Iustinus	XXVIII. 3.
Livius Titus	XXXIII. 19.
	XXXIX. 33.
	XXXIX. 44.
	XXXIX. 53—54.
	XL. 21.
	XLV. 29—32.
Malchus Philadelphensis	Fragment 18.
Marcelinus Comes	100.
Notitia Dignitatum	Ed. O. Seeck, pp. 1—7, 24—25.
Novelae Iustiniani	XI.
	CXXXI.
Patrum Niceanorum nomina	Ed. Gelzer, Hilgenfeld, Cuntz,
	I. 213.
	II. 213.
	III. 208, 216.
	IV. 192.
	V. 208.
	VIII. 210.
	IX. 217.
	XI. 207.
Plinius Secundus	Historia Naturalis IV. 10. 34.
Polybius	Historia V. 97—98.

Provinciae Macedoniae
Episcopi Dii   Michaelis Le Quien, *Oriens Christianus* (Paris 1750) 2, cols. 75—76.
Ptolomaeus   Geographia III. 12.
Ravennian Geographer   Ravenatis Anonymi Cosmographia IV. 196. 10.
Sacrorum Conciliorum   Mansi (Florence 1769)
                                II. 696; VI. 577D; VII. 161B;
                                XI. 645A, 614, 673; XI. 994D.
Salustius Crispus   Historia I. 133M, 134M.
                                Historia II. 36M.
Stephanus Byzantius   Ethnica.
Strabo   Geographia VIII. 389.
Tabula Peutingeriana   VII. 5.
Valerius Maximus   Memorabilia.

STUDIES OF SOURCES

Honigmann, E.   *Le Synekdémos d'Hiérokles et l'opuscule géographique de Chypre* (Bruxelles 1939) 15.
Katancsich, P.   *Orbis antiquus ex tabula itineria quae Theodosii Imp. et Peutingeri audit ad systema geographiae* (Buduae 1824) 465. II—654. VII.
Le Quien, M.   *Oriens Christianus* (Paris 1750) 2, cols. 73—76.
Liebe, C.   *Gotha Numaria* (Amstelaedami 1780) 158.VII.
Papazoglu, F.   *MGRD* 15—36.
Schwartz, E.   Ueber die Bischoflisten der Synode von Chalcedon, Nicea und Konstantinopel, *Abhandlungen der bayerischen Akademie der Wissenschaften*, 13 n. F. (1937) 12, 39.
Zumpt, W.   *De coloniis romanorum militaribus. Commentationes epigraphicae* I (Berlin 1850) 434, 481, 489.

HISTORICAL ACCOUNTS

Collart, P.   *Philippes, ville de Macédoine* (Paris 1937) 230, note 3.

Geyer, F.	Makedonia, *RE* XIV (1928) 669, 765—766.
Grujić, R.	Stobiska mitropolia, *NE* IV (1929) 491—492.
Heisterbergk, B.	Zum IUS ITALICUM. III. Angebliche Municipien mit Ius Italicum, *Philologus* 50 (1891) 648.
Heuzey, L.	Découverte des ruines de Stobi, *RA* (1873) pt. 2, 25—42.
Jones, A.	*The Greek City from Alexander to Justinian* (Oxford 1937) 325, note 3.
Kazarow, G.	Die ethnographische Stellung der Paeonen, *Klio* 18 (1923) 23.
Kornemann, E.	Coloniae, *RE* IV (1901) 549.
	Municipium, *RE* XVI (1933) 596, 609, 633.
Lenk B.	Paiones, *RE* XVIII (1942) 2403—2408.
Mommsen, T.	*Römisches Staatsrecht* III, p. 808, note 1.
Papazoglu, F.	La Macédoine Salutaire et la Macédoine Seconde, *Bulletin de la classe des lettres de l'académie royale de Belgique* 42 (1956) 115—124.
	MGRD 235—236.
	Natpis iz nemezejona i datovanje stobskog pozorišta, *ŽA* 1 (1951) 279—293.
	Srednjobalkanska plemena u predrimsko doba, Akademija nauka i umjetnosti Bosne i Hercegovine, knjiga XXX (Sarajevo 1969) 79, 122—123, 133, 137, 225, 348, 352—353.
Premerstein, A. von	Ius Italicum, *RE* X (1917) 1240, 1242.
Salmon, E.	*Roman Colonization under the Republic* (London 1969) note 321.
Saria, B.	Istraživanja u Stobima, topografija i istorija, *Glasnik* 5 (1929) 1—13.
	Pozorište u Stobima, *Godišnjak muzeja Južne Srbije* 1 (1937) 54.
	Stobi, *RE* IV (1932) 47—54.
	Stobi, *NE* IV (1929) 489—491. This article is almost identical with the former and henceforth only the one in *RE* will be cited.
Stein, E.	*Histoire du Bas Empire* II (Paris 1849) 661, 662, note 1.

Tod, M.   The Macedonian Era Reconsidered, *Studies Presented to D. M. Robinson* II (1953) 382—397.

Zeiller, J.   *Les origines chrétiennes dans les provinces danubiennes de l'empire romain* (Paris 1918) 144, 160, 163—164, 391, 399, 401, 600.

TOPOGRAPHICAL STUDIES

Hammond, N.   *A History of Macedonia* I (Oxford 1972) 66—67, 76—79, 171—172, 201—202, also see index.

Miller, K.   *Die Peutingerische Tafel* (repr. Stuttgart 1962) 10.

Saria, B.   Istraživanja u Stobima, topografija i istorija, *Glasnik* 5 (1929) 1—13.

Tomovski, T.   Prilog za rekonstrukcija na Tabula Peutingeriana na delnicata Scupi-Stobi, *ŽA* 11 (1961) 113—125.

Venedikov, I.   *Zemite po Srednı Vardar* (in Bulgarian) (Skopje 1943).

Vulić, N.   Geografija Južne Srbije u antičko doba, *Glasnik* 19 (1938) 1—15.

COINS

Crawford, M.   The Stobi Hoard of Roman Republican Denarii, *Studies in the Antiquities of Stobi* I (Beograd 1973).

Dušanić, S.   A Foundation-type on the Coinage of the Municipium Stobi, *RBN* 113 (1967) 11—29.

Keramitčiev, A.   Rimskata monetarnica vo Stobi, *Zbornik na arheološkiot muzej* 4-5 (Skopje 1961—1966) 39—58.

Mano-Zissi, Dj.   Bericht über die Ausgrabungen in Stobi, *Der 6. Kongress* (1940) 592.

Petrović, J.   Srpsko srednjevekovno blago u Stobima, *Umetnički pregled* 3 (1940) no. 4-5, pp. 108—109.
Stobi u numismatici, *Numizmatičar* 1 (Beograd 1933) 19—29.

Petrović, J.	U Stobima danas, *Glasnik Sarajevo* (1943) 516—520.
Simić, V.	Zusammensetzung der Münzen, die in der römischen Lokalgeldprägestätte Stobi aus Kupfer und seinen Legierungen geprägt wurden, *Jahrbuch der Numismatik und Geldgeschichte*, forthcoming.

INSCRIPTIONS

CIL	III, 629—631, 710a, 7325, 8203. VI, 2379B, line 40; 2382, line 25. X, 6096.
Dimitsas, M.	Ἡ Μακεδονία ἐν λίθοις φθεγγομένοις (Athens 1896) 327—328, 331—332.
Egger, R.	Der erste Theodosius, *Byzantion* 5 (1929) 9—32.
Engelhardt, M.	Inscriptions de la Mésie Supérieure, *RA* 26 (1873) 137.
Evans, J.	Antiquarian Researches in Illyricum, *Archaeologia* 49 (1886) 90, 114—115.
Hahn, J. G. von	Reise durch die Gebiete des Drin und Vardar, *DenkschrWien (phil-hist Kl.)* 15 (1867) part 2, pp. 160, 166, nos. 33—34.
Hald, Dr.	*Auf den Trümmern Stobis* (Stuttgart 1917) 41—48.
Keramitčiev, A.	A New Inscription from Stobi, *ŽA* 12 (1962) 315—317.
Macridy, T.	Antiquités de Notion II, *JÖAI* 15 (1912) 45, 52, 56.
Papazoglu, F.	Natpis iz nemezejona i datovanje stobskog pozorišta, *ŽA* 1 (1951) 279—293.
Petrović, J.	Stobi 1932, *Starinar* 8-9 (1933—1934) 174, 177, 180, 184.
Picard, C.	D'Ephèse à la Gaule et de Stobi (Macédoine) à Claros, *REG* 70 (1957) 112—117.
Premerstein, A. von and N. Vulić	Antike Denkmäler in Serbien und Macedonien, *JÖAI* 6 (1903) Beibl., 1—10.

Robert, J. and L.	Bulletin épigraphique, *REG* 71 (1958) 266—268. Bulletin épigraphique, *REG* 78 (1965) p. 123, no. 235.
Saria, B.	Die Inschriften des Theaters von Stobi, *JÖAI* 32 (1940) Beibl., 1—34. Ein Dionysosvotiv aus dem Konsulatsjahr des P. Dasumius Rusticus, *JÖAI* 26 (1930) 64—74. Epigrafski spomenici iz Južne Srbije, *Glasnik* 7—8 (1930) 293—299. Neue Funde in der Bischofskirche von Stobi, die Inschriften, *JÖAI* 28 (1933) 132—139. Novi nalasci u episkopskoj crkvi u Stobima, *Glasnik* 12 (1933) 25—32. This article is almost identical with the former and henceforth only the Serbian version will be cited.
SEG	XVII (1960) p. 86, no. 319. XXIV (1969) p. 174, no. 496.
Struck, A.	Inschriften aus Makedonien, *AM* 27 (1902) 317—319.
Truhelka, Ć.	Arheološke beleške iz Južne Srbije, *Glasnik* 3 (1927) 77.
Volkmann, H.	Neue Beiträge zum Nemesiskult, *Archiv für Religionswissenschaft* 31 (1934) 58—60.
Vulić, N.	Antički spomenici naše zemlje, *Spomenik* 71 (1931) pp. 44—48, nos. 100—110, p. 239, nos. 637—638. Antički spomenici naše zemlje, *Spomenik* 75 (1933) pp. 22—28, nos. 42—80. Antički spomenici naše zemlje, *Spomenik* 77 (1934) pp. 40—42, nos. 17—22, p. 63, nos. 71—72. Antički spomenici naše zemlje, *Spomenik* 98 (1941—1948) pp. 41—44, nos. 91—94.
Wiseman, J.	Gods, War and Plague in the Time of the Antonines, *Studies in the Antiquities of Stobi* I (Beograd 1973).

Wiseman and Mano-Zissi	W-MZ (1971) 399, 401, 402, 407, 408, 410.
	W-MZ (1972) note 68.
	W-MZ (1973) 397, 402—403.

POLYCHARMUS' INSCRIPTION

Danov, C.	Notizen zur grossen Synagogeninschrift aus Stobi, *BIABulg* 8 (1934) 101—105.
Frey, J.	*Corpus Inscriptionum Judicarum* I (1936) pp. 504—507, no. 694.
Hengel, M.	Die Synagogeninschrift von Stobi, *ZNTW* 57 (1966) 145—183.
Kitzinger, E.	Survey, pp. 141—146.
Klein, S.	Neues zum Fremdenhaus der Synagogue, *Monatsschrift für Geschichte und Wissenschaft des Judentums* 77 (1933) 81—84.
Lietzmann, H.	Notizen bei den Ausgrabungen in Stobi, *ZNTW* 32 (1933) 93—95.
Marmorstein, A.	The Synagogue of Claudius Tiberius Polycharmos in Stobi, *Jewish Quarterly Review* n. s. 27 (1937) 373—384.
Petrović, J.	U Stobima danas, *Glasnik Sarajevo* (1943) 497—499.
	Iskopavanje u Stobima 1931, *Starinar* 7 (1932) 81—86, 135—136.
Robert, J. and L.	Bulletin épigraphique, *REG* 81 (1968) 478—479.
Sukenik, E.	*Ancient Synagogues in Palestine and Greece* (London 1934) 79—81.
Vulić, N.	Antički spomenici naše zemlje, *Spomenik* 71 (1931) pp. 238—239, no. 636.
	Inscription grecque de Stobi, *BCH* 56 (1932) 291—298.
	Inscription grecque de Stobi, *Academie royale serbe, Bulletin de l'academie des lettres* 1 (1935) 169—175.

Vulić, N.	Jevrejski natpis iz Stobi, *Glas Srpske kraljevske akademije* (1933) 34—42.
Wiseman and Mano-Zissi	W-MZ (1971) 407.

TRAVELERS' ACCOUNTS

Hahn, J. G. von	Reise durch die Gebiete des Drin und Wardar, *DenkschrWien(phil-hist Kl.)* 15 (1867) pt. 2, 158—188. Reise von Belgrad nach Salonik, *Denkschr Wien(phil-hist Kl.)* 11 (1861) pt. 2, 175, 231—236.
Heuzey, L.	Découverte des ruines de Stobi, *RA* (1873) pt. 2, 25—42.
Heuzey, L. and H. Daumet	*Mission archéologique de Macédoine* (Paris 1876) 331—338.
Leake, W.	*Travels in Northern Greece* III (London 1835) 439—442.
Premerstein, A. von and N. Vulić	Antike Denkmäler in Serbien und Macedonien, *JÖAI* 6 (1903) Beibl., cols. 5—10.

GENERAL

Dušanić, S.	A Foundation-type on the Coinage of the Municipium Stobi, *RBN* 113 (1967) 11—29.
Goldman, H.	Excavations at Stobi in Jugoslavia, *AJA* 37 (1933) 297—301.
Hald, Dr.	*Auf den Trümmern Stobis* (Stuttgart 1917).
Josifovska, B.	*Vodič niz Stobi* (Skopje 1953).
Kašanin, M.	Fouilles à Stobi, *Jugoslovenski istoriski časopis* 1 (1935) 746—747. Otkopavanja u Stobima, *Umetnički pregled* 1 (1937) no. 2, p. 62.
Kitzinger	Survey, pp. 81—161.
L., R.	Les ruines de Stobi, *RA* (1930) pt. 2, p. 313.

Mano-Zissi, Dj.	Bemerkungen über die altbyzantinische Stadt von Stobi, *CISB* II (1940) 224—237.
	Bericht über die Ausgrabungen in Stobi, *Der 6. Kongress* (1940) 591—593.
	Department of Greek and Roman Antiquities, *National Museum Beograd Guidebook* (Beograd 1970) 25—35.
	K pitanju stratigraphije u Stobima, *Zbornik* 2 (1958—1959) 355—357.
	Pitanje kontinuiteta iz aspekta antičkog urbanizma u našim zemljama, *6. Kongress jugoslovenskih arheologa* (Beograd 1964) 95—99.
	Pogled na pitanja urbanizacije i urbanizma u Ilirikumu, *Zbornik* 4 (1964) 97—99, 107—108.
	Stratigraphic Problems and the Urban Development of Stobi, *Studies in the Antiquities of Stobi* I (Beograd 1973).
	Stobi, *Enciklopedija leksikografskog zavoda* (Zagreb 1971) VIII, 153—155.
	Urbanistički lik Stobija, *Umetnički pregled* 2 (1939) no. 9, p. 265.
Nestorović, B.	Iskopavanja u Stobima, *Starinar* 6 (1931) 109—114.
Nikolajević-Stojković, I.	Povodom najnovije diskusije o ranohrišćanskim krstionicama u Saloni, *Zbornik radova vizantološkog instituta* 14-15 (1973) 159—171.
	Ranovizantiska arhitektonska dekorativna plastika u Makedoniji, Srbiji i Crnoj Gori, SAN, knjiga 279 (Beograd 1957) 2—34.
Papazoglu, F.	MGRD 235—245.
Petrović, J.	Iskopine starog grada Stobi u Makedoniji, *Svijet*, knjiga 12, godina 6, broj 12 (September 19, 1931) 278—279, 288.
	U Stobima danas, *Glasnik Sarajevo* (1943) 463—525.
Saria, B.	Iskopavanje u Stobima, *Glasnik* 1 (1925) 287—300.
	Istraživanja u Stobima, *Glasnik* 5 (1929) 1—13.

Saria, B.	Stobi, *RE* IV (1932) 47—54.
	Vor- und frühgeschichtliche Forschung in Südserbien, *BRGK* (1925—1926) 97—104.
Vinčić Ž.	Stobi — antički grad. Lokalitet krečana — vila rustika. Antička nekropola, *Arheološki pregled* 12 (1970) 140—142.
Wiseman, J.	*Guide.*
Zwenger	Ausgrabungen in Stobi, *Berliner Lokalanzeiger* (3. Juni 1917).
Anonymous	*Die Weltkunst*, 6 (1932) no. 29, p. 2.

ARCHITECTURAL SCULPTURE

Dyggve, E.	*Den Senantike Faellesscene* (Kobenhavn 1938) 24.
Egger, R.	Ausgrabungen in Stobi - die frühchristliche Bischofskirche, *AA* (1927) 175—176.
	Gradska crkva u Stobima, *Glasnik* 5 (1929) 17—42.
Filow, B.	Altchristliches aus Mazedonien, *Studien zur Kunst des Ostens, Festschrift J. Strzygowski* (1923) 33—39.
	Early Bulgarian Art (Berne 1919) 6.
	Geschichte der altbulgarischen Kunst (Berlin 1932) 22.
Goldman, H.	Excavations at Stobi in Jugoslavia, *AJA* 37 (1933) pp. 298—300, figs. 1—6, 10—11.
Kautzsch, R.	*Kapitellstudien* (Leipzig 1936) 77—78, 83—84, 159, 163, 172.
Kitzinger, E.	The Horse and Lion Tapestry at Dumbarton Oaks, Appendix: List of Early Byzantine Animal and Bird Capitals, *DOPapers* 3 (1946) pp. 64, 68—71, nos. 30, 66, 74, 75, 76, 95, 96.
	Survey, pp. 98—107, 124, 132.
Kondakov, N.	*Ocherki i zamietki po istorii aredneviekovago iskusstva* (Praha 1929) 131—132.
Mano-Zissi, Dj.	Dekorativna plastika u Stobima, *Umetnički pregled* 3 (1940) no. 1—2, pp. 36—41.

Mano-Zissi, Dj.   Iskopavanje u Stobima 1933 i 1934 godine, *Starinar* 10-11 (1935-1936) 157—159.

Nikolajević-Stojković, I.   *Ranovizantiska arhitektonska dekorativna plastika u Makedoniji, Srbiji, i Crnoj Gori*, SAN, knjiga 279 (Beograd 1957) 2—34, 36, 38, 43—47, 49—51, 55, 61, 62, 64, 68, 71—73.

Saria, B.   Jedan rimski figuralni kapitel iz Stobija, *Starinar* 8-9 (1933—1934) 8—13.
Novi nalasci u episkopskoj crkvi u Stobima, *Glasnik* 12 (1933) 16—25.

FIGURAL SCULPTURE

Goldman, H.   Excavations at Stobi in Jugoslavia, *AJA* 37 (1933) p. 299, figs. 7, 8, 9.

Grbić, M.   Die Herkunft der römischen Porträts auf dem Gebiet des mittleren Balkans, *Archaeologia Jugoslavica* 3 (1959) p. 82, fig. 31.
Dva satira iz Stobia, *Umetnički pregled* 1 (1937—1938) no. 10, pp. 310—312.
Odabrana grčka i rimska plastika u narodnom muzeju u Beogradu (Beograd 1958) 29—30, 37—38, 42—44, 68—69, 80—81, 86, 89—93,96.
Rimski portreti u predjašnjem istorisko umetničkom muzeju u Beogradu, *Starinar* 10-11 (1935—1936) 137.

Mano-Zissi, Dj.   *Antika u narodnom muzeju u Beogradu* (Beograd 1954) 4.
Antiquité gréco-romaine, *L' Art en Yugoslavie de la préhistoire à nos jours* (Paris 1971) pp. 43—48, nos. 71, 73, 74, 92, 154, 155.
Iskopavanje u Stobima 1933 i 1934 godine, *Starinar* 10-11 (1935—1936) 155.

Petković, V.   Antičke skulpture iz Stobi, *Starinar* 12 (1937) 12—35.
Die neuentdeckten Skulpturen in Stobi, *Bericht über die Jahrhundertfeier des Deutschen Archäologischen Instituts* (1930) 192—193.

Petković, V.	*Report on 1927, *Godišnjak* 37 (1928) 191—192. *Report on 1928, *Godišnjak* 37 (1928) 220—221. *Report on 1929 *Godišnjak* 38 (1929) 234. *Report on 1930 *Godišnjak* 39 (1930) 189. *Report on 1931 *Godišnjak* 40 (1931) 225. *Report on 1932 *Godišnjak* 41 (1932) 209.
Petrović, J.	Stobi 1932, *Starinar* 8-9 (1933—1934) 179—180.
Picard, C.	Un bronze alexandrin importé à Stobi, *RA* 47 (1956) 217—220.
Reinach, S.	Sculpture, *RA* 29 (1929) 21, 330—338. Sculpture, *RA* 30 (1929) 87.
Saria, B.	Ein Dionysosvotiv aus dem Konsulatsjahr des P. Dasumius Rusticus, *JÖAI* 26 (1930) 64—68.
Anonymous	*Die Weltkunst* 6 (1932) p. 2, no. 29.

MOSAICS

Dragendorff, H.	Archäologische und kunstwissenschaftliche Arbeit während des Weltkrieges in Mazedonien, *Kunstschutz in Kriege* II (ed. P. Clemen) (1919) 162. Archäologische und kunstwissenschaftliche Arbeit während des Weltkrieges in Mazedonien, *Zeitschrift für bildende Kunst* n. F. 30 (1919) 266. This article is identical with the former and henceforth only one will be cited.
Kitzinger	Survey, pp. 107—108, 124—127, 135—138.
Mano-Zissi, Dj.	Mosaiken in Stobi, *BIABulg* 10 (1936) 277—297. Mozaici jedne kuće u Stobima, *Starinar* 8-9 (1933—1934) 249—254.

---

* Brief reports contained in the annual report of the Istorisko umetnički muzej.

Mano-Zissi, Dj.	Mozaici u Stobima, *Umetnički pregled* 1 (1937—1938) no. 1, pp. 8—10. Prolegomena uz probleme kasnoantičkog mozaika u Ilirikumu, *Zbornik* 2 (1958—1959) 83—109. La question des différentes écoles de mosaïques gréco-romaines de Yougoslavie et essai d'une esquisse de leur évolution, *La mosaïque gréco-romaine* (Paris 1963) 287—295.
Nestorović, B.	Iskopavanje u Stobima, *Starinar* 6 (1931) 111-112.
Nikolajević, I.	Povodom najnovije diskusije o ranohrišćanskim krstionicama u Saloni, *Zbornik radova vizantološkog instituta* 14—15 (1973) 164—166, 169—170.
Petković, V.	Report on 1927, *Godišnjak* 37 (1928) 189—190. Report on 1930, *Godišnjak* 39 (1930) 189. Report on 1931, *Godišnjak* 40 (1931) 221. Report on 1932, *Godišnjak* 41 (1932) 209—210.
Petrov, K.	Neobjasneti mesta na dve hristijanski alegoriski mozaični kompozicii, *Zbornik Skopje* 23 (1971) 299—305.
Saria, B.	Novi nalasci u episkopskoj crkvi u Stobima, *Glasnik* 12 (1933) 12—16.
Sodini, J.—P.	Mosaïques paléochrétiennes de Grèce, *BCH* 94 (1971) 747.
Wiseman, J.	*Guide*, Sections 5, 10, and 20; figs. 4, 6, 12, 13.
Wiseman and Mano-Zissi	W-MZ (1971) 398—400. W-MZ (1972) 422—423. W-MZ (1973) 393, 397—399.

WALL PAINTINGS

Djurić, M.	O skidanju zidnih slikariju u Stobi, *Starinar* 7 (1932) 86—87.
Kitzinger	Survey, pp. 108—110.

Mano-Zissi, Dj.   Freske u Stobima, *Starinar* 8-9 (1933—1934) 244—248.

Maksimović, J.   Contribution à l'étude des fresques de Stobi, *Cahiers archéologiques* 10 (1959) 207—216.

Petković, V.   Report on 1931, *Godišnjak* 40 (1931) 221—222.

Wiseman and Mano-Zissi

W-MZ (1971) 408.
W-MZ (1972) 411—413, 422—423.
W-MZ (1973) 394—397.

STUCCOS

Mano-Zissi, Dj.   Stukatura u Stobima, *Zbornik* 3 (1962) 101—107.

Wiseman and Mano-Zissi

W-MZ (1971) 410.
W-MZ (1973) 394—396.

TECHNICAL STUDIES

Davis, E. M. *et al.*   Radiocarbon Dates from Stobi: 1971 Season, *Studies in the Antiquities at Stobi* I (Beograd 1973).

Folk, R. L.   The Geologic Framework of Stobi, *Studies in the Antiquities at Stobi* I (Beograd 1973).

Srdoč, D. *et al.*   Rudjer Bošković Institute Radiocarbon Measurements II, *Radiocarbon* 15 (1837) 438—439.

MONUMENTS

AQUEDUCTS

Mano-Zissi, Dj.   Bemerkungen über die altbyzantinische Stadt von Stobi, *CISB* II (1940) 230—232.
Iskopavanja u Stobima 1933 i 1934 godine, *Starinar* 10-11 (1935—1936) 155, 159, 163.
Urbanistički lik Stobija, *Umetnički pregled* 2 (1939) no. 9, p. 265.

Nestorović, B.	Iskopavanja u Stobima, *Starinar* 6 (1931) 114.
Petković, V.	Report on 1930, *Godišnjak* 39 (1930) 190. Report on 1932, *Godišnjak* 41 (1932) 209—210.
Petrov, K.	Istražuvanja na vodovodniot sistem vo ranovizantiskiot Stobi, *Zbornik Skopje* 19 (1967) 267—306.
Petrović, J.	U Stobima danas, *Glasnik Sarajevo* (1943) 482, 483, 485, 486, 487, 502, 503.
Saria, B.	Pozorište u Stobima, *Godišnjak muzeja Južne Srbije* 1 (1937) 15.

BASILICA TRANS-ERIGON

Petrov, K.	Kon otvorenoto prašanje na šestata bazilika vo Stobi, *Zbornik Skopje* 22 (1970) 307—318.
Petrović, J.	Krstionice u Stobima, *Umetnički pregled* 3 (1940) no. 9, p. 265. U Stobima danas, *Glasnik Sarajevo* (1943) 472, 488.

CASA ROMANA
(Roman House)

Wiseman and Mano-Zissi	W-MZ (1972) 411—413. W-MZ (1973) 394—397.

CASINO

Petrović, J.	U Stobima danas, *Glasnik Sarajevo* (1943) pp. 473, 476, 487, figs. 11, 28, 29.
Wiseman, J.	*Guide*, Section 21.

CEMETERY BASILICA

Dragendorff, H.	Archäologische und kunstwissenschaftliche Arbeit während des Weltkrieges in Mazedonien, *Zeitschrift für bildende Kunst* n. F. 30 (1919) 265—267.
Egger, R.	Gradska crkva u Stobima, *Glasnik* 5 (1921) 14, 16.
Filow, B.	Altchristliches aus Mazedonien, *Studien zur Kunst des Ostens, Festschrift J. Strzygowski* (1923) 33—34.
Hald, Dr.	*Auf den Trümmern Stobis* (Stuttgart 1917) 24—25.
Hoddinott, R.	*Early Byzantine Churches in Macedonia and Southern Serbia* (London 1963) 167—168.
Kitzinger	Survey, p. 147, note 288.
Mano-Zissi, Dj.	Bericht über die Ausgrabungen in Stobi, *Der 6. Kongress* (1940) 593.
Petrov, K.	Pravata osnova i arhitektonskite osobenosti na grobišnata bazilika vo Stobi, *Zbornik Skopje* (1973) forthcoming.
Petrović, J.	Krstionice u Stobima *Umetnički pregled* 3 (1940) no. 9, p. 265. U Stobima danas, *Glasnik Sarajevo* (1943) 489—490.
Saria, B.	Novi nalasci u episkopskoj crkvi u Stobima, *Glasnik* 12 (1933) p. 29, no. 7. Stobi, *RE* IV (1931) 53.
Truhelka, Ć.	Arheološke beleške iz Južne Srbije, *Glasnik* 3 (1927) 78—81.
Wiseman, J.	*Guide*, Section 28.
Wiseman and Mano-Zissi	W-MZ (1971) 403—404. W-MZ (1973) 402.

CENTRAL FOUNTAIN

Mano-Zissi, Dj.	Bemerkungen über die altbyzantinische Stadt von Stobi, *CISB* II (1940) 230.

Petrović, J.	U Stobima danas, *Glasnik Sarajevo* (1943) 483.
Wiseman, J.	*Guide*, Section 7.

CITY WALLS

Hald, Dr.	*Auf den Trümmern Stobis* (Stuttgart 1917) 19—20.
Heuzey, L.	Découverte des ruines de Stobi, *RA* (1873) pt. 2, 34.
Heuzey, L. and H. Daumet	*Mission archéologique de Macédoine* (Paris 1876) 332.
Kitzinger	Survey, p. 111.
Mano-Zissi, Dj.	Bemerkungen über die altbyzantinische Stadt von Stobi, *CISB* II (1940) 225—227. Iskopavanja u Stobima 1933 i 1934 godine, *Starinar* 10-11 (1935—1936) 145. Report on 1932, *Godišnjak* 41 (1932) 235. Report on 1933 *Godišnjak* 42 (1933) 271.
Petrović, J.	U Stobima danas, *Glasnik Sarajevo* (1943) 471, 473.
Premerstein, A. von and N. Vulić	Antike Denkmäler in Serbien und Macedonien *JÖAI* 6 (1903) Beibl., 6.
Saria, B.	Report on 1926, *Godišnjak* 35 (1926) 310. Stobi, *RE* IV (1931) 48, 51.
Wiseman, J.	*Guide*, Sections 25 and 26.
Wiseman and Mano-Zissi	W-MZ (1972) 412—413. W-MZ (1973) 393—395, 399—400.

CIVIL BASILICA
(formerly Basilica Geminata)

Kitzinger	Survey, pp. 130, 144.
Koco, D. *et al.*	Izveštaj zo iskopuvanjata vo Stobi vo tekot na 1955 godina, *Zbornik na arheološkiot muzej* 3 (Skopje 1961) 71.
Mano-Zissi, Dj.	Bericht über die Ausgrabungen in Stobi, *Der 6. Kongress* (1940) 593.

Petrović, J.	Srpsko srednjovekovno blago u Stobima, *Umetnički pregled* 3 (1940) no. 4—5, pp. 108—109. U Stobima danas, *Glasnik Sarajevo* (1943) 486.
Wiseman, J.	*Guide*, Section 2.
Wiseman and Mano-Zissi	W-MZ (1972) 412. W-MZ (1973) 391—392.

EPISCOPAL BASILICA

Bošković, Dj.	Quelques remarques sur la grande basilique de Stobi et son rapport envers la structure urbaine de cette ville, *Charisterion eis Anastasion K. Orlandon* IV (Athens 1967—1968) 184—189.
Djurić, M.	O skidanju zidnih slikarija u Stobi, *Starinar* 7 (1932) 86—87.
Dragendorff, H.	Archäologische und kunstwissenschaftliche Arbeit während des Weltkrieges in Mazedonien, *Zeitschrift für bildende Kunst* n. F. 30 (1919) 266—267.
Egger, R.	Ausgrabungen in Stobi: die frühchristliche Bischofskirche, *AA* (1927) 174—178. Gradska crkva u Stobima, *Glasnik* 5 (1929) 14—44. Die städtische Kirche von Stobi, *JÖAI* 24 (1929) 42—87. This article is nearly identical to the former; henceforth only the Serbian version will be cited.
Filow, B.	Altchristliches aus Mazedonien, *Studien zur Kunst des Ostens, Festschrift J. Strzygowski* (1923) 33—39. *Early Bulgarian Art* (Berne 1919) 6. *Geschichte der altbulgarischen Kunst* (Berlin 1932) 22.
Goldman, H.	Excavations at Stobi in Jugoslavia, *AJA* 37 (1933) p. 298, figs. 1—5.
Grabar, A.	*Martyrium* (Paris 1946) 457—459.
Hald, Dr.	*Auf den Trümmern Stobis* (Stuttgart 1917) 13—19.

Hoddinott, R.	*Early Byzantine Churches in Macedonia and Southern Serbia* (London 1963) 161—167.
Kautzsch, R.	*Kapitellstudien* (Leipzig 1936) 77—78, 83—84, 159, 163, 172.
Kitzinger	Survey, pp. 87—109.
Kondakov, N.	*Ocherki i zamietki po istorii aredneviekovago iskusstva* (Praha 1929) 131—132.
Krautheimer, R.	*Early Christian and Byzantine Architecture* (London 1965) 95, 328.
Maksimović, J.	Contribution à l'étude des fresques de Stobi, *Cahiers archéologiques* 10 (1959) 207—216.
Mano-Zissi, Dj.	Bemerkungen über die altbyzantinische Stadt von Stobi, *CISB* II (1940) 235.
	Bericht über die Ausgrabungen in Stobi, *Der 6. Kongress* (1940) 592.
	Dekorativne plastika u Stobima, *Umetnički pregled* 3 (1940) no. 1—2, pp. 36—41.
	Freske u Stobima, *Starinar* 8-9 (1933—1934) 244—248.
	Iskopavanja u Stobima 1933 i 1934 godine, *Starinar* 9-10 (1935—1936) 164—169.
	Mosaiken in Stobi, *BIABulg* 10 (1936) 277—279, 286, 287, 289—292.
	Prolegomena uz probleme kasnoantičkog mozaika u Ilirikumu, *Zbornik* 2 (1958—1959) 93, 94, 96.
	La question des différentes écoles de mosaïques gréco-romaines de Yougoslavie et essai d'une esquisse de leur évolution, *La mosaïque gréco-romaine* (Paris 1963) 293.
	Report on 1933, *Godišnjak* 42 (1933) 262—263.
	Report on 1934, *Godišnjak* 43 (1934) 251—252.
Nikolajević-Stojković, I.	*Ranovizantiska arhitektonska dekorativna plastika u Makedoniji, Srbiji i Crnoj Gori*, SAN, knjiga 279 (Beograd 1957) 6—34, 46, 47, 49, 64, 68, 72, 73.

Orlandos, A. K.	Ἡ Ξυλόστεγος Παλαιοχριστιανικὴ Βασιλικὴ (Athens 1952—1954) 87, 205, 308—309, 320, 422, 437, 458, 460, 471, 503, 524.
Petković, V.	Report on 1927, *Godišnjak* 37 (1928) 188—190. Report on 1931, *Godišnjak* 40 (1931) 221—222. Report on 1933, *Godišnjak* 42 (1933) 251.
Petrović, J.	Krstionice u Stobima, *Umetnički pregled* 3 (1940) no. 9, 263 265—267. U Stobima danas, *Glasnik Sarajevo* (1943) 474—476.
Petrov, K.	Smešano zidanje vo nekolku zgradi vo Makedonija od III—VI vek, *Zbornik na arheološkiot muzej* (Skopje 1955) 75-77.
Saria, B.	Neue Funde in der Bischofskirche von Stobi, *IIIe Congrès international des études byzantines, Athens 1930* (1932) 213. Novi nalasci u episkopskoj crkvi u Stobima, *Glasnik* 12 (1933) 11—32. Pozorište u Stobima, *Godišnjak muzeja Južne Srbije* 1 (1937) 60. Report on 1925, *Godišnjak* 34 (1925) 321—325. Report on 1926, *Godišnjak* 35 (1926) 309—310. Stobi, *RE* IV (1932) 52—53. Das Theater von Stobi, *AA* (1938) cols. 138—139. This article is nearly identical to Pozorište u Stobima (see above) and henceforth only the Serbian version will be cited. Vor- und frühgeschichtliche Forschung in Südslavien, *BRGK* (1925—1926) 102—104.
Sotiriou, G.	Ἀι Παλαιοχριστιανικαὶ Βασιλικαὶ τῆς Ἑλλάδος, *Archaiologike Ephemeris* (1929) 124, note 3; 178—179.
Stričević, Dj.	I monumenti dell'arte paleobizantina in rapporto con la tradizione antica ed all'arte medioevale nelle régioni centrali dei Balcani, *Zbornik radova vizantološkog instituta* 8 (1964) 400—401.

Truhelka, Ć.	Katedralna bazilika u Stobi — Gradsko. Arheološka beleška iz Južne Srbije, *Glasnik* 3 (1927) 71—77.
Wiseman, J.	*Guide*, Section 19.
Wiseman and Mano-Zissi	W-MZ (1971) 398—401. W-MZ (1972) 420—422. W-MZ (1973) 397—399.

EPISCOPAL BASILICA BAPTISTERY

McKeen, V.	A New Baptistery at Stobi, *AJA* 76 (1972) 215 (Abstract).
Nikolajević, I.	Povodom najnovije diskusije o ranohrišćanskim krstionicama u Saloni, *Zbornik radova vizantološkog instituta* 14-15 (1973) 160, 163.
Wiseman, J.	*Guide*, Section 20.
Wiseman and Mano-Zissi	W-MZ (1972) 422—424. W-MZ (1973) 398—399.

EPISCOPAL RESIDENCE

Kitzinger	Survey, pp. 118, 128.
Mano Zissi, Dj.	Bemerkungen über die altbyzantinische Stadt von Stobi, CISB II (1940) 230. Iskopavanje u Stobima 1933 i 1934 godine, *Starinar* 10-11 (1935—1936) 161—162. Stukatura u Stobima, *Zbornik* 3 (1962) 101—107.
Petrović, J.	U Stobima danas, *Glasnik Sarajevo* (1943) pp. 473, 476, figs. 11, 14.
Wiseman, J.	*Guide*, Section 16.

HELLENISTIC CEMETERY

Mikulčić, I.	Peristerija — kasnohelenistički grobovi, *Arheološki pregled* 8 (1966) 113—114.

Sokolovska, V.   Peristerijeva palata, *Arheološki pregled* 7 (1965)
                          128—129.
Wiseman and
Mano-Zissi   W-MZ (1973) 401—402.

HORREUM

Petrović, J.   U Stobima danas, *Glasnik Sarajevo* (1943)
                          471.

HOUSE OF THE FULLER
(Formerly North Palace)

Egger, R.   Gradska crkva u Stobima, *Glasnik* 5 (1929) 15.
Mano-Zissi, Dj.   Iskopavanja u Stobima 1933 i 1934 godine,
                          Starinar 10-11 (1935—1936) 159—164.
                          Report on 1934, *Godišnjak* 34 (1934) 252.
Kitzinger   Survey, pp. 117—118.
Petrov, K.   Smešano zidanje vo nekolku zgradi vo Makedonija od III-VI vek, *Zbornik na arheološkiot muzej* 1 (Skopje 1955) 71—72, 77.
Petrović, J.   U Stobima danas, *Glasnik Sarajevo* (1943) 474.
Saria, B.   Report on 1925, *Godišnjak* 34 (1925) 325.
                          Report on 1926, *Godišnjak* 35 (1926) 310.
                          Vor- und frühgeschichtliche Forschung in Südslavien, *BRGK* (1925—1926) 104.
Wiseman, J.   *Guide*, Section 15.
Wiseman and
Mano-Zissi   W-MZ (1971) 402—403.
                          W-MZ (1972) 420.
                          W-MZ (1973) 397.

HOUSE OF PARTHENIUS

For bibliography see Theodosian Palace. The Theodosian Palace and the House of Parthenius were in the past considered a single complex.

HOUSE OF PERISTERIAS
(Formerly Double-apsed Building)

Kitzinger	Survey, p. 128.
Mano-Zissi, Dj.	Mosaiken in Stobi, *BIABulg* 10 (1936) 279—280, 283—289, 296—297.
	Prolegomena uz probleme kasnoantičkog mozaika u Illirikumu, *Zbornik* 2 (1958—1959) 91, 95. La question des différentes écoles de mosaïques gréco-romaines et essai d'une esquisse de leur évolution, *La mosaïque gréco-romaine* (Paris 1963) 292-293.
Mikulčić, I.	Peristerija — kasnohelenistički grobovi, *Arheološki pregled* 8 (1966) 113—114.
Nikolajević, I.	Povodom najnovije diskusije o ranohrišćanskim krstionicama u Saloni. *Zbornik radova vizantološkog instituta* 14-15 (1973) 165.
Petrov, K.	Smešano zidanje vo nekolku zgradi vo Makedonija od III-VI vek, *Zbornik na Arheološkiot muzej* 1 (Skopje 1955) 74—75, 77.
Petrović, J.	U Stobima danas, *Glasnik Sarajevo* (1943) 482—483.
Sokolovska, V.	Peristerijeva palata, *Arheološki pregled* 7 (1965) 128—129.
Vulić, N.	Antički spomenici naše zemlje, *Spomenik* 98 (1941-1948) p. 44, no. 94.
Wiseman, J.	*Guide*, Section 10.
Wiseman and Mano-Zissi	W-MZ (1973) 401.

HOUSE OF PSALMS
(formerly Palace of Polycharmus and Summer Palace)

Goldman, H.	Excavations at Stobi in Jugoslavia, *AJA* 37 (1933) p. 299, figs. 8, 10, 11.
Kitzinger	Survey, pp. 134—140.
Mano-Zissi, Dj.	Bemerkungen über die altbyzantinische Stadt von Stobi, *CISB* II (1940) 234.

Mano-Zissi, Dj.	Mozaici jedne kuće u Stobima, *Starinar* 8-9 (1933—1934) 249—254. Mosaiken in Stobi, *BIABulg* 10 (1936) 280—281, 283, 286—287, 290—292. Prolegomena uz probleme kasnoantičkog mozaika u Ilirikumu, *Zbornik* 2 (1958-1959) 93-96. La question des différentes écoles de mosaïques gréco-romaines et essai d'une esquisse de leur évolution, *La mosaïque gréco-romaine* (Paris 1963) 293. Report on 1932, *Godišnjak* 41 (1932) 234—235.
Nikolajević, I.	Povodom najnovije diskusije o ranohrišćanskim krstionicama u Saloni, *Zbornik radova vizantološkog instituta* 14—15 (1973) 165—166, 169.
Petković, V.	Report on 1931, *Godišnjak* 40 (1931) 222—224. Report on 1932, *Godišnjak* 41 (1932) 208—210.
Petrović, J.	Stobi 1932, *Starinar* 8-9 (1933—1934) 173—177, 182. U Stobima danas, *Glasnik Sarajevo* (1943) 484—486, 502.
Saria, B.	Jedan rimski figuralni kapitel iz Stobija, *Starinar* 8-9 (1933—1934) 8—13.
Vinčić, R.	Poliharmosova palata, Stobi, *Arheološki pregled* 5 (1963) 97—98. Arheološki ispituvanja na "Poliharmosovata palata," *Zbornik na arheološkiot muzej* (Skopje 1966) 67—75.
Wiseman, J.	*Guide*, Section 5.
Wiseman and Mano-Zissi	W-MZ (1971) 406—411.

LARGE BATH
(Formerly Winter Palace)

Kitzinger	*Survey*, pp. 140—141.

Mano-Zissi, Dj.	Bemerkungen über die altbyzantinische Stadt von Stobi, *CISB* II (1940) 232, 234.
Petrov, K.	Smešano zidanje vo nekolko zgradi vo Makedonije cd III-VI vek, *Zbornik na arheološkiot muzej* 1 (Skopje 1955) 72—73, 77.
Petrović, J.	Stobi 1932, *Starinar* 8-9 (1933—1934) 173, 177—183.
	U Stobima danas, *Glasnik Sarajevo* (1943) 484.
Vinčić, Ž.	Velike gradske terme, *Arheološki pregled* 5 (1963) 95—96.
Wiseman, J.	*Guide*, Section 8.

MEDIAEVAL GRAVES

B. Aleksova	Slovenska nekropola u Stobima, *Glasnik instituta za nacionalna istorija* (Skopje 1958).
Koco, D. *et al.*	Izveštaj za iskopuvanjata vo Stobi vo tekot no 1955 godina, *Zbornik na arheološkiot muzej* 3 (Skopje 1961) 71—72.
Petković, V.	Report on 1931, *Godišnjak* 40 (1931) 223.
Petrović, J.	Krstionice u Stobima, *Umetnički pregled* 3 (1940) no. 9, p. 263.
	Srpsko srednjovekovno blago u Stobima, *Umetnički pregled* 3 (1940) no. 4—5, pp. 108—109.
	U Stobima danas, *Glasnik Sarajevo* (1943) 472 (jewelry), 492 (coins).

NORTH BASILICA
(formerly called Basilica Geminata and Basilica of St. John)

Kitzinger	Survey, pp. 130, 144.
Koco, D.	Crkva i baptisterium sv. Jovana u Stobima, *Acts of the International Byzantine Congress* (Istambul 1955).

Koco, D.	O simboličnom značenju podnih mozaika ranohrišćanskih bazilika, *Peristil* (Zagreb 1957) 53—55.
	Ranohrišćanski baziliki vo oblasta na Ohridskoto ezero, *Zbornik na trudovi naroden muzej vo Ohrid* (1961) 25—26.
Koco, D. et al.	Izveštaj za iskopuvanjata vo Stobi vo tekot na 1955 godina, *Zbornik na arheološkiot muzej* 3 (Skopje 1961) 69—76.
Mano-Zissi, Dj.	Bericht über die Ausgrabungen in Stobi, *Der 6. Kongress* (1940) 593.
Nikolajević, I.	Povodom najnovije diskusije o ranohrišćanskim krstionicama u Saloni, *Zbornik radova vizantološkog instituta* 14-15 (1973) 160.
	Ranohrišćanske krtsionice u Jugoslaviji, *Zbornik radova vizantološkog instituta* 9 (1866) 223—225.
Petrović, J.	Krstionice u Stobima, *Umetnički pregled* 3 (1940) no. 9, pp. 263, 266—267.
	U Stobima danas, *Glasnik Sarajevo* (1943) 488, 490—496.
Tomovski, K.	Konzervacija i delumno rekonstrukcija vo bazilikate so krstilnica narečena Sv. Jovan krstitel vo Stobi, *Kulturno nasledstvo* 7 (Skopje 1961) 101.
Wiseman, J.	*Guide*, Section 1.

PALIKURA BASILICA

Dragendorff, H.	Archäologische und kunstwissenschaftliche Arbeit während des Weltkrieges in Mazedonien, *Zeitschrift für bildende Kunst* n. F. 30 (1919) 265—266.
Egger, R.	Gradska crkva u Stobima, *Glasnik* 5 (1929) 14.
Filow, B.	Altchristliches aus Mazedonien, *Studien zur Kunst des Ostens, Festschrift J. Strzygowski* (1923) 33—34.

Hald, Dr.	*Auf den Trümmern Stobis* (Stuttgart 1917) 29—40.
Hoddinott, R.	*Early Byzantine Churches in Macedonia and Southern Serbia* (London 1963) 185—186.
Kitzinger	Survey, p. 147, note 288.
Nikolajević, I.	Ranohrišćanske krstionice u Jugoslaviji *Zbornik radova vizantološkog instituta* 9 (1966) 227.
	Ranovizantiska arhitektonska dekorativna plastika u Makedoniji, Srbiji i Crnoj Gori, SAN, knjiga 279 (Beograd 1957) 36, 45—47, 90.
Petrović, J.	Krstionice u Stobima, *Umetnički pregled* 3 (1940) no. 9, pp. 263—265.
Saria, B.	Stobi, *RE* IV (1932) 53.
Truhelka, Ć.	Bazlika na čifluku Palikura. Arheolcške beleške iz Južne Srbije, *Glasnik* 3 (1927) 81—82.
Wiseman, J.	*Guide*, Section 29.

PALIKURA TOMB

Petrović, J.	U Stobima danas, *Glasnik Sarajevo* (1943) pp. 473, 510, fig. 47.
Vulić, N.	Antički spomenici naše zemlje, *Spomenik* 98 (1941—1948) pp. 41—42, no. 91.

PORTA HERACLEA

Kitzinger	Survey, pp. 111—114.
Mano-Zissi, Dj.	Bemerkungen über die altbyzantinische Stadt von Stobi, *CISB* II (1940) 226—227.
	Iskopavanje u Stobima 1933 i 1934 godine, *Starinar* 10-11 (1935—1936) 145—150.
	Report on 1932, *Godišnjak* 41 (1932) 235—236.
	Report on 1933, *Godišnjak* 42 (1933) 270—271.

Petković, V.	Report on 1932, *Godišnjak* 41 (1932) 211—212.
	Report on 1933, *Godišnjak* 42 (1933) 250—251.
Petrović, J.	U Stobima danas, *Glasnik Sarajevo* (1943) 473—474.
Wiseman, J.	*Guide*, Section 21.
Wiseman and Mano-Zissi	W-MZ (1973) 399—400.

PRISON

Kitzinger	Survey, p. 128.
Petković, V.	Report on 1931, *Godišnjak* 40 (1931) 225.
	Report on 1932, *Godišnjak* 41 (1932) 212.
Petrović, J.	U Stobima danas, *Glasnik Sarajevo* (1943) 477.
Wiseman, J.	*Guide*, Section 16.

SEMICIRCULAR COURT

Bošković, Dj.	Quelques remarques sur la grande basilique de Stobi et son rapport envers la structure urbaine de cette ville, *Charisterion eis Anastasion K. Orlandon* (Athens 1967—1968) 184—189.
Kitzinger	Survey, pp. 114—117.
Mano-Zissi, Dj.	Bemerkungen über die altbyzantinische Stadt von Stobi, *CISB* II (1940) 229.
	Bericht über die Ausgrabungen in Stobi, *Der 6. Kongress* (1940) 592.
	Iskopavanja u Stobima 1933 i 1934 godine, *Starinar* 10-11 (1935—1936) 156—159.
	Report on 1933, *Godišnjak* 42 (1933) 262—263, 270—271.
Petković, V.	Report on 1933, *Godišnjak* 42 (1933) 251.
Petrović, J.	U Stobima danas, *Glasnik Sarajevo* (1943) 474.
Wiseman, J.	*Guide*, Section 17.

SMALL BATH

Kitzinger	Survey, p. 146.
Mano-Zissi, Dj.	Bemerkungen über die altbyzantinische Stadt von Stobi, *CISB* II (1940) 232, 234.
Petković, V.	Report on 1931, *Godišnjak* 40 (1931) 233—234.
Petrović, J.	Iskopavanje u Stobima 1931, *Starinar* 7 (1932) 86.
	Report on 1931, *Godišnjak* 40 (1931) 232.
Vinčić, Ž.	Male gradske terme, *Arheološki pregled* 5 (1963) 96—97.
Wiseman, J.	*Guide*, Section 3.

SYNAGOGUE BASILICA

Hoddinott, R.	*Early Byzantine Churches in Macedonia and Southern Serbia* (London 1963) 179, 181.
Kitzinger	Survey, pp. 129—134, 139—146.
Mano-Zissi, Dj.	Report on 1932, *Godišnjak* 41 (1932) 234.
Petković, V.	Report on 1931, *Godišnjak* 40 (1931) 222—223.
	Report on 1932, *Godišnjak* 41 (1932) 208—209.
Petrov, K.	Smešano zidanje vo nekolku zgradi vo Makedonija od III-VI vek, *Zbornik na arheološkiot muzej* 1 (Skopje 1955) 73—74, 77.
Petrović, J.	Iskopine starog grada Stobi u Makedoniji, *Svijet*, knjiga 12, godina 6, broj 12 (September 19, 1931) 278—279, 288.
	Iskopavanje u Stobima 1931, *Starinar* 7 (1932) 81—86.
	Report on 1931, *Godišnjak* 40 (1931) 232.
	Stobi 1932, *Starinar* 8-9 (1933—1934) 169—191.
	U Stobima danas, *Glasnik Sarajevo* (1943) 496—503.
Vinčić, Ž. and R.	Sinagoga bazilika, *Arheološki pregled* 7 (1965) 129—131.

Wischnitzer, R. *The Architecture of the European Synagogue* (Philadelphia 1964) 7—9.
Wiseman, J. *Guide*, Section 4.
Wiseman and
Mano-Zissi W-MZ (1971) 408—411.
W-MZ (1972) 408—411.
W-MZ (1973) 391—393.
(See also Polycharmus' Inscription, above page 241)

THEATER

Dyggve, E. *De senantike Faellesscene belyst ved Teatret i Stobi og ved Diptychonfremstillinger* (Kobenhavn 1938).
La theâtre mixte du bas-empire d'après le theâtre de Stobi et les diptyques consulaires, *RA* (1958) 1, pp. 137—157; 2, pp. 20—37.
Egger, R. Gradska crkva u Stobima, *Glasnik* 5 (1929) 36—37.
Kitzinger Survey, pp. 151—153.
Neppi Modona, A. *Gli edifici teatrali greci e romani* (Firenze 1961) 230—233.
Papazoglu, F. Natpis iz nemezejona i datovanje stobskog pozorišta, *ŽA* 1 (1951) 279—293.
Petković, V. Report on 1925, *Godišnjak* 34 (1925) 320—321.
Report on 1926, *Godišnjak* 35 (1926) 307—308.
Report on 1927, *Godišnjak* 37 (1928) 188—189.
Report on 1928, *Godišnjak* 37 (1928) 221—222.
Petrović, J. U Stobima danas, *Glasnik Sarajevo* (1943) 479—482.
Saria, B. Die Inschriften des Theaters von Stobi, *JÖAI* 32 (1940) 1—34.
Iskopavanja u Stobima, *Glasnik* 1 (1925) 291—300.

Saria, B.	Pozorište u Stobima, *Godišnjak muzeja Južne Srbije* 1 (1937) 1—68. Vor- und frühgeschichtliche Forschung in Südslavien, *BRGK* (1925—1926) 97—102.
Saržoski, S.	Antičko pozorište, *Arheološki pregled* 7 (1965) 129.
Volkmann, H.	Neue Beiträge zum Nemesiskult, *Archiv frü Religionswissenschaft* 31 (1934) 58—61.
Wiseman, J.	*Guide*, Section 23.
Wiseman and Mano-Zissi	W-MZ (1970) 402. W-MZ (1972) 417—419. W-MZ (1973) 400—401.

THEODOSIAN PALACE AND HOUSE OF PARTHENIUS
(formerly Palace)

Goldman, H.	Excavations at Stobi in Jugoslavia, *AJA* 37 (1933) p. 299, fig. 7.
Kitzinger	Survey, pp. 118—129.
Lavin, I.	Antioch Hunting Mosaics and Their Sources, *DOPapers* 17 (1963) 256.
Mano-Zissi, Dj.	Bemerkungen über die altbyzantinische Stadt von Stobi, *CISB* II (1940) 231—233. Mosaiken in Stobi, *BIABulg* 10 (1936) 279, 282, 286, 290. Prolegomena uz probleme kasnoantičkog mozaika u Illirikumu, *Zbornik* 2 (1958—1959) 94—95. La question des différentes écoles de mosaïques gréco-romaines de Yougoslavia et essai d'une esquisse de leur évolution, *La mosaïque gréco-romaine* (Paris 1963) 293.
Nestorović, B.	Iskopavanja u Stobima, *Starinar* 6 (1931) 109—114. Un palais a Stobi, *BIABulg* 10 (1936) 173—183.

Petković, V.	Antičke skulpture iz Stobia, *Starinar* 12 (1937) 12—35. Die neuentdeckten skulpturen in Stobi, *Bericht über die Jahrhundertfeier des Deutschen Archäologischen Instituts* (1930) 192—193. Report on 1927, *Godišnjak* 37 (1928) 190—192. Report on 1928, *Godišnjak* 37 (1928) 220—221. Report on 1929, *Godišnjak* 38 (1929) 231—234. Report on 1930, *Godišnjak* 39 (1930) 188—191. Report on 1931, *Godišnjak* 40 (1931) 224—225.
Petrov, K.	Istražuvanja na vodovodniot sistem vo ranovizantiskiot Stobi, *Zbornik Skopje* 19 (1967) 267—268.
Petrović, J.	Report on 1931, *Godišnjak* 40 (1931) 232. U Stobima danas, *Glasnik Sarajevo* (1943) 478—479.
Reinach, S.	Sculpture, *RA* 29 (1929) 21, 330, 338. Sculpture, *RA* 30 (1929) 87.
Saria, B.	Ein Dionysosvotiv aus dem Konsulatsjahr des P. Dasumius Rusticus, *JÖAI* 26 (1930) 64—74. Epigrafski spomenici iz Južne Srbije, *Glasnik* 7—8 (1930) 293—299.
Vulić, N.	Antički spomenici naše zemlje, *Spomenik* 71 (1931) pp. 44—45, no. 101.
Wiseman, J.	*Guide*, Sections 12 and 13.
Anonymous	In *Die Weltkunst* 6 (1932) no. 29. p. 2.

VIA AXIA

Petrović, J.	U Stobima danas, *Glasnik Sarajevo* (1943) 484.
Wiseman, J.	*Guide*, Section 6.

VIA PRINCIPALIS INFERIOR

Kitzinger	Survey, p. 128.
Petković, V.	Report on 1930, *Godišnjak* 39 (1930) 190.
Wiseman, J.	*Guide*, Section 9.

VIA PRINCIPALIS SUPERIOR

Kitzinger Survey, pp. 117—118.
Mano-Zissi, Dj. Bemerkungen über die altbyzantinische Stadt von Stobi, *CISB* II (1940) 230.
Iskopavanje u Stobima 1933 i 1934 godine, *Starinar* 10-11 (1935—1936) 159.
Report on 1934, *Godišnjak* 43 (1934) 252.
Wiseman, J. *Guide*, Section 9.

VIA SACRA

Bošković, Dj. Quelques remarques sur la grande basilique de Stobi et son rapport envers la structure urbaine de cette ville, *Charisterion eis Anastasion K. Orlandon* (Athens 1967—1968) 184—189.
Kitzinger Survey, pp. 114—117.
Mano-Zissi, Dj. Bemerkungen über die altbyzantinische Stadt von Stobi, *CISB* II (1940) 228.
Bericht über die Ausgrabungen in Stobi, *Der 6. Kongress*, (1940) 592.
Iskopavanja u Stobima 1933 i 1934 godine, *Starinar* 10-11 (1935—1936) 150—159.
Report on 1932, *Godišnjak* 41 (1932) 236.
Report on 1933, *Godišnjak* 42 (1933) 262—263, 270—271.
Petković, V. Report on 1933, *Godišnjak* 42 (1933) 250—251.
Petrović, J. U Stobima danas, *Glasnik Sarajevo* (1943) 473—474.
Wiseman, J. *Guide*, Section 18.

VIA THEODOSIA

Kitzinger Survey, p. 128.
Petković, V. Report on 1930, *Godišnjak* 39 (1930) 190.

Petrović, J. U Stobima danas, *Glasnik Sarajevo* (1943) 478—479.
Wiseman, J. *Guide*, Section 11.

WEST CEMETERY

Aleksova, B. Stobi. Palikura, *Arheološki pregled* 1 (1959) 126—127.
Kitzinger Survey, p. 87.
Mano-Zissi, Dj. Iskopavanja u Stobima 1933 i 1934 godine, *Starinar* 10-11 (1935—1936) 145.
Mikulčić, I. The West Cemetery: Excavations in 1965, *Studies in the Antiquities of Stobi* I (Beograd 1973).
Mikulčić, I. and V. Dautovska Antička nekropola, *Arheološki pregled* 7 (1965) 126—128.
Petković, V. Report on 1932, *Godišnjak* 41 (1932) 211.
Vinčić, Ž. Stobi — antički grad. Lokalitet krčana — vila rustika. Antička nekropola, *Arheološki pregled* 12 (1970) 142.
Wesolowsky, A. Burial Customs in the West Cemetery, *Studies in the Antiquities of Stobi* I (Beograd 1973).
Wiseman, J. *Guide*, Section 22.
Wiseman and Mano-Zissi W-MZ (1971) 403—406.
W-MZ (1972) 413—416.